Robert C. Banks, Jr.

Anatomy of a Trial

ANATOMY OF A TRIAL

By ALAN E. MORRILL
of the Illinois Bar

COMMERCE CLEARING HOUSE, INC.
PUBLISHERS of TOPICAL LAW REPORTS

NEW YORK   CHICAGO   WASHINGTON
BOSTON   PHILADELPHIA   LOS ANGELES   SAN FRANCISCO

Anatomy of a Trial first appeared in the publisher's *Insurance Law Journal.*

Printed in the United States of America

Library of Congress Catalog Number: 68-26671

To P. K.

Table of Contents

Preface

WHAT DOES A LAWYER LEARN about the application of psychology after he has had considerable experience dealing with juries? We have seen lawyers consistently obtain poor results over the years. Other lawyers seem to captivate juries almost immediately. So, we ask ourselves at what point, either through innate ability or experience, does a lawyer suddenly leave the herd and become recognized by his contemporaries as a true professional?

It's true that any trial lawyer, given a good case of liability and the evidence to back it up, can get the verdict, barring a calamity. It's also equally true that the most experienced or skillful lawyer cannot successfully prosecute or defend a hopeless case without the intervention of a miracle. Therefore, an easy solution is simply to say, given the right set of facts, any lawyer should be able to obtain the desired verdict. However, there are a large percentage of cases that, even though all the evidence is known by both sides and after careful deliberation, no one can say with even the slightest degree of certainty what the verdict will be—let alone the amount if it's a plaintiff verdict.

The delicate art of applied psychology in jury persuasion is so vastly complex because of the unlimited variations in human beings that even the best trial lawyer can get only a momentary glimpse into the vast field of the psychological approach to jury persuasion. Brief as this might be, however, it is still sufficient to set him apart significantly from those trial lawyers who have not been so rewarded —it has been said that, "In the land of the blind, the one-eyed man is king." He must develop his own style to become a true professional. He should profit by the successful techniques of his colleagues, but at the same time he should keep in mind that there is no substitute for individuality. No man will ever become truly great by imitation. On the other hand, a lawyer can hardly improve significantly if he has no other model but himself to emulate.

The methods of persuading juries have become more widely varied since the turn of the century. These variations are ever in-creasing. In our rapidly growing space age, trial lawyers will find themselves turning more and more to highly sophisticated methods and evidence to persuade a jury that their position is correct. There are only a few trial lawyers who seem to blaze the trail for the rest of us to follow by opening up new avenues to assist juries in arriving at the truth. There will be found many lawyers and judges among our number who will resist change. These same men, learned in the law, are enamored with the doctrine of *stare decisis*. The courageous and imaginative trial lawyer, in fighting his way against the current, can establish a precedent which will some day be cited by those same men learned in the law. No precedent, no matter how long it has been on the books, can withstand the strength of a new precedent when its time has come. There will always be a few trial lawyers who possess the imagination and courage to lead us on in the battle for truth and justice. How many lawyers possess the courage to use a unique or novel approach in proving their cases, knowing that their offer of proof will bring strong criticism from the opponent as well as from the trial judge? To knowingly take on this battle without the comforting security of an authority to flourish may shorten this lawyer's life, but the contribution that he will leave to the trial bar will live forever. It is to those lonely and courageous men that this book is dedicated.

ALAN E. MORRILL

Chicago, June 1968

Foreword

FREQUENTLY books which arouse my interest cross my desk. While these works range a galaxy of topics, I am irresistibly drawn to those which seek to advance the art of advocacy. Our lives today are such that the need for trial lawyers has never been so great.

Yet law students are still being lured from trial litigation to the less formidable and more sedentary fields of law. "Service" to and for one's fellow man is not necessarily the gravamen in this more sophisticated "out of court" legal area.

More than ever there is need for encouragement and education in trial practice—"bread and butter" practice, down-to-earth trial law practice education. *Anatomy of a Trial* is a book of such encouragement and education.

Alan E. Morrill, a respected member of the trial bar, is eminently qualified to dissect and lay open the heart of a law trial. Having had past associations with him in the trial of complex lawsuits, I am not surprised by the informative quality of his *Anatomy of a Trial*. This book, aptly named, succinctly and totally demonstrates the art of jury persuasion. Specificity, through detail and example, is good law writing, and Morrill outstandingly illustrates the trial doctrines of which he writes.

But the outstanding feature of this treatise is that it conveys ideas —not precedents; it advances concepts—not stringed citations; it relates techniques—not stories. The trial lawyer cannot completely disown his role as a protagonist, but he should know how and when propitiously to recede into the shadows.

This book is more than a book; it is an actual trial. It begins with the *voir dire* examination, proceeds through the opening statements to direct and cross-examination, and concludes, as does the trial, with summation. How else to portray a trial other than by "telling it like it is"? Every chapter is rich with demonstrations from actual trials and pertinent inquiries to exemplify each technique or suggestion.

Clarity of style is a particular gift of Alan E. Morrill. He writes with the confidence of a master of his subject, yet with refreshing portrayal of each phase of the trial. He makes it understandable and interesting to both the profession and to the layman. Lawyers can and should look upon this book, written by a trial specialist in every sense of the term, as a significant contribution to the trial lawyer.

MELVIN M. BELLI
Los Angeles, June 1968

I. Voir Dire Examination

Appraisal of the *Voir Dire* Examination

COUNTRIES which have a "trial by jury" system stress the importance of having a fair and impartial jury. This concept is so deeply embedded in the American system of disposing of civil disputes between persons or corporations—to say nothing of crimes against a sovereign power—that lawyers can safely assume that this is the attitude and frame of mind in which jurors enter the jury box. Experience has taught us that the great majority of jurors generally want to uphold the tradition of the jury trial system which calls for fairness and impartiality to both sides. This being admittedly a fact stipulated to by lawyers, lay people will then ask: "Why, then, is the *voir dire* examination conducted by the trial lawyers a necessary part of our trial procedure? Is it not sufficient that the trial judge inquire of the prospective jurors if there is any reason why each cannot be fair and impartial to both sides, and to admonish each that his verdict should be free from sympathy or prejudice?"

It has been said by some lawyers that the *voir dire* examination is of little value. These lawyers contend that there is no reason why

a trial lawyer should not just take the first 12 jurors, submit the issues to them, and try the case. There are only two reasons for a
lawyer to take such a position: either he is lacking in aptitude
for jury trial work or he has had little or no trial experience. Who
is there who would dispute the wisdom in the statement of Thomas
Fuller: "A fox should not be one of the jury at a goose's trial."
Successful trial lawyers who have learned and applied the subtleties
of proven techniques in the battle of jury persuasion give this phase
of the lawsuit first priority in importance. There are too many
lawyers who do not rise up in the defense of the *voir dire* system
when movements are made to eliminate or curtail the lawyer's participation in the jury selection. There have been many attempts
by some to limit the interrogation of prospective jurors by lawyers
and, in many jurisdictions, these efforts have met with some success.
To the knowledge of this writer, the only reason that there has been
legislative interference with our jury selection method is to speed up
the trial. When one considers that the average *voir dire* in a case of
some consequence consumes on the average no more than two or
three hours of actual trial time, it would seem that the amount of
time necessary to carefully and properly select a jury is a small price
to pay to maintain our proven adversary system.

In large metropolitan areas which use an assignment system in
which a case is assigned to any one of a number of trial judges, it is
impossible to assign trial dates in advance. Therefore, trial lawyers
do not know the exact date when they are going to trial with any
particular case. A lawyer may be assigned to trial on any one of a
number of cases which are all subject to immediate trial and he cannot possibly be expected to have his witnesses for each case available
on the first day. This problem is peculiar to the plaintiff's lawyer only
—because he is the first up to bat. If he were expected to have his
clients and witnesses prepared to testify on a moment's notice, it
would be necessary that each and every one of his clients and witnesses remain home indefinitely or crowd into his office each morning
on a stand-by basis in the event that any one of a number of those
lawsuits would be assigned for immediate trial. Experienced trial
judges know that this is a physical impossibility. There often will be
no witnesses available to testify on the first day of trial, when the
jury is selected and when opening statements are made. When assigned to a trial judge, both the plaintiff and defense lawyers will, for
the first time, be able to put the machinery into motion toward gathering witnesses by having subpoenas served upon them, as well as lining
up other witnesses that each intends to use. More than likely, the

subpoenas will be served on the evening of the same day that the lawyers have selected the jury. Therefore, it can be seen that there is little practical value in squeezing the *voir dire* examination into a 20-minute procedure conducted by the trial judge, only to have the court adjourn until the following day because there are no witnesses available to testify.

In those jurisdictions where the trial judge conducts the entire *voir dire* examination, permitting only a limited participation by the trial lawyers, the result is often the selection of a less than satisfactory jury. There is no substitute for a conscientious, partisan lawyer rooting out any hidden background experiences or attitudes affecting the prospective juror's judgment. A limited *voir dire* examination also prevents a lawyer from extracting important promises from each juror in order that each be firmly committed on propositions important to the case.

The defense lawyer finds himself frustrated when he cannot require that each and every juror be committed and assure him that he will not let his natural feelings of sympathy toward an injured plaintiff interfere with his duty as a juror to find the defendant "not guilty" if the plaintiff fails to prove that the defendant was negligent. The factual situation may be such that great sympathy will be felt for the plaintiff, and perhaps even antagonism and prejudice against the defendant; whereas, on the other hand, if the jury properly follows the law, the plaintiff would not be entitled to a recovery. The plaintiff's lawyer can feel equally frustrated when he is thwarted in his desire to have a jury assure him that each will fully and adequately compensate his injured plaintiff by awarding damages for pain and suffering, even though they may not be in sympathy with the law that allows money damages for such an intangible. There are many points upon which both lawyers may want the jurors to give assurances while they are under oath before each can feel fairly comfortable with the jury. Experienced lawyers want a juror committed to a position that he will enter a verdict in favor of his client if such a finding is proper in accordance with the evidence and the law. During the closing arguments, the trial lawyer will find it most effective to remind the jury that each and every one of them assured him that they would do the very thing which the evidence now indicates to be fair and just.

Even though the voices that have spoken out against the *voir dire* examination by lawyers have been heard in some jurisdictions, the majority of our courts still permit the lawyers to select their own juries. Be that as it may, while this book is not written for the pur-

pose of expounding on the author's personal viewpoints with regard
to our jury trial procedure, the fact does remain that it is an important part of jury persuasion and the lawyer cannot afford to
neglect its proper application.

THE PREJUDICED JURY

All Jurors Are Prejudiced

Regardless of anything to the contrary, all human beings are
prejudiced. Not only are all human beings prejudiced, but these
feelings spill over into many areas. The reader can be quite certain
that he or she is biased or prejudiced in many fields. Inasmuch as
every one of us is prejudiced, it follows, therefore, that it is not possible for us to be completely objective in any area in which our
prejudice exists. To give but a few examples: we are all prejudiced
to some extent with regard to religion, politics, our concept of beauty,
a favorite news commentator or newspaper, good food, recreational
activities, proper child-rearing methods, and adequate income, proper
medical care, labor unions, and other examples that could go on ad
infinitum. Almost to a man, we would be prejudiced against those
who commit crimes of violence or prejudiced in favor of the person
who considers us to be astute. Certainly everyone will agree that
jurors who come into the jury box will have preconceived feelings on
many of the subjects mentioned. Given enough time and thought, a
list could be made of thousands of subjects upon which everyone
would have to honestly say that it would be difficult for him to be
completely objective. Then, of course, there are those with deep-
rooted prejudices directed in favor of or against nationality groups,
races, occupations, or simply, with a long-standing tradition of hate passed
down from generation to generation, such as hate directed toward
an old enemy of war. Even today there can be found, to some extent,
hard feelings resulting from the United States Civil War, even though
all of the participants have long been dead. "People hate, as they love,
unreasonably," said Thackeray.

Now that it has been established that we are all loaded with
prejudices or biased feelings, what about those little "quirks" that we
dislike to admit even to ourselves? These little "quirks," sometimes
called "idiosyncrasies," are the very things that influence the judgment of this most important fact-finding body known as the jury. Accepting now that it is impossible to select a jury free from preconceived feelings, it can be seen how naive legal writers have been in
penning the reams of articles written for trial lawyers describing

methods for selecting jurors who will be "free" from sympathy, passion, or bias. We can also see that a trial judge, by admonishing a jury that their verdict should be free from sympathy and prejudice, cannot make it so. A man's personality, prejudices, feelings, passions, bias, and beliefs go right along with him into the jury room when he passes judgment on the facts.

Therefore, it follows that if a lawyer, in questioning the prospective jurors, could be clairvoyant, he could select those jurors with preconceived feelings unfavorable to the other side of the case. The evidence and later arguments given by this lawyer would fall on sympathetic ears, and who is there that can deny that his side of the case would have a strong advantage? Someone once said: "A friend is one who dislikes the same people that you dislike." Most of us are not psychic, but with a little thought and effort, we can probably improve our "picking" by reflecting upon the probable or improbable. Surely we can estimate how a juror may feel on any given point based upon his background and experience. "Men willingly believe what they wish," said Julius Caesar.

The Examiner Must Surmise the Prejudice

As a class, the lawyer represents the least prejudiced of all groups since he is trained to acknowledge that there will usually be two sides to every story. Knowing the magnitude of his own prejudices, how then can this serve him in ascertaining preconceived feelings in the prospective juror? It is safe to say that he will never find a juror who will stand up and say, "I am prejudiced," and then start listing the categories in which he is prejudiced, for or against. The lawyer's job is to surmise the prejudices. This educated guess will be based upon facts already known about the juror, facts he learns from questioning him, his demeanor while answering questions, his attitude toward the questioner and his opponent, his physical appearance, his general attire, such as clothing and jewelry, and anything else that conveys information to the lawyer. Every human communicates recondite information about himself from which the attentive observer can draw conclusions.

Understanding What Motivates People

To enjoy success with juries, the trial lawyer must be genuinely interested in people so that he can understand why people think and act as they do under a given set of facts. Each of us has had the experience of becoming acquainted with members of ethnic groups quite different from our own. We have seen that members of these ethnic groups will often share the same convictions within their group in many areas such as religion, politics, nationalism, conservatism, liberalism, and other basic beliefs or philosophies. The more isolated this group is, the more uniformity will be found in their approach to many subjects. Strong feelings can be found, for example, on the importance of labor unions. A particular ethnic group may feel that unions are absolutely essential and every effort should be made to strengthen them in order to protect the laboring man against management who would exploit him. Members of another group will feel organized labor is dangerous because higher wages force prices up and the individual loses his initiative, to say nothing of his identity. There are ethnic groups that have strong feelings concerning the teachings of their particular religion as opposed to another group. Others will feel religion is merely an opiate for the masses. "Opinions founded on prejudice are always sustained with the greatest violence," said Jeffrey.

Every one of us is a product of his environment and background. Each of us belongs to various ethnic groups, starting with large groups and working down into smaller ones. As Americans, we are all members of an ethnic group. It can be anticipated that when the interests of our country come into conflict with those of another, we will be prejudiced in favor of our own country. Within that ethnic group, we are all members of other ethnic groups, such as residents of the Middle West, the South, a large city, a rural area, or perhaps a small town. As residents of a particular area, it can be anticipated that we would be more in sympathy with its problems when they come into conflict with those of a different area. The ambitious working man will find it difficult to appreciate why a good part of his tax dollar should be used to support the unemployed who live in a large city within his county. A good portion of the people trace their ancestry to some other country, tending to identify with members of that group. They are proud to say that their ancestry is German, Irish, or Greek.

In order to appreciate why members of an ethnic group have inclinations or even convictions on certain points, there must be an understanding of their background. They were molded through their experiences or lack of experiences. Did this ethnic group have a hard, difficult life? Was it the reverse? Did they have a pleasant, privileged life? It would be impossible for a juror who grew up in an exclusive suburban section, and attended the finest schools, to view life the same as another juror who grew up in a slum district and never finished grade school.

The trial lawyer must be aware of how these people feel on many issues, particularly in the big city, which has every conceivable ethnic group. In a local farming community the trial lawyer will find that there will be a limited variety of ethnic groups. This is a group unlike any found in the big city. A big city lawyer who never tried a case in a farming area would be at a decided disadvantage in not knowing preconceived feelings of the local residents as intimately as his opponent. His opponent can exploit these feelings in the battle of persuasion. The farmer who is concerned about the possibilities of a late frost or a rainfall, what Washington is doing with farm subsidies, and who listens to a broadcast on the livestock market, cannot view problems peculiar to the big city with the same objectivity as his cousin who resides in that city. A farmer who often works long hours earning less than $5,000 a year for his efforts certainly cannot be expected to award as large a verdict as a juror who works in the city earning twice that amount of money for a 40-hour week. In defending a Dram Shop case, would it be possible to receive a fair trial from a juror who is a member of the Women's Christian Temperance Union, or perhaps, a member of a group which is intent on obtaining legislation to make a particular area "dry"? This woman would likely be so prejudiced against tavern operators that she could not wait to get back into the jury room to explain to her fellow jurors that liquor is the devil's business and all engaged in it are *in pari delicto*. On the other hand, a lawyer representing a plaintiff bringing suit against his landlord for injuries received on the premises will find that jurors who are also landlords probably will identify with and be sympathetic toward the defendant. Therefore, recognizing that people have these feelings, why should a lawyer take on an up-hill battle when he can just as easily take a down-hill ride toward a verdict? Perhaps a lawyer with contrary feelings may have in mind the sentiments Corneille had when he wrote: "We triumph without glory when we conquer without danger."

Experiences Will Affect a Juror's Judgment

Aside from the molding and building that the personality and make-up of a person undergoes by his everyday exposure to the people around him, he is also affected by the experiences in life— both planned and unexpected. These experiences can have an effect all the way from a slight leaning toward one side or the other to a deep-rooted, unshakeable conviction, love, or faith, on a particular point which make him thoroughly and completely incapable of being objective on that specific point.

Assume that the plaintiff's lawyer in questioning a Mrs. Callaghan, who would otherwise make a wonderful juror since she has all of the attributes he would like, discovers that she has a daughter named

Cathleen living at home. Cathleen, her only child, works in the claims department of an insurance company and has been so employed for the past 15 years. In this situation, there is a distinct danger that Cathleen, because of her experience and association, has developed an antagonistic attitude toward claimants in general. This feeling may be strong as is found in many insurance claims employees who feel that most claims are phonies and most lawyers who represent plaintiffs have questionable ethics, if they are not downright crooks. Further, it is quite possible that after 15 years, Cathleen has "brainwashed" her mother. It is equally possible that Mrs. Callaghan will regard the entire plaintiff's case with suspicion. On the other hand, how would the plaintiff be likely to fare if the same Mrs. Callaghan instead has a daughter who is engaged to a lawyer whose practice is confined solely to representing plaintiffs? If this has been a long courtship, Cathleen's fiancé has surely explained to her how insurance companies are out to cheat the widows and orphans. It is probable that Mrs. Callaghan's exposure through Cathleen would make her a most desirable juror from the plaintiff's standpoint.

Based on the facts and personalities in his case, the lawyer should ask himself what kind of jury he should look for. For example, if the plaintiff's lawyer finds himself in the unfortunate position of having a chiropractor as his only medical witness to establish injuries, then he should be thinking in terms of jurors who are more prone to accept the testimony of a chiropractor. We have all had the experience of talking to people who have expressed confidence in chiropractors and who would not hesitate to seek out their services in preference to an orthopedic surgeon highly regarded in the medical profession. On the other hand, there are people who feel that all chiropractors are "quacks," pure and simple. Again, there are people who have no definite opinion because they have heard both favorable and unfavorable comments. Each lawyer will be conducting a guileful and subtle battle in an effort to get jurors with preconceived opinions. If the plaintiff's lawyer finds that he is trying such a case with a rather sophisticated jury, he should certainly bring out this fact immediately with the first juror. The juror can be asked specifically if he has ever gone to a chiropractor or if any member of his family has gone to one. This lead ought to get things started. There is no point in "tip-toeing" around. Some jurors will be completely "sold" on chiropractors, going on to cite experiences of marvelous results from treatments given to themselves or friends. Any dwelling upon the ability and reputation of a chiropractor should not, of course, be discouraged by the plaintiff's examiner since these testaments will influence some of the neutrals. On the other hand, those jurors who have strong feelings against chiropractors can be promptly dismissed before the words of contempt influence the unopinionated. In addition to "weeding out the garden," there should be a promise extracted from each juror that he will fairly and impartially weigh the testimony of the chiropractic physician.

Assume the Probable

We cannot establish as a fact that a person has a feeling for or against a particular subject or issue merely because we can identify him with a particular ethnic group. Human beings are, first and foremost, individuals capable of formulating their own opinions and feelings irrespective of how their peers may feel. However, it is not an easy matter for a lawyer, when identifying a particular member of an ethnic group, to determine if his viewpoints are different from the known viewpoints of that group. The prospective juror is certainly not going to lay his soul bare in the courtroom for the lawyer to examine in the presence of God and everyone. Therefore, the examiner should probably play the percentages. If it can be anticipated that the ethnic group to which the prospective juror belongs will react adversely to the client's interest, then he should be rejected.

CONDUCT OF EXAMINER

Be Informal

Experience has persuaded me that you can get a warmer relationship with people by avoiding formality. Formality has a tendency to prevent a close amity. However, I don't think that in order to encourage a more intimate relationship one has to sacrifice the respect that may be important. We can take a lesson from highly successful politicians who have the facility of being referred to by their first names, or even better—nicknames—in spite of the great prestige that their high office brings to them. Offhand, I cannot think of any United States president since Hoover or of any serious presidential contender who has not been referred to either by his first name, initials, or a nickname. These successful national figures have deliberately discouraged people from referring to them formally. Presidents of the United States have been affectionately referred to as "Jack," "Ike," "Harry," or "FDR." Presidential candidates have been known as "Barry," or "Rocky," and vice presidential office holders have been known as "Hubert," "Dick," or "Veep."

It can hardly be necessary in this era of informality that the lawyer and his client maintain an impersonal attitude with the jury. The extreme in observance of formality exists in the Armed Services. Elaborate measures are taken to avoid any informality between enlisted men and officers. If one wants to know how much warmth an enlisted man feels toward an officer, he has only to ask an enlisted man. The lawyer should personalize his client by referring to her as "Mary Smith." People will feel warmer toward "Mary" than they will toward "Mrs. Smith," or the "plaintiff" or the "defendant." I start right out by calling my client by his first name and refer to him that way throughout the trial. I have had occasion where the judge referred to my client by his first name in the presence of the jury, instead of formally. This is evidence of success in personalizing a client—to say nothing of the fact that you are enlisting the court's help in projecting a warmer relationship between your client and the jury.

While creating this "close friendship" between the jury and your client, you should be creating a formal relationship at the same time between the opposite party and the jury. Your opposing lawyer may even help you to keep it formal by referring to his client as "Mr. Jones." With the court acknowledging him as "Mr. Jones" and your maintaining this courtesy, the image that is being implanted in the jury's mind is that there is a controversy between "Mary" and "Mr. Jones."

The defense lawyer representing the "Fast-Way Taxi Cab Company, Inc.," will have some difficulty in personalizing his corporate client. If the driver of the taxi cab is also named as a party defendant, then the suggested procedure is to try to create a personal relationship between the driver and the jury. By referring to "our driver, John," the jury can identify with a live person who is seated right in the courtroom. If John happens to be a likeable, personable chap, they may think of that party to the lawsuit as "John."

However, care should be taken not to over-do personalization. The reference to your client should be with a natural, matter-of-fact manner so that the jurors will not be aware that you are deliberately creating a personal relationship between them and your client.

Explain the Reason for Questions

It must be remembered that this is an experience unlike any other experience a novice juror has ever had, or is likely ever to have. He must submit to personal questions and demands for promises in the presence of a considerable number of strangers. The courtroom itself is constructed in such a way as to create a mood of veneration. The judge is melodramatically elevated above everyone else in the courtroom. He wears black robes and sits behind a massive bench. Lawyers sit at tables staring at jurors intently as they answer questions. Prior to this, they were marched into the courtroom like an army platoon with a bailiff in charge. To top it all off, they were sworn to truthfully answer the questions which are about to be asked and they must suffer the indignities of highly personal questions. Any benignity or warmth at this point can bring forth a feeling of gratitude. The following should be routinely covered:

Q. You understand, Mr. Jones, that it is necessary that we ask questions touching upon your qualifications to serve as a juror in this case.

A. Yes.

Q. And, I'm sure you understand that these questions are not asked to satisfy a personal curiosity, but merely asked in an effort for us to determine if there is anything in a juror's background or experiences in life that might affect his fairness and impartiality to both sides.

A. I understand.

It may be necessary to inquire into an area in which he is quite sensitive and he may resent you for it. An explanation for the questioning doesn't mean that he will not continue to resent you, but you may have softened, if not completely eliminated, his resentment by apologetically explaining the reasons for your questions.

Don't Say "Hello"

After a great deal of effort is made toward building up a rapport between yourself and the jury as well as the client, a simple precaution should be taken in order that it not all be knocked down like a deck of cards merely because you did not nod or say "Hello" to a juror in the hallway or in a restaurant the following day. He may well interpret your failure to acknowledge him or initiate an exchange of greetings as an insult and penalize you for it. This failure on your part could be because of inadvertence or it may be deliberate because you were afraid it could be interpreted as an attempt to court favor with him.

This potential problem can easily be avoided by stating the following on the *voir dire* examination:

Q. I'm certain that you folks understand that under the Rules of Court we lawyers are not permitted to talk to any members of the jury. If we should happen to meet you from time to time outside of the courtroom, I take it that you will not consider it to be a personal affront if neither my opponent nor I speak to you. (There should be a warm smile on the face of the lawyer as this statement is made in order that he does not appear to be a "stuffed shirt.")

Ulterior Motives in Excusing a Juror

In those states where a peremptory challenge must be made in the presence of all the jurors, quite often it is desirable to invent some reason that is acceptable to the remaining jurors so as not to antagonize them. If a juror, by reason of his intelligence, experience, or background makes an apparently good juror and is well liked by the other jurors, it may seem strange to them that one with such obvious capabilities is not wanted by the lawyer who rejects him. There can be any one of a number of reactions in the minds of the remaining jurors. Perhaps the lawyer doesn't want intelligent jurors so he can "pull the wool over their eyes." Perhaps he doesn't want a juror who has experience in engineering and can see the weaknesses in the case. Worse yet, possibly there was a warm relationship between the rejected juror and one or two of the surviving jurors who will resent and possibly "hold it against" the rejecting lawyer.

If the rejected juror has been in a similar accident, or perhaps if some member of his family has had a similar injury or has been a party to a lawsuit, then this can be the ostensible reason for excusing him. A rejection under these circumstances will be readily understood and accepted by the balance of the jurors. To use an example, in defending an action brought by the parent of an injured child the defense lawyer would certainly prefer to have childless jurors. In excusing a mother with small children, he might imply that the reason for such dismissal is that she does not drive an automobile.

In those states that carefully guard the fact that the defendant has liability insurance, many plaintiff's attorneys excuse a person employed in a claims department of an insurance company and do not hide the fact that this is the reason they are excusing him. In those states that have adopted the position that the existence of insurance should be kept from the jury, invariably there will be a good deal of case law describing the degree of "hinting" as to the existence or nonexistence of liability insurance permitted by the lawyers for the plaintiff or defendant. It will be error if, in the opinion of the reviewing court, the suggestions were sufficiently strong enough that the jury "caught the hint." Therefore, it becomes necessary in many instances for a lawyer to practice subterfuge or downright deceit in attempting to convey indirectly the existence of insurance or the lack of it. An example of the game played by the defense lawyer is as follows:

Q. Now, in deciding the issues in this case, Mr. Smith, do you understand that there are only two parties to this lawsuit?

Q. The plaintiff has an interest in this lawsuit and certainly my client, John, has an interest in this lawsuit. Do you feel that you can be fair to both sides?

Q. If you were being sued and were defending yourself, would you want someone to decide your case who has the same frame of mind that you have right now?

As can be seen from these questions, the defense lawyer is subtly attempting to convey an impression that the defendant does not have liability insurance. The defense lawyer was the first to embark on this little "game." Now the plaintiff's lawyer feels compelled to do some "hinting" himself in an effort to let the jury know that there is liability insurance. Regardless of which one put the "game" into motion, both will now find it necessary to "hint" within the permissible bounds as set out by their own case law. In spite of everything said to the contrary, neither of these lawyers would feel secure if his opponent clearly left the jury with the impression that there was or was not liability insurance. Therefore, the trial lawyer who really has no stomach for the "game of deceit" will often feel compelled to enter into it as a precautionary step.

All of this Machiavellianism is in spite of the rule that fundamentally the *voir dire* examination should be conducted in good faith—not for the purpose of creating a false impression or of improperly conveying information that is clearly inadmissible. Whether this is a deliberate attempt on the part of the examiner or a good-faith inquiry is a "state of mind," and, therefore, it is not easily identified. I must allow that in those situations in which the lawyer is representing a severely injured plaintiff seeking substantial damages, he must be sorely tempted to let the jury know that the defendant factory worker, who earns $100 a week and has five children, did, in fact, carry liability insurance at the time of the accident. While again, the purpose of this book is not to expound on the writer's personal feelings, I cannot help but say in passing that in my judgment the existence or nonexistence of liability insurance should be made known to the jury. This would eliminate the need for subterfuge. Also, studies have established that in those states permitting the jury to know the "big secret," the size of judgments has not been materially affected. If there is an effect on jury verdicts, it is insignificant. In addition, it is more desirable for the insurance companies to adjust their rates, if necessary, rather than have lawyers engage in the "practice of deceit." It is an ironic twist because of this rule that success can come to those who lack integrity rather than to those possessing it.

There will be those instances in which a witness will blurt out "the insurance adjuster came to my house . . . ," or "he said he didn't have any insurance . . . ." Here again the test is whether this was sufficient to preclude the donee of such a remark from having a fair trial. There have been trials where I have felt quite certain that this "inadvertent" statement was deliberately made. The lawyer recipient of whatever prejudice may have been created by such a statement should not highlight it by immediately jumping up and demanding a mistrial. The better approach is to casually and quietly invent a reason for a conference in chambers. It can then be argued in seclusion without fear of creating further damage. If the statement made by the witness was sufficient to declare a mistrial and the motion is denied, you will have quietly made a record in the event that there is an adverse verdict without letting the jury know how much the punch hurt.

Indoctrinating the Panel

It is a good idea to address yourself to the entire panel after you have pretty well determined that you will accept them. The reason for this is that the balance of the *voir dire* examination is not really an examination at all—it is the commitment and indoctrination stage. Further analysis of each juror is not necessary. Searching questions have brought forth information which has, in good part, helped you to form an opinion as to the desirability of each juror. It is at this point, then, that you should strive to influence them to your side of the case and draw expressions of fidelity from them.

This can more effectively be done in panels of four rather than talking to each juror individually. The repetition would become not only tedious, but offensive. When you have arrived at this stage of the *voir dire* examination, you can commence by saying: "Now, I would like to address myself collectively to the four of you." Then you can proceed with the general commitments or perhaps with necessary tailor-made commitments peculiar to your case. An example of this might be a child dart-out case wherein the plaintiff's lawyer would want the jury to promise him that they would follow the law relative to the degree of care required of children. An example of this group of commitments and indoctrination is as follows:

Q. You folks understand that in the trial of a lawsuit there is a division of labor between the jury and the judge; that is, the jury decides the facts in the case and the judge decides what law is applicable to the case. Do you all understand that function? (There should be a nodding of the heads and perhaps an audible "yes" from each member of the panel. A positive reaction should be received from each member of the four. If one of the members of the panel neither nods in agreement nor makes an audible sound indicating an agreement or understanding, then that particular juror should be specifically asked if he understands or agrees. If there is any hesitancy or reluctance to give a comment, it should be followed up until the questioner either gets a positive commitment or the juror disqualifies himself.)

Q. In other words, the jury is the sole judge of the facts and His Honor is the sole judge of the law. After you have heard all of the evidence, His Honor will instruct you as to what the applicable law is in this case. Will you all agree that you will follow that law?

Q. As Americans, we all have the right, of course, to disagree with the law, but if we accept the responsibilities to serve as jurors, then we must follow the law. Will you follow the law even though your idea of what the law ought to be is different than what His Honor tells you it is?

Q. You understand that if juries disregard the law and decide a case irrespective of the law, then our jury system as we know it would cease to exist. Do you agree with that? Then, as the four of you sit there now, can each and every one of you assure me that you will follow the law that His Honor instructs you?

During closing arguments you can then remind the jury that each and every one of them assured you before they were selected to serve as jurors that they would follow the law. *"It was based upon that promise that you were accepted as jurors in the case."* After setting the stage with the *voir dire* examination and following up with a reminder of it during closing arguments, you can now most effectively anticipate the instructions of law. When the trial judge, after closing arguments, reads the law, the jurors should be properly prepared to discharge their sworn duty even though their natural inclination might be to enter a verdict which is the opposite of what they have been forced to do by this polite but firm reminder of what their sworn duty is as jurors. In those states in which the law is read to the jury before the closing arguments, the argument can be equally as effective by directing the jury's attention to the law relied upon and reminding them of their sworn duty.

This argument, of course, is more appropriate with defense tactics because of natural sympathy and a desire to help an injured person. This is especially true when the plaintiff is personable and has undergone great hardships as a result of his injuries. If, in addition, the defendant is a target defendant, such as a taxicab company, and there is little evidence of wrongdoing, the defense lawyer should remind the jury that it is their sworn duty to find his client "not guilty" if the plaintiff fails to prove that the defendant was negligent. There may be an inner struggle in the minds of the jurors. On one side, they want to follow their natural sympathies. On the other side, they want to perform their sworn duty as they promised they would do. It will make a powerful impression when they are reminded during closing arguments of their promise made under oath. In hard cases, the defense lawyer may not always force a "not guilty" from a jury, but this type of reminder can go a long way toward holding down the amount of the verdict.

There will be situations in which the plaintiff can use this type of argument to his advantage. An example of this would be a case in which contributory negligence is not chargeable to a plaintiff who was a passenger in an automobile which collided with a car driven by the defendant. If the evidence clearly establishes that both drivers failed to stop at a stop sign, then clearly as to each driver, there would be a "Mexican standoff." Yet, if the jury is made to understand that under the law the negligence of the driver is not imputed to the passenger, then the plaintiff will receive a full verdict in spite of natural feelings to the contrary.

Watch Your Peremptory Challenges

Keep track of your challenges. If your opponent has been saving his while you have been using yours, it's possible that he may be scheming to "pack" the last panel. At the same time that you are sizing up the jury you should have one eye on the reserves ready to fill the vacant chairs. For example, assume for one reason or another that both you and your opponent know that older men would be preferable as jurors for your side of the case. Assume further that while you are in the process of selecting your first panel, you see that the last panel in the jury box answers your needs because there are four elderly men. At the same time, you see that the reserve jurors in the back of the room are practically all young women except for two or three older men. With an opponent saving his challenges, it isn't difficult to anticipate that he may attempt to "pack" the last panel. At this point you should take a hard look at the first two panels with a view toward keeping them unless they are clearly undesirable. With the entire last panel excused, you could find yourself in a most uncomfortable position of having two or three dangerous jurors move into the box and being helpless to do anything about it. If, on the other hand, the reserve forces should appear to be what you want because they are practically all older men, you may want to use up your challenges early by getting rid of questionable jurors and stocking the first two panels with older men. There are numerous possibilities that can arise, depending upon the set of facts with which you find yourself working.

It is advisable to keep one reserve challenge tucked away to be used only in case of an emergency. There is the distinct danger that after all of your challenges are gone, a strong, forceful juror may step into the box who will be your most dangerous antagonist. If he is educated, articulate, and capable of influencing people and, together with all these attributes, is strongly in favor of the other side, your "boat has sprung a leak." In order to more graphically illustrate how this could be a very real problem, imagine how perplexed a plaintiff's attorney would be in a physician malpractice case if one of the jurors turns out to be a doctor's wife—a woman well respected and admired in the community who has strong feelings against malpractice cases. Perhaps there have been annoying and groundless claims presented against her husband in the past. If she is antagonistic toward malpractice claims because of conversations with and exposure to doctors, she not only will be prejudiced, but she undoubtedly will be influential with the jury. Another example is the defense lawyer who may be out of challenges and then finds that the last juror suffered a lesser injury than the plaintiff and received a substantial settlement for an accident identical to the one the lawyer is defending. Another example is the plaintiff's attorney, who, in a suit brought against a landlord, finds that the last juror is a landlord who has had numerous claims brought against him by tenants and who feels quite certain that these claims are unfair and groundless. A final example might be a mother whose son is a dedicated plaintiff's personal injury lawyer and she feels, first of all, that there is always liability insurance in these cases, and secondly, that insurance companies are always stalling.

COMMITMENTS

Commitment to Duty

An important function while talking to the jurors is to get each to pledge himself on specific points. The jurors have been sworn to answer truthfully all questions put to them by court or counsel. As I mentioned, a reminder of this during summation can invoke a strong duty or contract on the part of those who feel a strong moral obligation to "live up to their word." Most people enter the jury box with a strong desire to discharge their function as jurors honorably and with fairness to both sides. With this noble attitude coupled with

the austerity of the courtroom, these people are psychologically prepared to enter a verdict in spite of their natural prejudices or sympathies. This is especially true in the beginning days of their tour of
duty. After they have decided a few cases, they become more accustomed to their surroundings, lose some of their laudable principles,
and are less apt to be held in line because of their natural feelings to
the contrary.

In addition to special problems in his case, the plaintiff's lawyer
can get commitments on general points such as a promise that they
will bring in a verdict for the plaintiff if he establishes his case by
a greater weight of the evidence; that they will not hesitate to
award substantial damages if the evidence warrants it; that they will
agree to compensate the plaintiff for pain and suffering. The defense
lawyer, on the other hand, can require them to promise and commit
themselves to him that they will not let their natural sympathies
influence their verdict; that if the plaintiff fails to prove his case as
required by the law, that they will not hesitate to find his client "not
guilty"; or commitments on any special problems that he is facing.

When the jury is reminded by the defense lawyer during closing
arguments, "folks, you will recall that at the outset I asked each and
every one of you if you would enter a verdict in favor of John if the
plaintiff failed to prove his case by a greater weight of the evidence
and you assured me that you would. You also assured me that you
would do this in spite of your natural feelings of sympathy for the
plaintiff, just as anyone feels sorry for a person who has been injured,
and I am sure that we all feel sorry for the plaintiff for the injuries
he has sustained. However, before he can collect money for these
injuries, the law requires that he must prove that he is entitled to
damages from John. I now remind you folks again of your promise
and assurance to me. . . ." The promises that they made will mean a
great deal to them if sufficient groundwork is laid during the *voir dire*.

Commitment to Set Aside Prejudice

The *voir dire* examination is a good time to prepare the jury for
any problem that your case may have. If the client has a liability
such as an irritating speaking voice, a speech impediment, a nervous
twitch, facial disfigurement, or any other obvious problem, it should
be commented upon to meet the needs. To illustrate this, take the
client who has a heavy, foreign accent. It should be kept in mind that
there are some jurors who resent recent immigrants. An attitude
such as, "these foreigners come over here and figure they'll get rich
by suing an American . . . ," or "the first thing they do when they
get off the boat is buy a car, and the second thing they do is to run

somebody down. . . ." There are people who just plain do not like recent immigrants and particularly those who speak poor English. The *voir dire* examination should prepare the jury by telling them that one of the parties has not lived in this country long and does speak with an accent. There should also be a commitment received from the jurors concerning these facts. An example of receiving commitments from a panel is as follows:

Q. My client, Jesus Gonzalez, moved to this country a short time ago. Do you feel that because of this there would be any reason that you could not give him just as fair a trial as any other American?

Q. Now, it's possible, and I'm sure it's true, that there are jurors who do harbor prejudices against recent immigrants to a country. However, when people accept the responsibility to serve as jurors, I believe that they will decide a case fairly and squarely and set aside any feelings that they may have. The fact that my client comes from Mexico doesn't start him out at a disadvantage; does it?

Q. Our jury system as we know it would suffer if juries had favorites; isn't that so?

Q. It would, therefore, follow that pure justice should concern itself only with the evidence and with the jury calling the shots fairly and squarely. Do you folks agree?

Arthur Helps must have had juries in mind when he said: "Tolerance is the only real test of civilization."

Q. As you folks sit there now, do you know of any reason why my client cannot receive a fair trial?

Q. In other words, if any one of you folks were a party to this lawsuit, would you want someone to decide your case who has the same frame of mind as you do right now?

Q. Will you all assure me here and now that you will give this man a fair trial?

The same thing holds true with any minority group. For example, if you represent a Negro, an Indian, or an Oriental, you should insist that each juror commit himself by an unhesitating, unqualified "yes" or a nod of the head that he or she will give your client just as fair a trial as any other person.

The lawyer representing the "Fast-Way Taxi Cab Company, Inc." has the same type of problem. It isn't going to help this lawyer by remaining silent on the subject in hopes that it really isn't in the

minds of the jury and that perhaps there really isn't any prejudice
against his client. By remaining silent, he reasons he will not create
a prejudice that might not be there. He is only fooling himself since
there will always be a great deal of animosity against this type of
target defendant. The same thing is true with the trucks that deliver
newspapers throughout the big cities. These drivers have a tight
schedule to meet and often drive rapidly. Every motorist who has
driven through a big city knows this to be a fact. Because of past
experience in being "cut off" by newspaper trucks and taxicabs, or
some other frightening or irritating experience, there will be a natural
tendency to associate this type of driving in the case they are about
to decide. If a juror is subconsciously in this frame of mind, then it
is better that this fact be brought to his conscious mind so that he
can then control it better. He can then make an effort to consciously
not let it dominate his verdict.

A failure to clear the air will leave the unspoken thought hang-
ing over the courtroom like a heavy mist. A party to a motor vehicle
collision who was driving a motorcycle has at least one strike against
him—and probably two. It is a generally accepted feeling that motorcycles are dangerous and that anyone driving one should be prepared
to assume the risk if he is injured. Further, he ought to assume liability
if he injures someone else. People must, therefore, be literally torn
away from their fixed feelings. The examiner, by accepting the fact
that there is a prejudice, might create a better rapport between himself and the jury. He has a better chance to direct their thinking into
the proper channel by admitting to the jury during the *voir dire* examination that he, too, is prejudiced against motorcycles. An example
of this *voir dire* indoctrination to a panel is as follows:

Q. Now, the evidence will establish that my client was driving a
motorcycle. Quite frankly, I'm prejudiced to some extent against
motorcycles and I'd be surprised if you folks were not also—am
I right? If I were asked to sit on a jury to judge the facts,
admittedly it would be difficult for me to give a motorcycle
driver a fair trial, and yet that's precisely what you folks must
do. Do you feel that you can give my client, John, a fair trial?

Q. Certainly, we would all agree that the driver of a motorcycle
should observe the rules of traffic just as the driver of an automobile should observe the same rules. By the same token, the
driver of a motorcycle owes a duty of care to other motorists not
to injure them and the driver of an automobile owes that same
degree of care to a motorcycle driver, isn't that correct?

Q. That doesn't give him any special privileges merely because he is driving the car and the other person is driving a motorcycle; does it?

Q. You don't feel that merely because one of the parties to this occurrence was driving a motorcycle, that by that fact alone, he was responsible; do you?

Q. You would have to hear the evidence, wouldn't you, in order to make a determination as to where the fault lies in this occurrence; isn't that correct?

Q. If the evidence established that John was careful while driving his motorcycle and that this collision resulted from the negligence of the defendant, would you have any hesitancy in finding in favor of John?

Q. As you folks sit there, you may have feelings against motorcycles, but let me ask you here and now, while you are under oath, can you set aside any prejudicial feelings that you may have concerning motorcycles and decide this case solely on the evidence?

Q. In other words, can you decide this case with the same impartiality as you would decide a case where there were two automobiles involved instead of one automobile and one motorcycle, as in this instance?

Q. Will each and every one of you assure me that if you are selected to serve as jurors in this case, John will receive a fair trial in your hands?

Disclose the Weaknesses at Once

When you have explosive material in your case such as a client who has been convicted of a felony, who was driving under the influence of alcohol at the time of the accident, or some other dangerous point, it should be brought out as quickly as possible with the very first juror. The jury is going to be unquestionably shocked by this information and you can be quite sure that there will be some prejudice against your client. Nothing, however, softens the blow so much as the guilty party confessing his sins. As evidence of this, we have only to search our own memories to recall the impressions that were created in our own minds when we learned of the indiscretion of a person through others (as opposed to learning it from the person himself). No amount of wishful thinking will prevent a jury from learning of it. The inclination is to avoid talking about it because of the obvious prejudice that is going to be created against your client. By confessing, if nothing else, the jury cannot accuse you of being less than sincere and candid with them. This certainly would not be true if you gave the other lawyer the opportunity to disclose this information. To permit the other lawyer to enlighten the jury as to substantial unsavory facts would be tantamount to handing your opponent a bomb so that he can blow you up.

If you represent a man who previously was convicted of a felony there is no question that every juror will be prejudiced against your client. The degree of prejudice will vary from juror to juror. Some jurors will experience a mild prejudice, while others will be so affected that they will want to not only find against him, but make an effort to persuade their fellow jurors to do the same. You will not necessarily be able to "weed out" jurors who have this strong prejudice. Therefore, it is necessary to silence those highly prejudiced jurors and prevent them from spewing forth their hatred while deliberating and thereby contaminating the other jurors. Each juror should be forced to audibly agree that he will decide the case solely on the evidence and the law; that he will not be influenced or attempt to influence his fellow jurors to hold against your client because of the information you have just volunteered. The reason that he is restrained to some degree is because there will be a strong reluctance to "break his promise" in the presence of his fellow jurors. An oath in open court is a hard thing to forget after he has been reminded of it during the closing argument. Even though he may have a strong tendency to vote in line with his prejudice and may do so, his promise to you will help your side of the case by at least partially silencing him on the very thing that disturbs him so much. This will prevent some of the poison from spreading to the other jurors. By removing some of the powder from the bomb, it does not mean that you have eliminated a potentially lethal weapon that can destroy your case. However, you have at least reduced its potency so that perhaps your case can survive the blast.

I recall a case in which I represented a Negro plaintiff who had been convicted of murder and was serving a sentence in an Illinois prison. After serving some years, he was brought to the county jail to appear before the trial judge on a post-conviction hearing in an effort to obtain a new trial. In the process of transferring him from the courthouse back to the county jail in a paddy wagon, there was an intersection collision which resulted in a compound fracture to his leg. The only element of damage was the injury itself, since we did not have any medical bills—the care being provided by the state—and any evidence as to loss of income would have put me in the cell next to his. The problem that perplexed us was how an all-white jury would treat a convicted Negro murderer in the midst of the Negro Civil Rights marches in Chicago which were creating much adverse pub-

licity on a most controversial issue. We would hardly claim that he
was a useful, tax-paying member of society. Any small settlement
offer would have been tempting, but, as it turned out, we were
fortunate in letting the jury decide the issues because they gave us a
verdict of $44,500.

The *voir dire* examination with the first juror got into the problem
as quickly as possible as follows:

Q. Now, Mrs. White, I'm going to tell you something straight from
the shoulder. Walter was convicted of murder. Have you ever
known a convicted murderer?

A. No.

Q. Does the information which I have just given you so completely
shock you that you feel that you would rather not sit as a juror
on this case?

A. I don't think so.

Q. Do you feel that in spite of what I've just told you that you can
give Walter a fair trial?

A. I think so.

Q. It would be foolish of me to ask you to put this information out
of your mind when you consider your verdict. In spite of this,
do you feel that you can give substantial justice to both sides?

A. Yes.

Q. In other words, as you sit there now, you feel that you can decide
the issues in this case irrespective of any other facts outside of
this case?

A. Yes.

Q. This information which I have just given you isn't going to
disturb you so much that you would have it influence your decision?

A. No.

Q. You understand that the trial of a lawsuit is not a personality
contest where the jury decides for the person that they like
the most?

A. Yes.

Q. Certainly, if that were so, then we would not have equal justice
before the Bar; isn't that right?

A. Yes.

Q. I certainly wouldn't ask you to condone or even forgive Walter
for the crime that he has committed, but can you assure me that
Walter will receive a fair and impartial trial in your hands?

A. Yes.

Q. You won't try him again for this crime, will you? In other words, you are only going to decide the facts in this case?

A. Yes.

Q. And there isn't anything locked away in the deep crevices of your mind that you feel either side should know that might affect your fairness and impartiality in deciding this case?

A. No.

Q. Needless to say, you certainly would not try to influence your fellow jurors or try to poison their minds against Walter because of this fact we just discussed.

A. No.

Q. And would you be influenced if any other juror improperly tried to influence you against Walter because of this fact that has nothing to do with the case you will be asked to decide?

A. No.

Q. And if any juror violated his promise under oath and attempted to influence you against Walter because of his past indiscretion, you would recognize that juror for what he was, correct?

A. Yes.

Q. I am sure you want to discharge your sworn duty as a juror in accordance with the high standards that the law imposes on you.

A. Yes.

Q. And, once again, you can assure me that if we accept you as a juror in this case, that you will give Walter a fair trial.

A. Yes.

The promise and commitment from each juror that he will not hold a past indiscretion against your client is of little value unless he is reminded of his promise during closing arguments.

Don't Let Them Lean Too Far to Be Fair

If your opponent has had the jury commit themselves strongly that they will give his client a fair trial in spite of the natural feelings they may have against cab drivers, motorcycle drivers, parking lot attendants, bus drivers, truck drivers, drunken drivers, youthful drivers, drivers of advanced age, women drivers, ambulance drivers, fire truck drivers, police car drivers, delivery drivers, drivers with vision in only one eye, brand-new drivers, or other such problem cases, it is now possible that they will lean so far to show their fairness that they will literally lean in the direction of your opponent. Jurors who take their job quite seriously, and a large percentage answer this description, may try too hard to discharge their duty in not letting natural prejudices interfere with their verdict. Under these circumstances, Samuel Johnson summed up your feelings very nicely when he said: "I like a good hater." A suggested *voir dire* to cover this situation is as follows:

Q. You folks indicated to the defendant's lawyer that you will give his client a fair trial in spite of the fact that he was driving a motorcycle at the time of the occurrence. Now, in your effort to be fair to the defendant, I take it that you are not going to lean so far in his direction that you will not be completely objective and thereby not be completely fair to John. You won't do that; will you?

Q. The plaintiff is entitled to exactly the same consideration that you give the defendant. Will you call the shots exactly as you see them, regardless of any other consideration?

Q. People will differ as to their feelings about motorcycles, but certainly we all will agree that a motorcycle driver owes other people the same duty not to injure them as any other motor vehicle driver; isn't that correct?

Q. Will each and every one of you assure me that you will not set aside your experiences in the ordinary affairs of life during the entire time that you serve as jurors in this case? I guess that's just another way of asking, will you use your good "common sense" and will you give us the benefit of your experiences?

Q. I take it that if the evidence indicates that the defendant was negligent or careless while he was driving his motorcycle that you will call that shot just as you see it.

Don't Let the Opponent's Personality Win the Lawsuit

There will be those situations in which the other party is bubbling over with personality and charm, perhaps even contrasting to the complaining, sour type of personality which you represent. In defense of a person who has driven a taxicab, bus, or truck in a large city for a number of years—it could be that the public has made a snarling animal out of the man. Just to talk about traffic disputes with him is comparable to jabbing an exposed raw nerve. If the facts are such that the defendant should receive the verdict, then commitments should be obtained to help stop the plaintiff from winning the lawsuit by winning a personality contest and capitalizing on prejudice.

Q. You understand, of course, that lawsuits are determined by the evidence that is presented?

Q. An unfortunate manner of expression, "to win a lawsuit," has been used. You understand, Mrs. Jones, that we don't "win" lawsuits since that would imply a game of chance?

Q. If lawsuits were "won," then there wouldn't be any need in asking this jury to decide this case, and we lawyers could go out in the hallway and toss a coin to determine the outcome. As you sit there now, do you feel that you can decide this case solely on the evidence and law?

Q. Just because the plaintiff claims we did something wrong doesn't make it so; does it?

Q. And you will require that he prove these charges?

Q. And the outcome of this lawsuit will not depend upon the flip of a coin, but upon hard facts that establish where the truth lies?

Q. Because you might have a tendency to like one of the parties for one reason or another, this wouldn't cause you to enter a verdict in favor of him even though the evidence indicated otherwise; would it?

Q. And this would also apply to a situation where you might not like one of the parties to a lawsuit. This would not prevent you from finding in his favor if, under the facts, he was entitled to a verdict; would it?

Q. In other words, the outcome of this case will not be decided upon a popularity contest; will it?

Q. Certainly, you would all agree that we would not want lawsuits determined by which one was the most handsome—or on which one had the best personality. Our sense of justice would be repelled at such a suggestion, correct?

Q. Will you folks assure me that if the evidence indicates that my client is entitled to receive a verdict that you will find in his favor even though you may not like him personally?

Q. And will you just as candidly assure me that you will not enter a verdict for the other side merely because he's a nice, likeable person, when the evidence indicates that my client is entitled to the verdict?

Q. Then I take it that you folks are all assuring me that my client, Tom, will receive a fair trial in your hands and that this is not going to be a personality contest?

When the Trial Judge Is a Handicap

There are situations when, for one reason or another, the trial judge is a liability to the lawyer. Every trial lawyer has had the unhappy experience of trying a lawsuit before an incompetent judge. Some of the common characteristics found in unqualified judges are: difficulty in understanding the law, arrogance, pomposity, vacillation in making rulings, feeblemindedness, favoritism toward a lawyer, inability to refrain from becoming a partisan, unpleasant or antagonistic attitude toward a lawyer or party which is apparent to the jury, and other such characteristics.

These problems are more often found where the judiciary is closely tied in with politics. For that reason the judicial candidate is slated primarily as a reward for service or a campaign contribution to the party. If the area is completely dominated by one political party so that the nomination is the equivalent to being elected, it will be found that even less consideration is given to judicial qualifications in handing out "judgeships" as political plums to faithful members of the party. Be that as it may, this sad commentary on our judicial system is a fact in many counties, and the trial lawyer must be called upon to take this into consideration in his battle to persuade the jury. It must be remembered that jurors are generally not aware of this method of judicial selection and are quite often under the impression that judges are selected primarily because of their legal ability.

It will be necessary for the trial lawyer to anticipate these problems and prepare the jury for this eventuality during the *voir dire* examination. If experience has taught the advocate that he can expect the trial judge, for example, to favor his opponent for one reason or another, and that the judge will reflect this attitude in the presence of the jury, this will be a persuasive benefit to the opposition. The jury will often interpret the court's apparent favoritism to mean that he feels the other lawyer has the meritorious case. The degree of the court's persuasiveness with the jury will, of course, depend on the image he projects during the entire trial. If he obviously lacks admirable qualities then his persuasiveness will be minimal. If, on the other hand, he projects a seemingly pleasant, juridical temperament except for his obvious dislike for one lawyer or his case, this will, without a doubt, have an adverse effect on the lawyer who does not seem to enjoy the approval of the court. If the lawyer is forced to try a lawsuit under these conditions, then he must prepare the jury so that they will be expecting it. An example of such a *voir dire* examination to a panel is as follows:

Q. Now, I'm sure that you folks all know that the trial of a lawsuit is an adversary system. That is, it's a system where each lawyer represents one side of the lawsuit and we are adverse to each other. Certainly you're all familiar with that fact?

Q. There is, of course, a division of labor between the jury and the
    judge. The function of the judge is to decide the law which is
    applicable to this case and the function of the jury is to decide
    the facts. Do each of you feel that you can decide this case solely
    on the evidence and in accordance with the applicable law?

Q. I am sure that you will all agree that you will follow the instruc-
    tions of law that will be given to you by the judge at a later pro-
    ceeding of this trial?

Q. The function of the judge is, of course, to give the jury instruc-
    tions of law that are applicable to this particular case and to rule
    on the admissibility of evidence and other points of law. Do each
    of you feel that you can discharge your duty as a decider of the
    facts, irrespective of how anyone else who is not a member of
    the jury may feel this case should be decided?

Q. And that, of course, would include the judge; wouldn't it?

Q. Of course, the judge in this case is neutral and I am sure that
    he will not in any way, directly or indirectly, show any favoritism
    to either side or to either of the lawyers. But even if you thought
    he favored one side or the other, and I'm sure he would not, this
    wouldn't cause you to feel that the side you thought he favored
    must be the correct side; would it?

Q. For such a thing to happen would not only be unfair if the judge
    deliberately did it, but it would be just as unfair if the jury were
    permitted to let their judgment be influenced by the judge;
    wouldn't that be correct?

Q. I am certain that you would agree that Mary is entitled to have
    her case decided by you folks and that it would not be fair if the
    jury's judgment was affected by the attitude of a judge as to
    how he thought the case ought to be decided.

Q. If a jury permitted itself to be influenced by anyone—no matter
    how important—so that another person's judgment were sub-
    stituted for the judgment of the jury, then our jury system as
    we know it would be worthless; would you agree?

Q. Then, as you folks sit there now, will you each assure me that
    you will decide this case on the evidence and not permit your
    judgment to be influenced by the attitude of the judge toward
    either side of this lawsuit? And can you also assure me that you
    will give my client, Mary, a fair trial?

Q. I'm sure that you understand that all Mary wants, as does the
    other party to this lawsuit, is the benefit of your judgment as
    the sole judges of the facts.

Q. You also understand, of course, that the trial of a lawsuit is not
a personality contest between the lawyers or the parties to the
lawsuit, or for that matter, a question of whom the judge likes or
dislikes; isn't that correct?

Q. And you have no quarrel with the concept that the jury should
find on the side of the case where the truth is found, regardless
of whom they may like or dislike? Or whom they may think the
judge likes or dislikes?

Q. I take it that we can count on you folks to find on the side of
truth and justice, regardless of whom it may hurt or help? (At
this point, each member of the panel should be addressed by
name and asked specifically if he or she will decide this case on
the evidence, and the evidence alone.)

The trial judge may take it upon himself to stop this line of
questioning or sustain an objection by your opponent. However, the
inquiry is proper and the examiner is getting at the very heart of
what we expect of our jury trial system. Each side to a lawsuit is entitled
to have the jury decide the facts of the case without influence from the trial
judge. The purpose in having the jury decide the facts is to avoid the very
thing that the trial judge would attempt to do in curtailing this examination, only to follow it up with partisan efforts to influence the jury.
As much as possible should be done, however, to obtain commitments from the jurors. It might well be that in attempting to obtain
these commitments while struggling with a pugnacious judge, the
jury will sense the court's hostile conduct and take the side of the
"underdog." Thoughtful care should be taken in making a record
so that a reviewing court can get, as nearly as possible, an accurate
picture regarding the tactics used by an offending trial judge in the
presence of the jury. When the trial judge displays grimaces or assumes a look of disbelief or disgust at various times, then this should
be made a part of the record whenever committed by describing
such conduct in the form of a motion for a new trial. There will
always be an extremely small minority of trial judges who, by one
means or another, will attempt to influence the jury's verdict. Efforts
should be made to root out this evil, but the trial lawyer must also
accept the fact that it does exist just as incompetence will be found
in every walk of life.

Keep in mind that after you have let the jury know the shape
of things to come, you will have to be on your best behavior during
the entire course of the trial. An unpleasant demeanor or less than
fair tactics used later by the lawyer obtaining these commitments

will only serve to hurt his image. It may give a justifiable reason, in the minds of the jury, for the judge to show favoritism.

"Judges are but men, and are swayed like other men by vehement prejudices. This is corruption in reality, give it whatever other name you please."—David Dudley Field.

Commitment to Substantial Verdict

On those occasions when the plaintiff's lawyer is fortunate enough to have a lawsuit asking substantial damages and can logically anticipate a large amount if he gets the verdict, then the jury should be committed to a position that it will render a substantial verdict if the evidence warrants it.

There are always some people who will not award money commensurate with the damages if it would mean that in order to do so they would have to sign a verdict giving the plaintiff a large amount of money. The reasons for this attitude are varied. Perhaps there is a feeling that no one should receive a large amount of money simply because of a serious injury. After all, the money will not restore the leg. Or perhaps there is a feeling that money should be earned and saved, and that this method would be too easy for the plaintiff; or that a large verdict might cripple or create a hardship upon the defendant; or that there should be no compensation for pain and suffering; or simply that the whole idea of money damages is wrong and a lawsuit is merely a means of profiting at someone else's expense. One dogmatic and determined juror answering this description can substantially hold down the verdict. It, therefore, behooves the plaintiff's lawyer to make an effort to identify this person and root him out. Conversely, the defense lawyer would like to recognize him. If he is fortunate enough not to lose him to a peremptory challenge by his opponent, he should flatter him by directing a good part of the argument toward him. This is especially true when the defense lawyer has a case in which the only real issue is the damages. While questioning a panel, if the plaintiff's lawyer detects any hesitancy or reluctance on the part of a juror in agreeing that he will award substantial damages if warranted by the evidence, then that juror should be viewed with suspicion. Consideration should be given to his background and experiences, with a view toward determining if this might account for a hesitating or reluctant attitude. It is possible that follow-up questions will result in this juror's disqualifying himself without the need of exercising a peremptory challenge.

The Outnumbered Lawyer

There are occasions when one side of the table will have two or more lawyers, contrasted with only one lawyer at the other side of the table. Many trial lawyers like to be the solo. They feel that this will give them an advantage because the jury will want to neutralize what appears to be an unfair battle by helping the lawyer who is alone. This lawyer conducting the battle by himself may head up a large firm and have five lawyers working for him, but whenever the jury comes out, he has ordered his assistants away from the counsel table. In this way, he may project an image of a pathetically lonely, but courageous lawyer, battling a group of lawyers who have "ganged up" on him.

This type of handicap will probably not be a factor in a significant case where both sides are obviously well represented. It should not be overlooked, however, that in the spirit of fair play, there is apt to be some helping of the "underdog." For that reason, when the opposition is a lawyer "rowing the boat" by himself, a commitment must be received from the jurors. An example of this follows:

Q. Mr. Smith, I'm sure you understand that your function will be to decide the facts in this case.

Q. And whatever you decide will be based upon the evidence in the form of sworn testimony or exhibits that are permitted into evidence.

Q. You certainly wouldn't permit sympathy, prejudice, or some outside factor to influence your decision.

Q. I am sure that you want your verdict to be on the side of truth and justice regardless of any outside influences.

Q. (Smiling at the juror.) As you can see, there are two lawyers representing Fred Hansen and only one lawyer representing Mr. Black. This isn't going to start Fred off with a disadvantage in your hands; is it?

Q. (Still smiling at the juror.) Then, I take it, sir, that you are not going to feel that in the American spirit of fair play that the other side has a handicap and needs your help.

Q. And, I'm also sure that you would agree that the trial of a lawsuit is not a game of sport where one side wins and the other side loses, but it is a place where the jury makes an effort to find their verdict on the side of truth and justice.

Q. Regardless of how many lawyers may be on one side or the other, your verdict will be on the side of truth regardless of personalities or lawyers.

Q. Will you assure me that your verdict will be on the side of truth and justice alone, and will not be influenced by the number of lawyers on one side or the other?

ANTICIPATED REACTIONS

The Previously Injured Juror

There is quite often a juror or some member of his immediate family who has sustained a rather substantial injury in an accident. This experience will affect this person's objectivity to some extent. No one having undergone this experience can come away from it with the same feeling that he had before the accident. For example, he may have received a serious injury in an automobile collision and employed a lawyer to attempt a collection from the other driver's insurance company. It may have been a long and rocky battle during which time this juror was forced to deplete his savings because of his inability to work and his mounting medical expenses. He may have developed a feeling that insurance companies are unscrupulous and treacherous and do not hesitate to spend a great deal of money to defeat a just claim. Another juror may have been unfortunate enough to have been seriously injured by an uninsured and financially irresponsible motorist. This bitterness in having exhausted his own savings, and perhaps having gone into debt, may be so strong that it would be difficult for him to award damages to someone similarly situated. If a juror received a similar or even more serious injury than the plaintiff and received a sum of money in settlement of this injury, the chances are that this will be the gauge he will use to assess damages. Not only will he use that as a guideline, but he will advise his fellow jurors and may influence them in determining damages. Depending on the amount of money he received, he may be favorable or unfavorable to either side of the case.

Therefore, a certain amount of care should be used to ascertain from this person's background whether his experience has left him favorable or unfavorable to your side of the case. The lawyer should first ascertain if he employed a lawyer. If the answer is "no," then it should be asked if the case was settled to his satisfaction. If the answer is "yes," then it is pretty certain that the other driver's insurance company entered into direct settlement with the juror. This information adds up to a conclusion that the juror probably received a modest amount and will think in those terms. If a juror explains that the other driver did not have insurance and nothing came of it, then this will be a factor to consider in evaluating the juror. From the plaintiff's standpoint, this would be a minus to put on one side of the scale to be weighed against the plusses on the other side. If the juror otherwise seems happy and well adjusted with no apparent bitterness from his experience, he is probably a good risk for the plaintiff. If the juror engaged a lawyer and ultimately received money, and he was satisfied with the results, then the chances are that this is a plaintiff's juror.

There is, of course, another possibility—such as the juror who was involved in an accident and who conspired with a doctor to make it appear that the injuries were worse than they really were in order to obtain a favorable settlement. This person will usually be a hypocrite who will suspect a similar situation and rise up to condemn the plaintiff if the injuries are not objective and obvious.

A Juror Who Was Once a Defendant

The juror who has had a claim or lawsuit brought against him will also have a different feeling because of his experience. Ordinarily, this man should be looked upon as a defendant's juror and he probably is, although this is a risky assumption for the defendant. The defense lawyer should not accept it without some inquiry as to the circumstances surrounding the disposition of this case. The juror might well feel that the other fellow made an attempt to take advantage of his insurance company by filing a false claim or was guilty of exaggerating his injuries. He may even have learned later that his insurance company made a settlement which he felt was outrageous in order to avoid a lawsuit. On the other hand, he could have had an accident where he felt he was completely at fault and expected his insurance company to do the honorable thing and settle with the other party. Instead of settling as he expected, they refused to pay, and the result was a lawsuit in which he was named defendant. This could have resulted in an annoyance to himself and perhaps even some danger with an *ad damnum* in excess of his insurance coverage. As can be seen, it would be an error for a lawyer to come to any conclusion without some examination into the circumstances.

When Opposing Party Projects Poor Image

Sometimes one of the opposition's key witnesses or perhaps even the other party himself may project a repulsive or undesirable image. This could be in the form of any one of a number of undesirable characteristics, such as the "shifty-eyed witness," "the thinker," "the argumentative type," or other such burdensome traits. If it is an obvious personality defect and this information is known by you in advance, it might be well to tell the jury that it is the judge of the truth and to have each promise that if they are accepted as jurors, they will closely observe the demeanor of the witnesses. If you can get the jurors thinking in terms of watching for this "sign," a witness with the unfortunate characteristic of looking down at the floor while on the witness stand will be received in an even more skeptical mood. Another example is the opponent's witness who cannot tell the same story twice. When he gives his estimate of speed or distances, he alters it like the changing winds. A reminder that it is the jury's function to listen attentively to the testimony with a view toward determining its accuracy will serve to highlight the anticipated inconsistencies.

A Juror with Previous Experience

If the prospective jurors have served on juries immediately preceding your case during their tour of duty, then some consideration should be given to this fact. It becomes especially important if they have gone to verdict. For example, I can recall a case a few years ago in a neighboring county in which I represented a plaintiff who admittedly had a good case of liability which was easily established through the occurrence witnesses. The only real issue in the case was the amount of damages and it became necessary that the jury decide this issue since at no time during the trial could we get together on a settlement figure acceptable to both sides. The jury came back with an extremely modest verdict which surprised all of us. In fact, it was small enough that the trial judge indicated that he would be obliged to set it aside, although it was subsequently settled without the need of a new trial. I was at a loss to understand why the verdict amounted to approximately the out-of-pocket expenses, without any apparent consideration being given to the tangible aspects of the case. The puzzle was answered when it was discovered that a week before this same jury decided a case involving an injured man who lost the sight of both eyes, together with other serious and permanent injuries, substantial medical expenses, and loss of income. The liability in this case was nil and the trial judge should have directed a verdict for the defendant at the close of the plaintiff's case, but he did let it go to the jury, who awarded a $1,500 verdict to the plaintiff. The jury had obviously decided that the defendant was not guilty, but they decided to take it upon themselves to give the plaintiff a "little something" to cover the expenses of trial. After giving $1,500 to a plaintiff suffering from injuries of this magnitude, they just simply could not bring themselves to award a proper verdict for my client whose injuries were far less serious.

There can be numerous variations of this type of problem, especially in the smaller counties where the number of prospective jurors is limited in number. Regardless of which party you represent, if the jury has been contaminated by some factor, it could seriously affect the success of your case. Certainly, it would be better to forego a trial with this jury, if possible.

The Minority Juror Identifying with Client

If a lawyer finds himself representing a person who is a member of a clearly identifiable small ethnic group and runs across a person in the jury who is also a member of this group, it is a mistake to accept that juror. Clearly, this person identifies with the client, and may even perhaps be in complete sympathy with him, but the problem is that he will be quite self-conscious of the great similarity between himself and the client. For that reason he will want to demonstrate to his fellow jurors his fairness and impartiality. In his desire to convey this image, he actually leans to the other side and becomes the opponent's juror.

This will be found most noticeably between races when we will have one Negro on a jury who will feel that his fellow white jurors are watching him carefully because one of the parties to the lawsuit is a Negro. The same analogy will hold true with any identifiable group, such as a person speaking with a heavy Greek or German accent, or perhaps just a name, where it is obvious to the juror that he is the only one who closely identifies with a party to the lawsuit. The same thing is true in occupations where one of the parties to the lawsuit has an unusual occupation, such as an airline pilot, a police officer, a perfume salesman, or any other such unusual occupation where the prospective juror is acutely aware of the similarity. To a lesser extent, the same thing is true when there are two such members on the jury because these two are still quite conscious of the fact that they are peculiarly identified with one of the parties. If there is any number more than this, the probability is that they will then rationalize that they are being objective, when, in fact, the loyalties to their own would result in that party's having an advantage.

There is a good chance that your opponent will excuse that solitary juror who identifies with your client. For that reason, hang on to your peremptory challenge until the last minute. There is even a better chance that when your opponent finds a unique juror who closely identified with his client, like most lawyers, he will keep that self-conscious juror and will be quite confident that the juror belongs to him. Given this opportunity, you can even strengthen this juror for you by showing that you have confidence in him and that you will accept him in spite of the fact that the natural inclination would be to let him go. If it is an obvious identity such as a Negro, everyone in the court is keenly aware that one of the parties to the lawsuit is a Negro and that there is only one Negro in the group of prospective jurors. No one is more aware of this fact than the prospective juror who is surrounded by all white jurors and who is being questioned by white lawyers in a courtroom conducted by a white judge. The probabilities are that he will be pleased and flattered when a white lawyer representing a white client shows he has the confidence to accept him. The probabilities are that he will not want to betray this confidence, and in his zeal to prove it, he will lean in the direction opposite of his own. Suggested questions would be as follows:

Q. Mr. Robinson, the fact that you are a Negro and that the other party to the lawsuit is a Negro does not start him out with an unfair advantage over my client; does it?
A. No.

Q. Regardless of the fact that you belong to the same race as Mr. Jones, would this prevent you from calling the shots just as you see them?
A. No.

Q. I'm certain that you would agree with me that prejudice should play no part in the trial of a lawsuit.
A. Yes.

Q. As you sit there now, Mr. Robinson, do you have the same frame of mind that you would want jurors to have if you were a party to a lawsuit? In other words, if we select you to serve on this jury, are we getting a juror who will decide this case on the evidence and not let that decision be influenced by any other factor?
A. Yes.

Q. Then you can assure me that if we accept you as a juror, we will receive a fair trial at your hands?
A. Yes.

It is not recommended that the obvious be politely ignored. If there is an obvious identity between the prospective juror and the other party, no one will take offense if polite reference is made to this fact.

Happy Spouse for Plaintiff in Death Case

When trying a death case, the ideal juror, from the standpoint of a plaintiff, is a housewife who has a successful marriage. If the woman has a house in the suburbs with children and a successful husband who pays the bills, she will place a good sized price tag on her husband. With a happy, contented husband who gives every sign of continuing on with his marriage and has productive years ahead of him, there is no question that she and the family have a large financial stake in his life. On the other hand, a woman whose husband has a spasmodic employment career, spends his money on liquor and women, beats her up regularly, stays away from the home for days at a time, or is separated from her, will have a price tag that is much less than her counterpart. Questions to the prospective women jurors can pretty well determine the situation, such as the number of years they have been married, whether they own their own homes, whether the wife has had to work during her married years, the type of work her husband does and the number of years he has stayed with the same type of employment, the advantages that their children have had, such as college, whether the prospective juror has a happy, relaxed air about her, and other such details. Of course, the same is true in the death of a woman. Men who have had a happy, successful marriage and deeply feel the value of a housewife and mother will make a good plaintiff's choice.

Getting the Juror to Disqualify Himself

There are times when it becomes immediately obvious to the lawyer that the juror he is questioning is definitely not his man. This juror may be constituted emotionally in such a way that he just simply could not give a plaintiff or defendant a fair trial. Without any reason to challenge this juror for cause, there is no alternative but to use a peremptory challenge unless the lawyer can get the juror to disqualify himself. Surprisingly enough, it is quite easy to get this juror to say that he would prefer not to sit on the jury because he cannot give both sides a fair trial. There are many people who feel it is basically wrong to award a plaintiff money damages for pain and suffering. To their way of thinking, damages should be limited only to money expenses actually incurred or likely to occur in the future. To give a plaintiff money for an intangible is almost immoral, encouraging exaggeration and dishonesty. Perhaps these people are the strong and defiant type who have had a great deal of pain themselves and accept it as a part of life. Perhaps they are young, and having had little experience with pain, attach less significance to it. In getting the juror to disqualify himself, a *voir dire* might be conducted as follows:

Q. You understand, of course, Mr. Jones, that if you accept the responsibility to serve as a juror in this case, you must obligate yourself to follow the instructions of law given to you by the judge.

Q. As Americans, we are accustomed to finding fault with the law and disagreeing with it, just like every person in this courtroom has done from time to time in the past. People who have strong feelings that the law is wrong on a particular point would have some difficulty in discharging their responsibilities as a juror; isn't that so?

Q. Both sides to this lawsuit are entitled to know that if you accept the job to serve as a juror, you will follow every law as given to you by His Honor. That's certainly fair; isn't it, Mr. Jones?

Q. My client, Bill Thompson, is entitled to know that you will apply the law in this case even though it's completely contrary to what you feel the law ought to be. You understand, of course, that this is a lawsuit in which Bill is asking for money compensation for damages that he sustained?

Q. Part of those damages is for pain and suffering. If you decide that Bill Thompson is entitled to a verdict, part of your responsibility will be to award him money for pain and suffering; isn't that correct?

Q. If you feel that it would be difficult for you to accept the law with regard to awarding money to an injured party for pain and suffering, I am sure that you would admit it here and now rather than conceal that fact and be unfair to anybody in this lawsuit; am I correct?

At this point, you have made it easy for the prospective juror to disqualify himself. You have also made it difficult for him to insist that he can be fair. A few more follow-up questions and you may get the man to agree that he would rather not sit on this jury. In jurisdictions that prohibit the lawyer from going into matters of law during *voir dire,* it should not interfere with this type of an examination. The prospective juror has not been given the plaintiff's lawyer's interpretation of the law, nor has he heard any law for that matter. A plaintiff is entitled to know that a juror is psychologically and emotionally prepared to award money damages for pain and suffering just as much as a defense lawyer is entitled to know that these elements will not create so much sympathy that the law of liability will be ignored.

Those prospective jurors who are so crammed full of compassion and sympathy for a suffering plaintiff are even more easily recognized. A defense lawyer can, more often than not, get these people to disqualify themselves with an understanding and sympathetic approach. In defending a case where the plaintiff is a severely injured child, a defense lawyer almost has to resort to this technique. In this situation he can quickly use up his peremptory challenges on those people who obviously will have a strong compulsion to award money in spite of liability. The material for laying this groundwork can often be supplied by the prospective juror himself. If he or a relative or friend has had a tragic experience involving a child, he will have great sympathy for the parents of the plaintiff because of the torment he has witnessed or experienced. The *voir dire* might be something as follows:

Q. Mr. Smith, I realize that because of the experience that your friend had when his child was injured, you had a great deal of sympathy for the parents and the child. You understand that a juror, when he accepts his responsibility to serve, must not let sympathy interfere with his decision.

Q. I'm sure that you will agree that my client, Bob Miller, is entitled to have a jury hear his case which will decide the facts fairly, regardless of natural sympathies for the plaintiff.

Q. I am sure that we all feel sympathy for this little girl and her parents because she was injured, but if that were allowed to interfere with the jury decision, then Bob Miller would not be getting a fair trial; isn't that correct?

Q. My client is, of course, entitled to have a juror decide his case on cold, hard facts and not sympathy. You would agree with that; wouldn't you?

Q. If you felt that your natural feelings of sympathy for this little girl and her parents would be very strong, you would tell us about that; wouldn't you?

Q. Do you feel that because of this other tragic experience that you have told to us and the sympathies for this family, you would find it difficult to decide this case on cold, hard facts?

As can be seen, it is now easy for this prospective juror to disqualify himself. There is nothing unmanly about having difficulty in deciding a case on "cold, hard facts" and ignoring one's sympathy for a little girl. Women will more quickly disqualify themselves and the examining lawyer can thank them for their honesty and fairness so that it will make it easy for other prospective jurors to disqualify themselves.

The plaintiff's lawyer should be careful not to lose sympathetic jurors who may even disqualify themselves without any prompting at all. Some of the finest plaintiff jurors are immediately siphoned off if the first prospective juror, with tears in her eyes, states that she feels so sorry for the little girl that she would rather not sit on the jury. If both lawyers graciously thank her for her honesty and candor and the trial judge treats her with great respect and admiration, some of the other sweet old gals witnessing all that will be encouraged to follow suit when their turns come. When the plaintiff's lawyer recognizes a plaintiff juror, he can make it difficult for her to disqualify

herself, as well as other prospective jurors who must listen. The
questioning should go something as follows:

Q. Now, Mrs. Kindly, there will be some evidence that the little
   girl I represent was rather severely injured. I am sure that you
   will agree that we all have a natural sympathy for this little girl.

Q. I am sure that you will also agree that both sides of this lawsuit
   are entitled to a fair trial.

Q. As a juror, you will surely want to discharge your duties in such
   a manner that both sides to this lawsuit will receive fair treatment
   in your hands.

Q. Do you feel that you can discharge your duty as a juror properly?

Q. And when I say "properly," that, of course, means that the defendant is treated with the same fairness and impartiality as the
   plaintiff; isn't that so?

Q. Do you have any quarrel with the concept that a lawsuit should
   be tried free from any sympathy, passion or prejudice?

Q. Do you have any prejudice against either side of this lawsuit as
   you sit there now?

Q. Do you know of any reason why you cannot give both sides to
   this lawsuit a fair trial?

Q. As you sit there now, if there were any reason at all that you felt
   you could not give my client as well as the defendant a fair
   trial, would you tell us here and now?

Q. Then, there is nothing that you are withholding or hiding from
   us that would cause you to have any undue sympathy or prejudice for either side?

Q. I gather that as you sit there now, you feel that it is a duty and
   a privilege for Americans to serve on a jury. I gather that as
   an adult, you will not be influenced by sympathy or prejudice
   and you will call the shots fairly and squarely exactly as they
   come in.

Q. If you had any undue sympathy or, for that matter, prejudice, you
   certainly would have volunteered this information by this time.

Q. Will you assure me, here and now, that you are the type of person
   that will give both sides of this lawsuit a fair trial?

As can be seen, this prospective juror has been led into a "call
to duty"—step by step. It would now be extremely difficult for her
to admit that her natural sympathies are such that both sides cannot
receive a fair trial. She cannot now, of course, volunteer that she
cannot give both sides a fair trial. Those other ideal plaintiff jurors
waiting for their turn have found nothing rewarding in volunteering
their natural sympathies for an injured plaintiff.

Is He a Plaintiff or Defendant Juror?

In spite of anything said to the contrary, I feel that the ethnic background of prospective jurors is important in determining their desirability from the standpoint of the plaintiff or defendant. It would be a dangerous generalization, however, to make a selection solely on that basis. Understand that the trial lawyer can only put this as a plus or minus among other information that he receives in response to his questions or from conclusions that are obvious from looking at and talking to the juror himself.

From the standpoint of the defense lawyer, a mark should be put in the plus column when a prospective juror has a name and mannerism that identifies him as having an ethnic background originating in the northern countries of Europe. Italy, Greece, the Slavic countries, and Spain, as well as countries generally closer to the Mediterranean produce people who act more through emotions than their cousins from the northern countries. Perhaps the everyday battle for existence in colder climates such as Norway produce a hardened, self-sufficient person who is more emotionally capable of accepting the hardships of life.

Certainly the plaintiff will fare better in the hands of a jury who would be more prone to be swayed through their emotions. Most of us have a stereotype picture of an excitable, emotional Italian man who would have great difficulty in following the law if it got in the way of awarding damages to an appealing plaintiff.

An occupation or experience, however, can completely nullify a plus or a minus due to ethnic background. If a Mr. Giovanni has been employed as a claims investigator for the past 17 years, it's a good bet that he's a defendant's juror. The same might well be true if that were the occupation of his father who, during the evening meals at home, talked about the exaggerated plaintiff claims that he encountered, thereby indoctrinating young Giovanni into becoming a skeptic of any personal injury claim.

My experience has also taught me that older jurors, generally speaking, are more prone toward the plaintiff. Experience probably has taught these jurors that human beings make many mistakes as they pass through life. They also have experienced pain, and identify more easily with an injured plaintiff. Younger people are more apt to be less forgiving, and not having experienced as much pain, will have a tendency to place a lower value on it. Jurors who are parents will usually make better plaintiff's jurors when the plaintiff is a child.

Because of their experience as parents, they are made more aware of the complete unpredictability of children. They are more apt to anticipate that a child standing at the side of a road may suddenly and without warning dart into the road. Instinctively, they will be more apt to be prepared for this eventuality and will slow down or even put their foot on the brake as they approach the child. These jurors will hold a defendant to a higher standard of care than the childless adult who is less likely to anticipate such a completely irresponsible act.

Most jurors have a tendency to be less forgiving of their own sex. Women have more of a tendency to believe a man, as opposed to a woman, especially if he presents a good appearance. If the woman is attractive, she will even receive less consideration. The same attitude is found in the well-adjusted male, although not quite as strongly as in the female. The typical training of the male is to favor the woman with a bit more courteousness and respect. The male looks more to the woman as the "keeper of the keys" to virtue in our society. Virtue, of course, includes veracity, which will give the edge to a woman in disputed questions of fact in the hands of a male juror.

I suspect that among jurors, the men exercise greater influence, in spite of Kipling who said, "A woman's guess is much more accurate than a man's certainty."

The following suggestions can be considered when weighing the probabilities in selecting jurors:

(1) **Ethnic background.**—People whose name and appearance indicate an origin of a southern European country are more apt to be plaintiff jurors. People of Oriental extraction or of other extremely small minorities exercise moderate influence on a jury. They are more apt to go along with the majority's expression in order to avoid dissension.

(2) **Age.**—Older jurors are generally favorable to the plaintiff. It should be kept in mind that some people become cantankerous in their old age and would, therefore, be an exception to the rule. They may also be less tolerant of teen-aged drivers.

(3) **Marital status.**—Men and women who have never been married are more apt to be introverted, maladjusted, severe, or have an unhappy outlook on life and should be considered defendant jurors. Happy, contented, well-adjusted people will have a greater tendency to want to make other people happy. The fact that a juror has been divorced should not reflect one way or the other.

(4) **Parents.**—People who have children obviously make better jurors when the plaintiff is a child. In addition to this, these people are more apt to be happy and well-adjusted. After all, adults who plan for children have to be more unselfish than adults who plan never to have them.

(5) **Occupation.**—This is too vast a topic to cover all contingencies. Generally speaking, the plaintiff's lawyer should avoid civil service workers, insurance company employees, and those who have an occupation that would appeal to a "loner" or introvert. Engineers and accountants do not deal with human beings and are trained to think in terms of tangible facts. An accountant is less apt to be impressed with an intangible such as pain when the only dollar values that he is accustomed to are those assigned to tangible, capital assets. A nurse must learn to administer to people suffering from pain and to do it without becoming emotionally involved. An efficient nurse must, therefore, become hardened to the pain and suffering she observes in others, otherwise her mind would become unstable and she would be unable to work properly under such disconcerting surroundings. A nurse or another person with a similar occupation will be less moved by pain and suffering. Salesmen are often the plaintiff's best bet. They are sympathetic with the plaintiff because he is trying to "sell" them, and salesmen, themselves, are easiest to sell. They will, in turn, become salesmen for the plaintiff in the jury room.

(6) **Occupation of other members of the juror's family.**—Depending upon the facts and circumstances, the occupation of a spouse, parent, uncle, child, or brother may well influence the thinking of a juror. The judgment of the lawyer will differ, based upon the facts and circumstances as certainly there are too many contingencies to anticipate. For example, a plaintiff in a medical malpractice case would not want a juror whose parent is a physician, nor would he want a landlord when the plaintiff is a tenant suing his landlord because of a fall down the front stairs.

(7) **Previous experience as party to a lawsuit.**—If he was once a party himself, then it's a good bet that he will be very much in sympathy with that side of the case.

(8) **Previous injuries.**—Any past history of injuries where the juror employed a lawyer, who brought about a satisfactory settlement, is a good sign for the plaintiff. It indicates that he respects lawyers and is not anticlaim-minded. If he had a fairly serious injury, but settled it himself without the services of a lawyer, then this fact should become a mark on the plus side for the defendant. It would

indicate that he does not think the services of a lawyer are important, in addition to which the sum of money he received was probably quite conservative.

(9) **Residence.**—Generally speaking, the big city dweller is more liberal with the size of the verdict than the country boy.

(10) **Physical appearance.**—Plump people, or if you prefer "fat," who are quick to smile will lean toward the plaintiff. Thin people who have a grim, unsmiling demeanor and are not responsive make good defendant jurors. The latter people are skeptical of others and will bring their skepticism with them into the jury box and view the selling job of the plaintiff with suspicion.

(11) **Identity with a party.**—The same membership in a club, church, community, occupation, or some other ethnic group should be considered as a favorable mark. There can be innumerable background experiences that would have a tendency to identify with a party. Because of the unlimited possibilities here, again, with practice and thought, the lawyer will find himself selecting a better juror to try the facts in his case. When in the course of acquiring information from the juror it develops that his father was killed by a drunken driver, it should become immediately apparent that if there is some evidence of drinking on the part of a party, there may be significant prejudice directed toward him.

It is easier for a defense lawyer to elicit background facts bearing on the desirability of the juror. The reasons for this are that the court and jury will understand and give more leeway to a defense lawyer looking for background experiences that would prevent his client from receiving a fair trial. He is defending a target which the plaintiff is shooting at and ought to have a little more leeway in being certain that a juror will call the shots fair and square. It's a little easier for the defense lawyer to ask in a child dart-out case, whether the juror himself has ever had the experience of almost hitting a child running out from between parked cars. This type of question can invite some opinions which will influence the other jurors. When the plaintiff asks such a question and gets an unfavorable answer, he must exercise a peremptory challenge. The defense lawyer, on the other hand, can be the "nice guy" and say:

Q. In spite of your experience, do you feel that you can give both sides to this lawsuit a fair trial?

Q. Will you give us the benefit of your everyday experience in life in helping to determine what is probable and improbable?

II. Opening Statements

How Valuable Is the Opening Statement?

JUST HOW VALUABLE is an opening statement in the battle of persuasion? In spite of the admonition to the jury to refrain from allowing "lawyer's talk" to influence them, an effective opening statement can be a valuable contribution to the aggregate. It is claimed to be a most valuable tool in the hands of a lawyer capable of painting a picture in the mind's eye through the use of words.

Proponents of the opening statement cite a recent study by The University of Chicago Law School which established that 65 per cent of the jurors ultimately decided the case consistent with their first impressions immediately following the opening statements. This survey unfortunately makes no attempt to evaluate their worth in determining the amount of damages. Many defense lawyers will keep the liability in issue only as a means of holding down the damages. This survey does not take into account that the defense lawyer, in many cases, fully expected a guilty verdict. An example of this would be a case where a personable defendant is guilty of a mild error of judgment, and a plaintiff projects a disagreeable attitude. Even though the jury is compelled to enter a verdict in favor of the plaintiff, it will be niggardly with the amount. The defense lawyer wants to be sure the jury sees the full unpleasantness of the plaintiff. By creating only a damage issue, the defense lawyer would not be able to parade this man or drag out the time for the plaintiff to be in the witness chair. There are also those cases involving injuries of a significant nature with only questionable liability at best. These types of cases will further reduce the value of the survey since it is difficult for the plaintiff's lawyer to settle for "nuisance value" with a client suffering from serious and permanent injuries. When the plaintiff's lawyer goes to the jury with a case of this nature, he is "playing a long shot." He knows the facts are against him, but he is looking for a lucky break during the trial. Therefore, the impression that the jury will have following opening statements is almost certain to be reflected in their finding unless something unusual and unexpected occurs during the course of the trial.

From the standpoint of many trial lawyers, this is the most uninteresting part of the trial, and as a result it suffers from lack of preparation more than any other phase of the lawsuit. It is common to find lawyers making a dull, tedious, and disjointed representation of the facts. The same lawyer may spend hours preparing the cross-examination of an expert witness and allow only two minutes for his opening. Even though there is little information evaluating its importance, there are experienced trial lawyers who contend that it is the most overlooked weapon in the trial lawyer's arsenal.

Opening Statement Is Easy to Improve

Fortunately, self-improvement in giving an opening statement comes quickly since it is the easiest phase of the trial in which to develop proficiency. The principal reason for this is that one does not need the gift of a quick mind that can seize upon an opportunity that comes and goes in a moment, such as occurs during the taking of evidence. All that is required is that the representation of facts be given in a clear manner. Anyone with a voice that can be heard can, by advance preparation, take whatever time is necessary to put together an effective opening statement. One of the best ways to improve on it is to impose on a group of friends by summarizing a given set of facts and then asking what each understood the facts to be, in addition to what impression he gained. It is interesting to note that each friend will have his own impression and understanding as to what you narrated. With effort you can quickly narrow the variance in the minds of the listeners, fill in the voids, and leave them with a clear understanding of the facts.

In addition to learning how to paint a picture in the mind's eye through the use of words, the lawyer, also by practicing with friends, will discover that certain words will create different pictures or moods. Just to give a few examples, the word "accident" will denote in the minds of many people an unavoidable occurrence. The plaintiff, by substituting the words "collision," "impact," "crash," or "smash-up," will be more effective in painting his picture. For a lawyer to say that his client was "involved" in an automobile collision will create a different impression than to say "the defendant's car smashed into Mary's car." When a lawyer describes his client as having been "involved" in a collision, he conjures up an unconscious impression in the minds of the jury that perhaps his client somehow contributed to the accident. He is unknowingly creating a weak first impression. Thought should be given to the proper use of words, just as the word "accident" should be deleted from the vocabulary of the plaintiff's attorney.

Describing Opening Statement to Jury

When the purpose of the opening statement is explained to the jury, together with a brief explanation as to the mechanics of a trial, it will function better as a jury. There is no advantage to either side in having a jury that is uninformed as to the procedure of a trial. Once having at least an introduction into the ground rules, they are less apt to become confused. I suppose that it is conceivable that a lawyer might want a jury to be confused, but if he finds himself in that frame of mind, then he should make every possible effort to settle his case. It can be explained to the jury that an opening statement can be compared to a book review in which it is possible to get a synopsis or condensation of the entire book first, thus making it easier to follow when it is heard in the unabridged form. Further, it can be explained that in this way, if they hear evidence out of its logical sequence, it will be easier to follow since it will be comparable to hearing an advance chapter and then going back to an earlier chapter until all of the chapters have been heard. It can be explained that if it becomes necessary during the trial for the lawyer to use witnesses in an illogical order, the jury will be in a better position to understand the purpose of evidence given by a witness who contributes a small but integral part of the entire case.

If the defense attorney has just witnessed an effective opening statement by his opponent, it is wise for him to emphasize that the purpose of an opening statement is to acquaint the jury with what the lawyers expect the evidence will be; that an opening statement, or "lawyer's talk," is not evidence; ". . . that the only evidence they will hear will come to them in the form of sworn testimony from witnesses or exhibits properly received into evidence." In some states, the jurors are given an instruction pamphlet when they first report for duty. These pamphlets attempt to describe evidence and phases of a trial. In describing opening statements and closing arguments, it is invariably mentioned that they are not evidence, but only an aid to help the jury. It will be stated that they are an attempt by the lawyers to persuade them. For this reason, they may revere the lawyer who, during opening statements, is candid enough to say: "What I may say, or for that matter, what my opponent may say, is not to be considered by you as evidence."

Is There Advantage in Waiving Opening Statement?

It is an unusual situation in which there is an advantage to waiving an opening statement. Any advantage gained would not be because it would help in the battle of persuasion. It could only be a situation where the lawyer, declining the opportunity for one reason or another, does not know how the evidence will come in, and for that reason he is afraid of making a misrepresentation. If the lawyer does not know the case and must "play it by ear," then he is hardly in a position to represent to the jury what the evidence will establish. This is more often done by the defense lawyer, not because he is more likely to be unprepared than the plaintiff's lawyer (actually the opposite is more often true), but because such strategy would be awkward for a plaintiff. From the plaintiff's standpoint, the jury almost has to have at least a general idea of what the case is all about or the jury may lose its way, which usually will work to the defendant's advantage. Another equally important reason is that in most jurisdictions, by waiving his opening statement, the plaintiff also waives his right to closing arguments if the defendant chooses not to argue.

The rules governing opening statements and closing arguments are persuasive advantages enjoyed by the plaintiff. Trial by jury emerged through the centuries into its present form wherein the plaintiff is given the advantage of being heard from first and last, while on the other hand the defendant is given the advantage of not being required to prove a thing.

There is, therefore, almost no reason from a strategic standpoint for the plaintiff to pass up an opportunity to state his case, other than, perhaps, a case which is poorly prepared or in which there is uncertainty as to what evidence will be admissible. The latter situation can come about for a limited number of reasons. An example would be the death of one of the parties, which makes the surviving party incompetent to testify as to the occurrence under the "Dead Man's Act," but there is a question as to whether the opposing lawyer will waive incompetency either deliberately or by accident. Another common example is where there is a question in the mind of the lawyer as to whether a witness he intends to offer will be sufficiently qualified as an expert to give an opinion in an area where only an expert is permitted to testify.

Even in those cases where the lawyer is not properly acquainted with the facts of the case or is in doubt as to the availability or admissibility of certain evidence, there should be at least a fairly detailed explanation given in those areas where there is certainty. Having done this, the lawyer puts himself in the position of being able to remind the jury during his summation that he did say at the outset that the evidence would show some points that were in fact borne out by the testimony and exhibits. The opening statement is, then, an integral part of the entire logical theory being advanced, rather than a disjointed or even irrelevant segment of the case.

TECHNIQUES EMPLOYED

Do Not Overstate

Avoid overstating the case since nothing falls so flat as an unfulfilled promise. The overextended lawyer may come on strong, creating a tremendous first impression, only to have his empty promises still ringing in the ears of the jury when they retire to consider the verdict. A good first impression should be painted, but it should be artistically underpainted just a shade so that the jury will never feel that the representations were anything less than accurate. First impressions are significant in most facets of human relations. Human beings are aware of this, as can readily be demonstrated from the concern people have for their personal appearance. An example of this is a doctor who assumes a professional pose with a patient or a schoolboy who hangs by his heels from the limb of a tree for a new girl. All of us, therefore, go through life receiving and dispensing first impressions.

Often there is a deliberate attempt to distort or convey an impression that is different from the facts. It probably is not important that we project an accurate first impression in our daily contact with other people. In fact, in our society it is considered boorish to accurately state the facts in many situations. How often do we deliberately distort the truth when we tell the hostess how delicious the dessert was, admire a friend's new baby, or tell someone how well he looks, when the facts are quite the opposite. These benevolent inaccuracies play no part in the trial of a lawsuit.

When a trial lawyer first appears before the jury to represent the facts, he will, as in any other confrontation, create a first impression. It becomes important that the word picture be an accurate impression since the jury will become intimately acquainted with the facts before they retire to consider whether the picture painted for them is still strong and clear. A favorable first impression created by an accurate opening statement properly maintained and supported by the evidence as promised contributes appreciably in the battle of persuasion.

Be Sure It's Admissible Before You Promise

If there is doubt as to the admissibility of certain evidence that you intend to use, then caution must be exercised so that you will not find yourself guilty of making unfulfilled promises. A conference in chambers with the trial judge and opponent immediately preceding the trial can help resolve this problem. Once having obtained the trial court's advance commitment as to what the ruling will be, the danger of being guilty of misrepresentation is removed and a more effective opening statement can be delivered. If such a pretrial conference or commitment is not possible, then the lawyer should be reasonably sure of his grounds before he proceeds to go out on a limb. Otherwise he should refrain from representing to the jury that he will deliver that evidence. If the evidence is essential to the success of the case, however, then it must be mentioned and a record made in the event of an adverse ruling.

Be Careful of Inconsistent Witnesses

There are times (and not too infrequently) when, after the lawyer has interviewed a witness in order to learn to what facts he can testify, his testimony on the stand is at variance with the interview. This type of witness can often be recognized during the initial interview. If there is a suspicion that this person you intend to present answers that description, then the representations made to the jury should be less detailed in regard to his proposed testimony. When interviewing a witness who vacillates in his description of the facts, then consideration should be given as to whether this witness should be used at all. If it is necessary that he testify, the opening statement should be framed carefully in order that the witness does not make the lawyer guilty of a misrepresentation.

On those occasions where the lawyer does get caught in a misrepresentation for one reason or another, then he should apologize to the jury during the summation and point out that this was a mistake on his part, but that the mistake in no way affects the merits of his case.

An Opponent's Admission Can Help

Listen carefully for any admissions or concessions that your opponent makes during his opening statement. In most jurisdictions a clear, unqualified admission made during this phase of the trial is binding upon that party. An admission on a point that was in issue no longer makes it necessary to present evidence on that point. If the evidence you have which was to be presented to establish that point was weak or undesirable, it may strengthen the case not to present it. If, on the other hand, the evidence that was intended to be presented is highly favorable and might even create feelings of antagonism toward the other side, then the use of this evidence should not be abandoned.

Aside from the legal effects of a concession if not classified as an admission, it might be useful to remind the jury in closing arguments that the opponent did concede this to be a fact at the outset. This concession could be all the more important if the evidence presented was not strong enough to establish the point that the opponent already conceded during his opening statement.

Be Certain Jury Knows Proof Required

Care should be taken to not create an erroneous concept in the minds of the jury as to the amount of evidence required to establish a fact. This is especially true of the plaintiff's lawyer who may be so impressed with the amount of evidence that he has available to establish a point that he may find himself saying such things as: "We will prove beyond any doubt . . . ." Perhaps he will, thereby, inadvertently plant an erroneous idea in the minds of the jury as to the amount of proof required.

While more often the plaintiff's lawyer is apt to make such statements, even a defense lawyer will, on occasion, make such a representation when he is exuberant over the evidence he has for rebuttal on a major point. The proper tactic for a defense lawyer is to never deviate from the concept that it is the plaintiff who has the burden of proof. If the defense lawyer is in possession of some good affirmative evidence that should establish that he is entitled to the verdict, it will not necessarily help his cause if he inadvertently should plant an erroneous concept in the minds of the jury that he, himself, must prove something in order to be entitled to the verdict. From the defense standpoint, favorable evidence will always be favorable. No representations of its value by a defense lawyer will add anything more to it. There is the danger, however, that it will not come across as effectively as the defense lawyer anticipates and the jury may think that he has failed to "prove" a representation he was required to prove.

The plaintiff's lawyer, on the other hand, should use such expressions as: "The more believable evidence . . .," or "The greater weight of the evidence . . . ." In most jurisdictions the lawyers are not permitted to go into matters of law during opening statements—such matters being confined to the closing arguments. So, while the plaintiff's lawyer may not define the "measuring stick" as to what constitutes proof in a civil case, he can at least inject the words, "by the greater weight of the evidence . . . ."

The defense lawyer should not concern himself with any attempt to distinguish burden of proof requirements in civil and criminal cases. His interests lie in building up the traditional American concept that before the defendant can be found guilty, the plaintiff is required by law "to prove the charges . . ." made against the defendant.

Summarizing the Pleadings

Summarizing the pleadings is especially helpful where there are issues created in which the lawyer feels he has the necessary evidence to definitely resolve those issues in his favor. It has been a long-standing practice of many defense lawyers to deny all of the material allegations set out in the plaintiff's Complaint. Many allegations are denied, not because the defense counsel believes that the plaintiff cannot prove the allegations, but because his training and experience tell him that he should make it as difficult as possible for the plaintiff to prove his case. Wherever the defendant chooses to make issues by simply denying allegations, the plaintiff must then go forward with evidence to prove his allegations. It will work to the advantage of the plaintiff when the defendant arbitrarily denies an allegation in which the plaintiff has abundant evidence to easily establish that issue. For example, it is a mistake for the defense lawyer to deny that the defendant drove his car over the center line when all of the physical evidence and testimony of witnesses, including his own client, confirm that it is a fact. He has only weakened his position if there is evidence tending to justify this conduct or cast doubts on the alleged injuries. Permitting a case to go to trial with the pleadings in this state of affairs will create doubts as to the sincerity of the defense lawyer and perhaps give credence to all the allegations of the plaintiff. To give an example, assume that the plaintiff claims he has been enduring back pains ever since the accident, although there are no objective findings through X rays or any other laboratory tests to substantiate the pains in his back. In the absence of any medical evidence to support the subjective complaints of pain in the back, the plaintiff's lawyer can anticipate a rather skeptical jury. He can, however, improve his chances if he can create some animosity toward the defendant and his lawyer for being less than honest in their denial of allegations. Seeds of hate and prejudice can be planted somewhat as follows:

As was previously pointed out, you folks are being asked to decide certain issues or questions in this case. These questions or issues were created by allegations or claims that we made which were denied by the defendant. The claims or allegations are made by an official court document that we filed known as the "Complaint." The Complaint sets forth with some particularity all of the allegations that Henry claims concerning his automobile collision and the injuries resulting to him because of it. The purpose of the Complaint is to adequately inform the defendant of the charges brought by Henry and to give the defendant an opportunity to either admit or deny those charges or allegations. Whatever allegations are denied by the defendant are the very questions you folks will be asked to decide. Your decision, of course, will be based upon the evidence that you hear or exhibits that are received into evidence.

One of the questions that you folks are going to be asked to decide is the manner in which the collision occurred. In the Complaint that we filed, we alleged that the defendant drove his automobile over the yellow line and smashed into the automobile being driven by Henry. The defendant has filed his formal Answer and has denied this charge. It, therefore, becomes necessary that we prove this allegation by a greater weight of the evidence. I would not, of course, presume to anticipate what evidence will be submitted to establish that the defendant did not drive the car over the center line, but I submit that the allegations that we have made will be supported by the evidence that the defendant's car did drive over the center line and strike Henry's automobile; that Henry did receive injuries to his back as a result of that smash-up; that he has suffered pain in his back and is still suffering pain in his back. The evidence will further show that the practice of medicine is not an exact science; that there will not be any X rays or other laboratory tests to establish the fact that Henry has pain in his back. Although the doctor who has treated Henry cannot see or feel anything wrong with the back, he will testify that there are many conditions of the back that will be painful, although there will not be any visible signs to the doctor to confirm the pain.

If the defense lawyer knows that his client, on cross-examination, is going to have to admit that he crossed the center line (to say nothing of the fact that the debris from the impact places him on the wrong side of the line, as well as testimony from occurrence witnesses and the plaintiff), the defense lawyer must attempt to "explain away" the Answer which he filed. This starts him out under a cloud of suspicion since surely anything so important as an official court document should not have been prepared in such a careless or flippant manner. If the defense lawyer says nothing to soften the blow, the jury now is prepared to receive evidence in order to establish the truth of the allegation that the defendant did go over the center line. It would not be hard to anticipate the feelings in the minds of the jurors when all of the evidence clearly establishes that the plaintiff's allegation as to the occurrence itself is completely accurate. The defendant, on cross-examination can be asked if his automobile did, in fact, go over the center line. When he answers in the affirmative, then he can be asked: "Then, the 'Answer' that was filed by your lawyer wherein you denied that your automobile went over the center line was not true?" This can cause the jury to feel that the lawyer and the defendant were less than honest in the preparation and filing of the court document described to them by the plaintiff's lawyer. There will be a tendency to want to penalize the dishonest side and accept the plaintiff's allegation as to damages.

It should be kept in mind that the defendant, by admitting certain allegations, can effectively prevent the plaintiff's lawyer from putting on evidence to substantiate those allegations. By preventing the plaintiff's lawyer from putting on this evidence, oftentimes, the defense lawyer can prevent a jury from hearing evidence that would create prejudice in favor of the plaintiff or against the defendant. I recall a case that I defended where my client was a 17-year-old youth who, while driving his father's car, ran the plaintiff down in the crosswalk after failing to stop for a stop sign. He had testified previously in a discovery deposition that he had not even seen the woman until he hit her, although at the time of the impact, she was more than halfway across the street on a bright, sunny day. By admitting these allegations, the plaintiff was unable to present this prejudicial evidence and was confined to evidence relative only to the damage issue. Had the jury heard the evidence of the accident itself, there would have been a strong tendency for them to penalize the defendant by awarding damages much in excess of compensatory damages. Of course, an allegation as to willful and wanton conduct would have permitted this type of evidence even if it fell short, since a defense lawyer would be most reluctant to admit that his client acted in a willful and wanton manner.

The same technique can be used by the defense lawyer when the plaintiff makes numerous and unnecessary allegations which will simply not be borne out by the evidence. These allegations will often be centered around the damages where the plaintiff alleges that he suffered multiple bone fractures and the injuries are permanent, when, as a matter of fact, there were no fractures at all and all of the medical evidence indicates that the plaintiff made a complete recovery.

Using Visual Aids

The use of visual aids, such as charts drawn to scale, photographs of machinery or an intersection, and even freehand drawing on a blackboard during opening statements, will give the jury a more accurate picture in their minds. The difficulty of painting a picture in the mind's eye through the use of words is apparent. If it is important to the advocate that the jury have an accurate concept in their minds of the scene of an accident because accuracy favors his side of the case, then every effort should be made to employ visual aids during opening statements. Most state courts permit the use of visual aids as do the federal courts if it can be demonstrated in advance that these aids can properly be used and it is counsel's intention to use them during the taking of evidence.

A diagram of a street intersection drawn freehand on a blackboard with chalk will help clarify the spoken word and accurately convey the theory of the case from both the plaintiff's and the defendant's standpoints. It will also greatly enhance the ability of the jury to follow the evidence. To most people, it is difficult, if not impossible, to follow the testimony of a witness as he describes the movements of his car as well as the movements of other cars at a complicated street or highway intersection. Even an experienced trial lawyer accustomed to understanding and communicating to others the details of an intersection collision, such as distances, directions, and speeds, becomes confused when the lawsuit involves a situation with three or four streets converging into one intersection. With anything more than a simple set of facts involving an intersection collision, it is probably safe to say that following opening statements through words alone, not one juror has a clear picture in his mind as to how the accident occurred. It is a good bet that about half of the jury is completely lost, and perhaps some of them have a completely erroneous picture created in the mind's eye. This jury must now depend upon the testimony of the occurrence witnesses and, hopefully, visual aids during the taking of evidence. Any arguments against the use of visual aids during opening statements are without merit when such aids can and will be used during the trial. The same drawing used during opening statements should be left in a prominent place for the jury to observe as the occurrence witnesses are testifying as to details of the accident. Therefore, it is possible, in spite of a complicated intersection, piece of machinery, or other subject matter of a lawsuit, to convey an accurate picture into the juror's brain through the use of his eyes as well as his ears.

There is a natural tendency for many lawyers to become argumentative when using visual aids. Aside from the fact that this is objectionable, any variance from an unemotional and matter-of-fact manner of delivery will detract from the clarity.

Don't Know Opponent's Case

It's better not to know too much about the other guy's case. Jurors are certainly not aware of the discovery procedure available to lawyers, and it may seem to them that something is out of balance if one lawyer knows too much about the other lawyer's case. They may not consciously put their finger on what is troubling them when they hear a lawyer describe the evidence of his opponent, but a "feeling," or "vague suspicion" can be created concerning such a lawyer. It is not that they would consciously suspect the lawyer of peeking into his opponent's file, but a "feeling" can be created that something is not just right. There is, in addition, a certain presumptuousness in a lawyer's speaking for his opponent, when certainly his opponent ought to know his own case and can certainly speak for himself.

It might, at first blush, be argued that anticipating the testimony of an occurrence witness for the other side and then contrasting it with the expected testimony of your witness might have the effect of reducing the value of your opponent's witness. The reasoning for this conclusion is based upon the then anticlimactic testimony of the opponent's witness and creating a mood wherein the jury may receive his testimony with some skepticism. Experience has now convinced me, however, that as a matter of fact, the effectiveness of your own occurrence witness is reduced because he is identified with the presumptuous side of the lawsuit.

Keep Your Damaging Evidence a Surprise

When an attorney has some damaging evidence unknown to his opponent, he should consider carefully before he shows his hand. This would apply to such situations as a damaging statement of his opponent's client or an important witness, medical information showing that the plaintiff suffered the same injury on a prior occasion, photographs contradicting anticipated evidence to be offered by his opponent, or other such potential "dynamite." The real value in possessing this type of evidence is the complete, sledgehammer effect that it will have at exactly the right moment. For the defendant, the right moment may be during the time the plaintiff is putting on his case in chief, or it may be wise to wait until the defendant is putting on his own case. As for the plaintiff, if he possesses this type of evidence, he must decide whether it should be used immediately while the defendant is putting on his case or whether he should wait until rebuttal.

In a sincere effort to settle the case many a lawyer has informed his opponent of the impeaching evidence, only to be robbed of its value when the case did not settle. The opposing lawyer, once aware of the danger, can then steer a course to avoid the mine that otherwise would have sunk his ship. Examples of this are found when the defendant has photographs or occurrence witnesses establishing that a plaintiff was bowling, dancing, horseback riding, repairing his house, or engaging in other such physical activities when he was supposed to be flat on his back. The plaintiff, who may have been prepared to vehemently deny that he engaged in any physical activities such as those mentioned, can now volunteer on direct examination that he did engage in these activities in spite of the pain. Whatever impeaching value such evidence heretofore had is, of course, now gone. The hurried conference with the client relative to the changes that are now necessary in his testimony, coupled with an opening statement representing to the jury that his client has engaged in these activities in spite of the pain, has rendered the impeaching evidence not only worthless, but actually damaging to the lawyer daring to introduce it at this point.

Highlight Opponent's Overstatement

One of the more effective ways of capitalizing on an opponent who has overstated his case is to highlight the overstatement, if you are confident that the evidence will bear this out. Try to use as closely as possible the exact words that the opponent used in order to underscore in "red ink" the statement that he has made which you know will turn out to be a misrepresentation. For example, if the defense lawyer has photographs of two automobiles which were involved in a collision that were taken immediately after the accident demonstrating little or no property damage, these photographs can be quite effective after the plaintiff's attorney has described to the jury the tremendous impact that caused injuries to his client's back. In highlighting this misrepresentation, it is more effective for the defense lawyer to say:

> My opponent has represented to this jury that the injuries suffered by his client were caused by a severe impact between the two automobiles. Whether it is a fact that there was a severe impact between the automobiles cannot be established as a fact, merely by stating it to be a fact. It is easy to say something, but I am sure that the members of the jury will require evidence on this point as well as on any other point, and then you will ask yourselves if this point was proven as my opponent says he will prove it.

Another common example is the situation wherein the lawyer, with his human desire to make a good first impression, overstates or exaggerates the testimony that a witness is prepared to give. It may be an occurrence witness or a doctor who simply cannot and will not testify to the extent claimed, and the opposing counsel can highlight this by repeating the exaggerated representation, followed up by a statement that he is sure the jury will prefer to let the witness do his own talking.

Don't Spend Energy on a Dead Issue

From the defendant's standpoint, when the plaintiff has accurately stated the damages but has a weak liability case, the opening statement should be confined to the liability issue. If the defense lawyer is quite certain that the evidence, as represented by the plaintiff's attorney, will establish that the plaintiff did in fact suffer specific injuries and incur specific financial obligations as a result of the injuries, then it would be a mistake to dignify the entire case by discussing the damages. If, on the other hand, it appears the plaintiff will be able to establish the liability, but the damages are open to doubt for one reason or another, then the defense lawyer should draw the jury's attention only to the vulnerable area of the plaintiff's case.

Deliberately Throwing in Inadmissible Evidence

There are lawyers who will deliberately or in ignorance represent that the jury will hear certain evidence when, in fact, such evidence is inadmissible. Examples of this are that the other driver received a traffic ticket, evidence of a party's background which is not material to the issues, previous injuries not related to the ones in question, and other incompetent evidence. Once this inadmissible evidence has been stated, it is locked within the brain of the juror and cannot magically be removed by a few words from the trial judge directing them to disregard the statement made by counsel. As a matter of fact, an objection at this point by an outraged lawyer, followed by an instruction from the judge that the remarks just made should be disregarded, will cause it to be even further implanted in the minds of the jurors. It is possible for a lawyer using these tactics to obtain a verdict when he would otherwise probably not have been successful. To many people, the fact that one of the drivers in a two-car collision received a traffic ticket by a policeman who arrived at the scene 30 minutes later is most significant. By and large, however, these unfair tactics deliberately committed work to the detriment of the lawyer using them. The jury will be quick to sense that this really was unethical and may even resent it, especially if it was obviously designed to prejudice them against the other party by reason of a past indiscretion. If the other party had once been an alcoholic, had a venereal disease, was divorced, stole a car in his youth, or has any other such skeletons in his closet, an improper rattling of these skeletons will react adversely on the lawyer employing this tactic. There are times, however, when the damage could be severe, and the recipient of such tactics should strongly urge a mistrial in order to avoid an unnecessary appeal.

EXAMPLES OF OPENING STATEMENTS

The following example of an opening statement by the plaintiff is given by way of suggestion and not for the purpose of laying down any inflexible dogmatic rules. Because the conditions in each case can vary so greatly, one must be flexible and even agile in his approach to the particular strengths and weaknesses of his case. To use but a few examples, the opposing lawyer may habitually overstate his case, he may be impersonable or antagonistic, his client or your client may be more or less than ideal as a witness, the judge may smile upon the opponent or his client while frowning upon your side of the table, the cause that you are selling or defending may be popular or unpopular, you may or may not want the jury to follow the law notwithstanding their natural sympathies, or a multitude of other problems or strong points.

May it please the Court, counsel, and may it please you, ladies and gentlemen of the jury. It is at this stage of the proceedings that the attorneys for each side have an opportunity to make what is known as an opening statement. An opening statement is something like a preview in that each lawyer can give the jury an outline of what he expects the evidence to establish. This preview that we give you might be something like a friend telling you what a movie was all about before you actually viewed it. His recounting of the details of the movie might not be appreciated but, nonetheless, you would probably get more out of the movie if you knew in advance approximately what to expect. A significant difference in the trial of a lawsuit is that the evidence sometimes is introduced out of its logical sequence, such as in an erratic reading of a book. If one were to read an advance chapter and then skip back to an earlier chapter until all the chapters are read in such a manner, he would probably comprehend the meaning if it were outlined in advance. By giving you a resumé of the case now, it will be easier to follow.

As was mentioned earlier, the jury's duty will be to weigh the evidence. Evidence consists of the testimony of sworn witnesses or exhibits that are received into evidence. What I say or what my colleague, Mr. Ironpanz, says is, of course, not evidence.

This lawsuit started by the filing of a document known as a Complaint. The purpose of a Complaint is to inform the defendant in precise language of the details upon which the plaintiff bases his lawsuit. In this case, Jesse's family lawyer, Mr. Robinson, filed such a Complaint. This Complaint is divided into paragraphs with each paragraph being numbered. The defendant has filed a document known as an Answer. The purpose of the Answer is to either admit or deny the allegations made by the plaintiff. Any of the allegations which are denied by the defendant thereby become issues of fact. It is these issues of fact that the jury is asked to decide. If any allegation is admitted, then it is not necessary for the jury to decide that allegation as it is agreed by both sides that it is a fact. In this lawsuit a Complaint was filed wherein Jesse alleges that on January 15, 1967, at about 5:00 P. M. he was driving his automobile south on Austin Boulevard approximately 200 feet north of Irving Park Road. The defendant in this case in his Answer admits this to be a fact. Jesse also alleges that at that same time and place the defendant was driving his automobile in a northerly direction. The defendant in his Answer admits this to be a fact. Jesse also alleges that Austin Boulevard at that point is a two-lane street which consists of one lane for northbound traffic and one lane for southbound traffic and that the speed limit in existence at that time was 35 miles per hour. The defendant in his Answer admits this to be a fact. Jesse also alleges that the defendant in the operation of his automobile had a duty to exercise ordinary care to avoid injuring Jesse. The defendant in his Answer admits this to be a fact. It is also alleged by Jesse that at the time of this occurrence he was in the exercise of ordinary care for his own safety. The defendant denies this allegation and has thereby created an issue of fact for the jury to decide. In addition to this, Jesse has also alleged that the defendant was negligent at the time of and shortly before this occurrence, and that the defendant negligently came over on to the wrong side of the road, causing a head-on collision in the southbound lane in which Jesse was traveling. The defendant in his Answer denies that he was negligent and denies that Jesse was injured in the manner and to extent claimed. The evidence presented on these questions of fact must, therefore, be weighed by the jury in order that the issues in this case be resolved.

Now, let me take you back in your mind's eye to January 15, 1967. The evidence will show that Jesse had finished his day's work as an accountant for the Holiday Manufacturing Company. The day's work had ended for Jesse, just as it had on many days during the 20 years that he has been employed there. He has said "good-night" to his co-employees and has driven his automobile out of the factory parking lot, just the same as he has done for the past 20 years. His car is again traveling the same route which has now become a fixed habit from the years that have now gone by. As he drives along Austin Boulevard, he finds a typical winter day in Chicago. It is cold, the heater is on, and signs of darkness are beginning to come since the sun will be setting soon. Jesse turns on his headlights just as headlights are beginning to appear on other automobiles. Jesse isn't in any hurry since there is nothing planned other than a routine evening at home. There will be supper with the family, followed by the normal activities before retiring. As he continues on his way through the intersection at Irving Park Road, Jesse has reason to be satisfied with life. He has good health, a satisfying job, and all the things that contribute to a contented life. As he continues along his way well within the speed limit, a car coming from the opposite direction approximately 150 feet in front of him suddenly comes into his lane of traffic. The gap narrows quickly and Jesse realizes that there is going to be an impact. He slams on his brakes, attempts to veer to the right, and then suddenly—there's darkness.

From that moment on, Jesse's life has become entirely different. He is now a handicapped man who must walk with a mild limp for the rest of his life. He has endured headaches from that moment on, and the evidence will be that he will endure headaches for the balance of his life. He has paid numerous medical bills and has become obligated to pay other bills. He is no longer employed by the Holiday Manufacturing Company and has not as yet returned to any form of work.

In addition to the testimony of Jesse, we will call to the stand Chicago police officer Patrick O'Sullivan. Patrick

O'Sullivan has been employed as a traffic policeman trained in the technique of investigating the details of traffic collisions. Officer O'Sullivan was called to the scene, arriving approximately ten minutes after the occurrence. After rendering first aid and summoning an ambulance on his squad car radio, he proceeded to make his investigation. He first determined that there were no known occurrence witnesses. He then viewed the physical evidence and found signs of debris, which, in his opinion, established the point of impact. This debris consisted of an accumulation of street dirt typically found on the underside of fenders. A severe impact will cause this debris to dislodge and fall to the pavement below. In addition to this, he found broken glass which he identified as belonging to the headlights of the automobiles involved. There were other physical signs which he noted that accumulated together led to his opinion as to the location of the impact itself. It was his opinion, based upon his investigation, that the collision occurred in the southbound lane, or the lane in which Jesse was traveling. By means of a tape measure, he also measured skid marks of the northbound vehicle where they commenced to where they ended at the point of impact. The skid marks measured 178 feet. Officer O'Sullivan was able to observe that the skid marks traversed the center line, terminating on Jesse's side of the road at the point of impact. Photographs of the automobiles will be introduced into evidence. The photographs will show the severity of the impact and the speed that obviously prevailed at that time.

Following the collision, Jesse was taken by police ambulance to the Lincoln Hospital. It was there that he came under the care of Doctor Handy. Doctor Handy, a general practitioner, as a member of the staff was called into the case immediately to render care to Jesse. After making an initial examination, Doctor Handy came to the conclusion that a specialist was required. He requested assistance from Doctor Bones, an orthopedic surgeon, and Doctor Cebral, a neurosurgeon. Jesse was taken almost at once to the operating room where Doctor Bones, assisted by Doctor Smith, cut open the lower part of his leg. The purpose of cutting open the leg was to expose the bones which were considerably separated. Then with their hands, they manually brought the bones together into the proper position. While in this position, they drilled holes in the bones with an electric drill so that screws could be screwed into the bones. The purpose of the screws was to hold the bones in position so that they could heal or knit in proper alignment. This operative procedure, I believe, is known as an open reduction. More important, however, was the second operation on the same leg at the knee joint itself. The kneecap was found to be fractured in many places. Rather than attempt to save the kneecap, Doctor Bones and Doctor Handy decided to remove the entire kneecap, which was done. Doctor Bones and Doctor Handy will be called to the witness stand to describe these procedures in more detail.

Following this, Doctor Handy in his treatment of Jesse called in Doctor Cebral, the neurosurgeon, because of headaches Jesse experienced. Doctor Handy will testify that when Jesse was brought into the hospital he was unconscious. Doctor Handy, as part of his routine examination, found a large hematoma on his forehead. He was able to determine that this was of recent origin, indicating that Jesse sustained a severe trauma to the head itself. Within a few minutes after this examination, Jesse did regain consciousness while exhibiting many of the symptoms of a man suffering from a brain concussion. Doctor Handy will describe that examination and the findings that he made at that time. Doctor Cebral, who examined Jesse two days after the automobile crash, was able to make a diagnosis of a brain concussion. Jesse did not exhibit nor could Doctor Cebral find what are known as objective findings. Doctor Cebral was able to make his diagnosis based upon the history of the injury itself. The history, coupled with the description of headaches Jesse was experiencing, was sufficient for Doctor Cebral to make his diagnosis. The diagnosis was an injury to the brain itself. Both Doctor Bones and Doctor Cebral are eminently well qualified—each having contributed significantly to his profession. Doctor Handy is also well qualified as a practicing physician in this community.

Following this, Jesse remained in the hospital under the care of these doctors. He actually remained at the hospital 19 days and underwent various treatments and diagnostic tests. One of the diagnostic procedures performed on Jesse was an electroencephalogram, oftentimes referred to as a brain wave test. This is a means of attempting to test the brain by a complicated system of electricity and measuring the brain waves on a graph. Unfortunately, this test is not always sufficiently reliable to discover an injury to the brain. The evidence will show that the results of this examination were negative. Doctor Cebral will describe the shortcomings of this diagnostic procedure in more detail.

In attempting to cure Jesse, physiotherapy treatments were prescribed by Doctor Bones. These were treatments given in the hospital in an effort to strengthen the leg and restore proper motion. These physiotherapy treatments were continued by Jesse as an outpatient of the hospital twice a week for a period of two months following his discharge from the hospital. The headaches that Jesse experienced following his brain injury have continued up to the present time. These headaches occur almost daily—the duration being as long as an hour or two.

Jesse has been discharged from further medical treatment by all of the doctors. It is their opinion that he has reached the maximum recovery that he will ever reach and that whatever condition he has today will remain with him for the balance of his life. Doctor Handy released Jesse from his care approximately two months after his discharge from the hospital. He has not had occasion to examine or treat Jesse since that time. Neither of the specialists has had occasion to see Jesse for the purpose of treatment since his discharge from the hospital. However, at my request, all of the doctors did examine Jesse last week so that the jury could have the benefit of a current medical evaluation from all of these doctors.

We will also call to the stand Jesse's wife, Mary. She will testify as to the things she has noticed about Jesse which are different since his injury. She has observed Jesse taking aspirin on many occasions. She has noticed a marked difference in his attitude in that he is now a nervous, preoccupied man when previously he was a happy, thoughtful husband. She has massaged his leg daily since his release from the hospital and often applies a heating pad to it.

The jury will also hear from the oldest daughter, Jane, who has also observed numerous differences in her dad. Ten-year-old Jane remembers her dad as a happy man interested in her activities. She remembers the evenings that her dad helped her with her homework and shared with her the laughter and humor of recounting the day's activities.

This is substantially what we expect the evidence to show. Thank you.

As can be seen from this opening statement, the plaintiff's attorney has pretty well laid his cards on the table. Most of the groundwork was devoted to preparing the jury for a generous damage award. An experienced defense trial lawyer can immediately recognize that this lawyer feels pretty good about his liability issue, but is trying to prepare the jury in advance for the shortage of medical evidence. Further medical treatment to the leg is also conspicuous by its absence. Both lawyers know that the plaintiff's claimed loss of income up to now, as well as any future claim, must be supported by these headaches. The plaintiff's attorney obviously has a big job to do with a limited number of tools. The plaintiff himself, as well as his wife and daughter, must be most persuasive in the absence of any reliable medical evidence to substantiate the claimed headaches.

The plaintiff's attorney has already served notice that his strategy will be to minimize the value of the electroencephalogram. The only avenue open toward accomplishing this end will be to bring it out through the testimony of Doctor Cebral. It would certainly seem obvious that the defense lawyer at this point would want to know what the authorities have to say about the reliability of electroencephalogram tests. This will be one of the important points of cross-examination since Doctor Cebral is going to have to admit that there isn't one single objective finding that he can observe about the plaintiff to substantiate the subjective complaints of pain. Doctor Cebral obviously has had to make his diagnosis entirely upon what the plaintiff has told him. The defense lawyer, by knowing all of the tests made by a neurosurgeon in a neurological examination, can make quite a dramatic impact on the jury when Doctor Cebral testifies on cross-examination that he performed each of these tests and that each test was negative.

The defense lawyer should, of course, be keenly aware of the type of impression the plaintiff's wife and daughter will make. If he has not already met them or taken their depositions, he will be anxiously waiting to observe their demeanor on the witness stand. Of course, he knows the demeanor of the plaintiff. If the plaintiff is the antagonistic, exaggerating, shifty-eyed type, or possesses some other undesirable personality trait, the defense lawyer will want to remind the jury that their function is to closely observe the demeanor of the witnesses.

Assuming that the plaintiff makes an average impression and that the demeanor of the wife and daughter is unknown to the defense lawyer, a suggested opening statement for the defense might be as follows:

May it please the Court, counsel, ladies and gentlemen of the jury. Mr. Windy has just explained to you folks what he expects to prove. He has also informed us of the witnesses he intends to use in order to prove the charges that have been brought against my client John. He has also told us of the witnesses he intends to use to prove the disability that is claimed by Mr. Whiney. At the risk of some repetition, let me also say that you folks must decide this case on the evidence—not on what lawyers say. While at this state of the proceedings we do not discuss the law with the jury, let me just say in passing that the law requires a plaintiff to prove the things that he claims. Proof, of course, consists of the testimony of sworn witnesses and not of lawyer's talk.

The facts of the accident are relatively uncomplicated. There was a head-on collision at the place and time described. I was not at the scene of the accident so it would be a useless gesture to pretend that I know how this accident happened. The police officer who came to the scene 10 minutes later does not know how the accident happened. I am sure that the jury will call the shots fair and square in deciding whether the plaintiff has proven that the accident happened as he claims. Now, with regard to the injury, there is no question that the evidence will show that the plaintiff did suffer a broken leg and had his kneecap removed. I am also confident that the evidence will show that he sustained a bump on his forehead and was rendered unconscious because of it. I would suggest that the jury listen very carefully to the evidence presented by the plaintiff to prove his claim for headaches. Thank you.

As can be seen, this opening statement was brief and ended on the weakest point of the plaintiff's case. If the last thought sticks with the jury, the defense lawyer may have set the stage for a generally skeptical jury. If the claim for headaches falls with a thud, much of the loss of income to date also goes with it, to say nothing of any claimed future loss of income. As it is falling, it will drag down the plaintiff's entire case, resulting in a rather modest verdict. It is even conceivable that if the police officer does not hold up on cross-examination or if the defense lawyer can cast doubts on the plaintiff's testimony, while at the same time being aided by a persuasive defendant, the jury could bring back a verdict of "not guilty."

III. Direct Examination

Let the Witness Travel the Road by Himself

L AWYERS MAY DIFFER as to the importance to be placed on skill and preparation in direct examination, as compared to other phases of the trial. However, any lawyer who has ever tried a lawsuit will have to agree that this phase can be the most frustrating. The rules of direct examination require that the witness do the testifying without help or suggestions from the examiner. The cross-examiner, however, can compel "yes" or "no" answers. He can prevent a witness from being unresponsive or from giving narrative-type answers. He can also deter a witness from testifying in a field where the witness would be more comfortable. In short, the cross-examiner has the power to be in complete control. Upon direct examination, the complete opposite prevails since the rules require that the examiner let the witness "travel the road by himself." We might compare the lawyer's role on direct examination with that of the captain of a ship who must temporarily turn over its control to a layman while the ship is in difficult waters.

No Substitute for a Good Witness

So far as the plaintiff is concerned, it is safe to say that most law-suits are won or lost by direct testimony. It is rare for a plaintiff examiner to win a contested liability case by cross-examination alone. The lawyer may be the most brilliant cross-examiner in the country, but he cannot win his lawsuit unless he presents his evidence in a believable and powerful manner or unless his opponent falters. We are all familiar with the criminal defense lawyer on television who scores a success, by adept cross-examination, with what would other-wise appear to be a "sure loser." During this brilliant display of cross-examination, one of the State's witnesses usually breaks down and admits committing the murder himself. But in real life, most lawsuits are won or lost as a result of direct testimony. If the exam-iner heeds the basic rules set forth in this chapter, he will probably win those cases which can be won.

Now, if we accept the fact that this is the dangerous period during the trial of a lawsuit—and, more often than not, the most important phase in establishing the case—how, then, can the skillful examiner take steps to get the most from a witness and avoid a sudden reverse? The experienced or inexperienced lawyer must, in large part, accept the witness as he is. The witness must contribute a part—some-times a major part—in establishing the theory of the case. The wit-ness may be a likeable, convincing, articulate person who projects well, or he may be the complete opposite. The trial examiner will be greatly comforted when he is handed a bonus in a witness who can capture not only the interest of the jury, but its sympathy and under-standing as well. Fortunately, these delightful witnesses come into the life of a trial lawyer from time to time, for constantly working with sluggish or antagonistic witnesses would be too great an ordeal for the average lawyer to bear. I recall the murder trial some years ago in which the daughter of a famous movie star, Lana Turner, was on trial for killing her mother's lover. What a refreshing experience it must have been for the direct examiner to submit a few words to the star witness, who then proceeded to keep the jury completely spellbound while she sold it on the defense side of the case.

Let the Danger Be Understood

The witness should be informed that the direct examination is the most vulnerable period during the course of the lawsuit. It is vulnerable because control over its conduct must be loosened. The witness should be made fully aware of the fact that an unfortunate or inaccurate statement may do irreparable damage to the case. Because of this lack of control over the witness on direct examination, the trial lawyer quite often finds himself in an apprehensive mood because of unfortunate experiences in the past. Every trial lawyer has had the frustrating experience of going to court with a case that looks good, only to be "blown out of the water" or to have the results of the trial materially affected by unexpected testimony of his client or an important witness.

The Defense Lawyer Wins a Rear-Ender

Every once in a while a defense lawyer will get a "not guilty" verdict in a rear-end case. His fame and reputation will rapidly spread among the insurance carriers because he has won a hopeless case. It must be, they feel, that he possesses some mysterious power or ability if he can persuade a jury that the defendant was not guilty in a fact situation in which the trial judge should have even directed a verdict for the plaintiff.

The explanation of this victory is quite simple. The defense lawyer is not a superman—it is just that the plaintiff lost his own case. Too often a plaintiff treats a rear-ender as if his ship had come in, and now that he has the insurance company right where he wants it, all he has to do is provide the damages. But anything smacking of a "buildup" will usually be recognized by the jury. An extended leave of absence from a job that consists of sitting behind a desk and pushing a heavy pencil will insult the intelligence of the jury—especially when the plaintiff continues a healthy, vigorous life of bowling, swimming, tennis, and golf. Add his catching up with repairs and painting around the house to the athletic endeavors, and you have an antagonistic jury. A doctor who testifies that he treated the plaintiff for the injuries, but who mistakenly inserts in his records dates of treatments on Sundays and legal holidays, will not add to the authenticity of the plaintiff's case. Top it off with a photograph of the defendant's car, indicating that the damage was less than $5, after the plaintiff testified to extensive damage to his own car, and we have an angry jury. A case consisting of all the examples used above would be extreme. It is difficult for a trial lawyer to be objective, and many shades of "manufactured evidence" may blind his perceptive abilities. If there is even the slightest suspicion that the damage evidence is not completely fair, the outcome of the lawsuit is in danger. Therefore, it can be seen that a defense lawyer does not win a rear-end case. The jury is simply showing its displeasure by giving a verdict to the defendant, or perhaps by giving the plaintiff a $5 award. Anything less than complete honesty in presenting the damage evidence will probably be recognized by the jury. Greed should never be allowed to become so overwhelming that it prevents the plaintiff or his attorney from recognizing the fact that the jury is not composed of idiots.

PREPARING THE WITNESS

Why Consider the Immediate Impression?

All of us form immediate, tentative opinions upon first meeting a person, and sometimes these opinions are based upon only the sketchiest evidence. As we get to know the person better, we may alter our tentative opinions, and then again sometimes they are confirmed. Some people make a conscious effort to keep an "open mind" and try not to form an opinion one way or the other, but I believe that it is not humanly possible to avoid forming an immediate impression of a person to some degree. Physical characteristics and mannerisms of persons whom we meet for the first time will probably remind us of others we have known in the past, and we have a tendency to identify a new person with them. Sometimes a person bears a striking resemblance to someone we know. It is rare indeed to meet a person who does not provoke some impression. As we look at his face, listen to his voice, and note his choice of words and his mannerisms, we begin to subconsciously categorize this person with people who have touched our lives in the past.

People do not uniformly agree on what are desirable or undesirable characteristics, but there are some areas in which everyone does agree. In conversing with someone we intend to put on the witness stand, we can observe him closely and begin to predict the type of impression that he will make. When a person is on the witness stand the jurors are both consciously and unconsciously forming impressions about him. These impressions come from many things. Foremost is the testimony. The witness paints a picture of the occurrence in the minds of the jurors through his choice of words and through his speaking voice. Does he answer questions promptly, or does he hesitate? Does he exaggerate, or does he play down? Is he forceful in manner, or meek? The jurors also take into consideration the witness' entire physical appearance. Is he pleasant or unpleasant? His sincerity or lack of it, his politeness or crudeness, his posture—all these things which go to make up a total person—create impressions in the minds of all who are observing the witness.

Evaluating Your Witness

As the trial lawyer interviews the witness, he comes to conclusions and forms impressions as to the accuracy of the statements of the witness. He begins to get a picture of how the jury would receive this witness if he were to appear just as he is. He begins to size up the strong points and recognize the weak points of the witness. The amount of time that will have to be spent in preparing him is becoming apparent. This amount of time will be directly related to the importance of the witness in the case, together with the amount of "cleaning up" necessary to smooth over any undesirable characteristics he may have. There may be obvious problem characteristics or mannerisms that will have to be improved. For example, improvement may be necessary in his general attire. A trial lawyer wouldn't want an essential male witness to show up in a suit similar to one worn by a gambler on a Mississippi River boat. A woman witness wearing a mini-skirt and long, flashing earrings would also cause her lawyer some concern. An obvious lack of courteousness in conversing may come through and it must be worked on. A lawyer would have to be quite unsophisticated in his understanding of juries if he failed to see that certain obvious characteristics could have an adverse effect on his selling job.

We must always bear in mind that the witnesses are produced for their persuasive value and their ability to satisfy the skeptic. The lawyer may pin his expectations optimistically on the inability of his opponent to effectively persuade the jury due to annoying characteristics or reckless attire of *his* witnesses. This is especially true if cross-examination can highlight these characteristics.

The most profitable time devoted to preparing the case is often spent in "cleaning up" the demeanor of the plaintiff and the witnesses. Careful preparation, combined with brilliant cross-examination, closing arguments, and other skillful work, is sometimes not sufficient to correct an undesirable image an important witness projects. This witness may have developed a habit of which he is unaware. This habit may seriously detract from an otherwise truthful and earnest appearance. An annoying habit can begin and grow until it is a part of him. A Spanish proverb states: "Habits are at first cobwebs, then cables." The lawyer must figuratively saw the cables away from the witness.

Common Problem Characteristics of Witnesses

In an effort to systematize the improvement of some of the undesirable characteristics found in witnesses, I have prepared a list of the most common ones and have suggested measures to help reduce the problem.

The Long-Winded Witness.—This is the witness who feels that every answer to a question requires a speech. He always provides a great deal of background material as a preliminary to answering the question.

This type of witness is dangerous because he invariably supplies abundant material for cross-examination that can create doubts and sometimes problems that otherwise would not exist. In addition, an overly talkative person is the least persuasive. The jury will have a tendency to discount much of what he has to say, which may involve some important segments of the case. In addition to creating a poor impression, he is difficult to examine if your opponent is making numerous objections that the trial judge sustains. In sheer desperation, the examining lawyer may find himself resorting to leading questions, which are in turn objected to. The result is an entire examination that is a clumsy, weak contribution to the case in chief.

Patience and time are required to reduce this problem to an acceptable minimum. By repeating practice questions and answers in your office, you will have to painstakingly point out that the answers are not responsive to the questions. The amount of repetition will depend upon the dimension of the problem. You can't expect to eliminate a practice that has been developed over a lifetime, but you can expect to obtain some improvement with this type of witness.

The Short-Winded Witness.—While in the office this witness may cause the lawyer's heart to leap with optimism. Unfortunately, when he takes the witness stand, he chooses that time to imitate a sphinx. By giving one-word answers, he forces the examiner to "drag it out of him," and thereby completely loses his effectiveness. The examiner may find himself resorting to leading questions. Assuming that the examiner overcomes the barrage of objections and somehow "drags it out" of the witness bit by bit, he will find that this contribution of evidence has been considerably depreciated, although it would have been of significant value otherwise. An impression may even be created that the lawyer is attempting to prod the witness into testifying to something that he is not quite prepared to say.

It is sometimes difficult to recognize this type of witness when you first interview him. I think that every witness, as a routine matter, should be educated on what a leading question is and why his testimony is of value only if it comes from him, rather than in the form of a simple "yes" or "no" in answer to a question. If a witness gives any indication of falling into this category, then spend enough time preparing him so that he knows he must give a sufficiently detailed answer to cover the particular point.

The Opinionated Witness.—This is the type of person who feels that a good partisan argument is essential to success in the trial of a lawsuit. He often uses adjectives, metaphors, and hyperbole. On cross-examination, these exaggerations can be shown for what they are, and the witness may have little persuasive value with the jury although the evidence that he could have contributed might have been significant.

This type of person is usually easy to recognize, and with patience he can be made into a more valuable witness. By repeatedly urging him to omit the adjectives and exaggerations, you will quite often find that you can obtain a relatively good result. It was Colton who said: "If a cause be good, the most violent attack of its enemies will not injure it so much as an injudicious defense of it by its friends."

The Antagonistic Witness.—This is the type of person who views a lawsuit as a personal affront. If he is a party to a lawsuit or is testifying on behalf of a party, then he views the other side as the enemy who has committed a serious and deliberate wrong. He cannot conceal his hatred and contempt for everyone connected with the other side and he does not hesitate to lash out at anyone he identifies as belonging in the "enemy camp." The opposing lawyer is certainly the object of his wrath because he identifies the lawyer as the principal antagonist.

This man's obviously partisan attitude will cause a jury to discount a great deal of his testimony, to say nothing of the fact that he will not project well. If the other lawyer, on cross-examination, meets this attitude with candor, then the bitter lack of neutrality is even further highlighted.

This witness should be made to understand that fury can dim the lamp of the mind and that his violent words may indicate that his side has a weak case. If the witness is intelligent enough to understand the problem that is gnawing at him, he can probably be "cleaned up" sufficiently. This witness is devoted to the cause and can be expected to work harder than most witnesses to help correct a wrong. If, however, this witness is so imbued with hatred that it is spilling over, he should be used sparingly—if at all.

The Dull Witness.—This witness is probably the most frustrating because there is little that can be done to "clean him up" for trial. In addition to being the most frustrating type of witness, he is invariably the most dangerous. If he happens to be an important witness, it won't take your opponent long to recognize that he is the soft "underbelly" of your case. So long as this person occupies the witness stand, your case is exposed and vulnerable. For example, he may be a key occurrence witness on a matter in issue who can testify to important details, but he has erroneous conclusions on one or two points that he cannot disregard in spite of all logic to the contrary. If anything becomes even slightly complicated, he is almost certain to come up with a wrong conclusion on a point or two during cross-examination, and often on direct examination.

When the examiner recognizes the danger, he can only prepare this witness as well as he can and hope the opponent will not inflict a mortal wound to the case while it is exposed. If this witness must be used, then the examination should be as brief as possible in order to create a minimum of target area for cross-examination. In areas in which distances or speeds are important, ample time should be spent in reviewing these facts with this witness. The examiner should expect unforeseen problems with this witness. An attempt to rehabilitate the witness on redirect examination may only serve to re-emphasize and highlight the errors, thus creating a dangerous or false picture in the minds of the jury. If there are other witnesses who can be used to correct these obviously incorrect assertions, they should be used rather than any further effort made with this witness.

> "Peter was dull; he was at first
> Dull,—Oh, so dull—so very dull!
> Whether he talked, wrote, or rehearsed—
> Still with his dullness was he cursed—
> Dull—beyond all conception—dull."—Shelley.

The Ham.—This type of person is a frustrated actor and usually lacks any talent. The witness stand becomes a stage in the courtroom from which to "act" out his role. He has seen great acting on the witness stand in the movies and on television; therefore, he knows what is expected from him. This witness will use exaggerated speech, grimaces, and words with which he is not particularly familiar—in general, he "hams it up." His "acting" causes him to come across to the jury as a complete phony and may even cause the jury to completely discount the attempted contribution toward a "sale" from this witness.

Fortunately, this characteristic is the least common and is the easiest to identify. This witness can usually be "cleaned up" by asking him to use standard words and strongly reminding him that if he uses the witness stand to demonstrate his dramatic ability, his testimony will add little to the case. Caricature expressions and mannerisms should be discouraged by showing him how ridiculous they are.

The Witness with Stage-Fright.—This witness is similar to the "short-winded witness," except that it is only a temporary condition that causes him to completely "freeze" on the witness stand. He may be a talkative person naturally, but suddenly he is panic stricken and unable to communicate intelligently. His mind is numb with fear. There are varying degrees of panic, but they all lead to irrational answers caused by his unnatural frame of mind. Preliminary questions pertaining to his place of residence, the number of years he has resided at each location, his employment, and so forth, will help to relax him so that he will become more prolific and possibly bear fruit.

If you recognize that you have a witness answering this description, it may be a good idea to take him to court and let him go through a "trial run" in an empty courtroom. I don't know of anything more you can do to prepare this witness, other than perhaps recommend a tranquilizer. This witness is only slightly dangerous because his obvious mistakes in answers will usually be recognized for what they are and a gentle, patient examination can usually amend his faulty testimony.

The Shifty-Eyed Witness.—This is the person who has great difficulty in looking in the face of anyone in the courtroom. He will look at the ceiling, the opposite wall, or any other place in order to avoid looking into anyone's eyes. Worse yet—and more often than not—he will look at the floor. These members of the "society of floor watchers" often are not aware of their idiosyncrasy. Invariably, there will be a number of jurors who will regard this as most significant. They have heard, and perhaps have been taught, that people who do not look them in the eye are liars. These same jurors may now regard it as their duty to identify the deceitful fellow and enlighten their fellow jurors at the first opportunity.

Much to a lawyer's chagrin, he may find himself with a client or important witness who answers questions while he is absorbed in studying the floor. The lawyer can be quite certain that this witness is not helping the cause. Coaching and guidance are necessary before presenting this witness to the jury.

The Very Important Person.—This type of person makes it clear that he is condescending to bestow some of his valuable time on the jury in spite of an important and busy schedule. He usually intimates that his station in life is obviously higher than that of any present in the courtroom.

If this characteristic is found in a client, then this attitude must be completely "cleaned up" or the jury will be looking for reasons to find against him. If this attitude is found in a witness, it will require patience and tact on the part of the lawyer to at least partially redeem this situation. A complete restoration cannot be expected because this man has spent a lifetime building up his ego, but with effort from you, it can be temporarily veiled.

The "Thinker."—Some persons allow considerable time to elapse between the time a question is asked and the time the answer is given. This characteristic is often interpreted as indicating either that the witness is not too sure of himself or perhaps that he is thinking up a lie. Extreme slowness is unconvincing and lacks spontaneity.

If there is a long period of thinking before the witness answers during your interview, you will be alerted to the problem. This type of problem can be corrected with very little effort. If you explain how this characteristic creates a problem and let the witness know what questions you are going to ask, he can be made to sound convincing.

The Disorganized Thinker.—Some persons have difficulty putting their thoughts into words, even though oftentimes they are intelligent. Before such a person can make a point, there will be other points that he considers prerequisites. The prerequisite points will have preliminary points. Before he ever gets to the important preliminary points —to say nothing of the main point—the listener has "tuned him out." This type of person may suddenly go off on a tangent and must be forcibly led back to the point in order to keep any continuity at all. If you know such persons well, you will find that they share other traits because they usually have disorganized minds. They are constantly misplacing things, their desks are disorganized, their work keeps piling up, and things in general are in a state of confusion. This type of person may be bright, but there is a distinct danger that the jury may not get the import or significance of his testimony.

When interviewing a person who displays his knowledge of the matter with wordy preliminaries, you probably have this type of individual on your hands. By constantly reviewing his answers and getting to the heart of them, you can probably get him "cleaned up" sufficiently so that the jury will take the trouble to follow him.

The Qualifier.—This type of witness is cautious by nature and finds it difficult to give an unqualified, responsive answer. He constantly uses such expressions as: "I think it was that way," or "As I recall it . . .," or "I believe it was . . . ." When interviewing a witness who has this characteristic, caution him that the trial of a lawsuit does not deal in speculation, guess or conjecture. More often than not, it is merely a habit that he has developed even though he feels quite sure of his position.

When you detect this characteristic in an opponent's witness, it is a good idea to resist the temptation to object on the ground that the answer is only speculation. The jury may be aware of the fact that the witness is noncommittal in that he continually qualifies his answers. By objecting, you may educate the witness and thus increase his probative value for your opposition.

Everyone's Friend.—There are persons who scrupulously try to avoid offending anyone. They want to be everyone's pal. This type of person will want to please even the opposing lawyer; so in order to do this, he will give him the kind of answers that he wants. Therefore, the suggestions given to him on cross-examination will be readily accepted, even though his answers may be contrary to the testimony he gave on direct examination. You can recognize this type of witness at the interview by his extreme eagerness to please you and help the cause.

Never put your money on this type of person unless he can be strengthened and indoctrinated in the facts in your case. He must be made to understand that he will be worse than useless if he does not stand up to his testimony and that even though he might choose to accommodate the opposing lawyer, he will not have the respect of anyone in the courtroom—including the other lawyer—if he does not have the courage of his convictions. Therefore, any potential witness that the trial lawyer interviews who easily accepts suggestions should immediately be suspect. Not long ago I had a prime example in a

65-year-old woman plaintiff who wanted to help the nice young man representing the insurance company. A question was asked of her in a pleasant, almost solicitous manner:

Q. Now, Mrs. Sweet, before you started to cross the street, you really didn't look at all, did you?

A. I guess I didn't.

The Vacillator.—A trait frequently found in prospective witnesses is the tendency to change the facts that they relate. From moment to moment, they will alter their versions of distances, time, speed, amounts, and other essential facts to suit their fancy. All of us can recall interviewing or conversing with people who answer this description. This trait is so dominant in such a personality that others have a tendency to consciously discount much of what he says. We are quickly able to conclude that this person is careless with the facts. For example, the estimate of the speed of one of the automobiles involved in an accident may be 20 M.P.H., but upon repetition it could suddenly be boosted to 35 M.P.H.

Juries are impressed by testimony that appears accurate and free from exaggeration or passion. When a witness changes his statement on the witness stand, he contributes little in the battle of persuasion. This person's contribution not only is worthless, but can be the road to ruin. Not only is he vulnerable to impeachment, but he injects doubts into the entire case. Unless this characteristic can be "cleaned up," the witness should be used only if it is absolutely necessary.

It's OK to Talk to the Lawyer

Breathes there a lawyer who has not had the experience of having a witness testify to the facts, hold up well under cross-examination, and then, in response to a question from the opponent as to whether he has ever talked to a lawyer about the case, steadfastly deny that he has ever discussed the facts with the lawyer who put him on the witness stand? This type of question was not anticipated by the witness and his immediate reaction was to avoid giving the impression that a conspiracy existed between him and the lawyer. The paradox is that this type of witness is probably testifying honestly and accurately to the facts as he recalls them. His conscience would not permit him to do otherwise. He feels that he has helped establish the truth and does not want his contribution to the cause suddenly destroyed or injured by making it appear that a lawyer told him what to say. Because of his zeal to help establish the truth, he can now be backed into a corner, and with a few follow-up questions it can be established that he is lying on this point. He has inadvertently cast doubt upon his entire testimony because it has been demonstrated to the jury that he is capable of lying on at least one point. This damage cannot be corrected merely by submitting an instruction of law advising the jury that it is perfectly proper for an attorney to interview a witness in order to determine what facts he can testify to before placing him on the stand. During closing arguments the opposing lawyer can point out how ridiculous it would be for an attorney to place a witness on the stand without having any idea of what facts he could testify to. Afterward, the witness will admit that it was a ridiculous answer and that he cannot imagine what possessed him to react that way.

Any problem such as this is the fault of the lawyer because he failed to prepare the witness adequately for cross-examination. It takes only a few seconds to explain to him that it is perfectly proper for an attorney to interview a witness and that it would be absurd not to do so. The witness should also be advised that it is perfectly understandable if he talked to other people, even a great many people, about the details of his testimony. It is only logical and it can certainly be anticipated that a witness will give such an unfortunate, unthinking answer in the face of such an unexpected question because once having testified, the human tendency is to become a sympathizer to the cause even if not previously a partisan.

Can You Recall Anything Else?

It is common to find that a witness will forget an important point while under direct examination. If the lawyer directs his attention to that point, an objection may be raised that the question is leading and it will properly be sustained by the trial judge. Depending on how bright the witness is, the examiner can usually drag the information out of him after a series of attempts and many objections. But the value of the testimony may be weakened since it comes to the jury in a clumsy, awkward manner. This is more often true if the witness is a party to the lawsuit or if he is very much a partisan. If the point is so unimportant as to be overlooked by the witness, then certainly the jury may feel justified in not attaching much significance to it. If, on the other hand, the witness is obviously impartial and the testimony does come forth after a futile attempt to block it by the opposing lawyer, it will be all the more significant.

Thus, a party or a partisan witness should be advised that there may be an important point he may forget and that it may be necessary for the lawyer to remind him. He should understand that the prohibition against asking leading questions prevents the lawyer from merely asking him whether he remembers a particular point so that groundwork must be laid before the examiner can remind him of it. He should understand that the question, "Is there anything else you can recall?" is the signal that he has omitted something. For him to answer "That's all there was . . .," or "There isn't any more . . .," puts up a roadblock that prevents the examiner from going any further. When the answer "That's all that I can recall at this moment . . ." is made, this permits the questioner to ask a follow-up question that will include a suggestion as to the point that has been overlooked by the witness. For example, suppose a witness testified as to all of the facts of an automobile collision, but neglected to mention that he saw ice on the pavement. The questioning might be something as follows:

Q. Do you recall anything else that you may have noticed?

A. That's all I can recall at this moment.

Q. Can you recall anything else with regard to the condition of the pavement?

A. I would still have to say that that's all I can recall at this moment.

Q. Did you notice any condition or substance upon the pavement itself?

A. Oh yes, now I remember that there was ice and . . . .

General Instructions to the Witness

When preparing your client or a witness you intend to use on the stand, give him general instructions. These instructions will be nothing more than basic rules of common sense in the art of persuasion. Too often those rules are violated, so the instructions should be given as a matter of routine in every case. Explain to a witness, whether he be partial or impartial, that his purpose in being on the stand is to help 12 impartial persons correctly decide the facts so that justice may be served. The partisan witness is, of course, eager to have the jury decide the issue for his side and he will be most receptive to these instructions. The impartial witness will do a better selling job if he understands that he is there to insure a fair verdict. If the following rules are observed, careless habits of the witness are less likely to diminish the value of his testimony.

(1) The witness should not chew gum.

(2) Women should not smoke where they can be seen by the jury because there is still some prejudice against women's smoking.

(3) Flashy jewelry should be avoided, especially long, dangling earrings.

(4) General grooming should be in conformance with local practice. Men should not have unusually long hair. Women should avoid unusual hairdos or extremely dramatic grooming.

(5) The witness should not slouch in the chair because this has a tendency to show indifference and even disrespect.

(6) There should be a pleasant look on the witness' face because people have a tendency to like pleasant people. There should be a ready smile or laugh when a situation calls for a sense of humor. However, this does not mean that the witness should maintain an idiotic smile during the entire time he is in the presence of the jury.

(7) There should be no attempt to talk to the jurors or to communicate with them by winking or waving. It is not that the exchange of winks between the client and one of the jurors would be harmful with that particular juror. The danger would arise if any of the other jurors should observe the silent communication.

(8) A party or a witness should, at all times, appear to be attentive and interested in the course of the trial.

(9) If an adverse witness testifies to something that is untrue or displeasing, there should be no demonstrative actions or words spoken by the client. (A delicate and careful shake of the head by the client, almost as if he cannot believe his ears, may be all right if he can carry it off convincingly.)

(10) When answering important questions, the witness should look at the jury to create an aura of sincerity.

(11) The witness should maintain a pleasant attitude and be extremely courteous to everyone in the courtroom at all times.

(12) Make certain that if the witness has given an oral deposition on a previous occasion, he has read the transcript carefully and knows it well. The consequences of giving answers at variance with the testimony in his deposition should be explained to him.

(13) The witness should use words with which he is familiar. Any attempt to use unfamiliar words to be in keeping with the solemnity of the occasion will probably come across as insincerity. Be careful not to insist upon or even suggest the use of certain words—let the witness be as natural as possible.

(14) Explain that the trial of a lawsuit is an adversary system that will inevitably bring about arguments and sharp differences of opinion. Explain that he is not a participant in the battle and that any harsh words or battling should be left to the professionals. The witness should understand that the lawyer is a professional "battler" in the courtroom arena and that he will be outmatched if he attempts to spar with the lawyer. Not only will he be outmatched, but he will be playing right into the lawyer's hands by projecting an undesirable personality. A smart aleck answer is quickly seized upon by the jury and identified with a particular witness in their deliberations.

(15) The witness should not attempt to outsmart the opposing lawyer by giving tricky answers. A witness should be advised that his function is to accurately testify to the facts as he understands them. An

unsuccessful attempt to outdo the lawyer may provide the weapon he needs to destroy that witness' entire testimony and perhaps the case itself.

(16) Explain that the question "Can you recall anything else?" is a preliminary question to help refresh his memory, as discussed on page 78.

(17) The witness should understand that any inquiry as to whether he talked to a lawyer or anyone else about the case is only a trick question, as discussed on page 77.

(18) Explain the rule as to hearsay testimony to the witness to prevent unnecessary objections and chopped-up testimony.

Preparing Witnesses with Similar Testimony

When preparing two or more occurrence witnesses, it is a good idea not to interview them in each other's presence. There is always the danger that one articulate and forceful witness will use words that will be adopted by the other witnesses. If two or more witnesses use the same words to describe an accident, an immediate suspicion will be created in the minds of the jurors—to say nothing of the ammunition supplied to the other lawyer for his closing arguments. The lawyer should also refrain from using any descriptive words while interviewing the witnesses because his words may be picked up and parroted. If the witness lacks the imagination for using descriptive words, then continue cross-examining him in the hope that he himself will come forth with acceptable words. If a witness testifies as to the things he has noticed about the plaintiff since he sustained injuries, he must use his own words no matter how inadequate they may be. It will sound like a speech prepared by the lawyer if each member of the family testifies that he noticed that the mother no longer scrubs floors, irons, vacuums rugs, washes windows, or bends down to wash her face in the basin, and that she is constantly holding her back, always lying on the couch, taking aspirins, and so forth, in the same order and in the same words.

The correct method in this circumstance is to have each member of the family jot down privately all of the things he noticed that are different about the injured person and ask him not to exchange observations with other members of the family. When each is asked the question, the result will be a spontaneous and sincere answer that will give the impression of being completely extemporaneous.

Conveying the Message of Pain

Pain can be produced when one touches the point of a pin and pain can be produced when an arm is torn off in slowly grinding gears. The words "pain and suffering" roll off the tongue easily. These words correctly describe the subjective messages delivered to the brain when a body is forced to undergo an intrusion on its normal routine. The words themselves cannot possibly describe the degree of torment suffered by the one subjected to pain and suffering. Yet this is one of the basic elements that the jury must measure. How can one weigh or measure such an intangible? We are limited to words in painting a picture in the minds of the listener. In order for the jury to "measure the damages," the plaintiff, to a marked degree, must create an image in the minds of the jurors through the use of words. If the jurors accept the fact that the plaintiff has justification for his complaints of pain in the back, how can they possibly know the quantity of pain if the plaintiff says he has "pain in his back"? The jury has a sworn duty to allocate a sum of money to compensate the plaintiff for the "pain in his back." If the jury is to properly discharge its duty, it necessarily follows that the picture must be painted accurately.

The task of creating this picture is just as important for the defense lawyer as for the plaintiff's lawyer. While the plaintiff's side is busy painting this picture through the use of words, demonstrations, or analogies, the defense side, by using the same methods should be just as busy in making certain that the picture is not over-colored. An attempt to paint this picture exclusively through the use of words is totally inadequate. The thoughts, sensations, and instincts of human beings can never be communicated through such an imperfect system as mere sound waves created through the use of vocal cords. The human being has five senses to help him receive messages from another human being. Obviously, the most accurate picture would be painted through the use of all five senses. There should be no reason why a trial lawyer must feel that he is confined to the sense of hearing as an instrument to convey the degree of pain experienced by the plaintiff; nor, for that matter, should he be content with the use of worn-out clichés.

While interviewing his client, the plaintiff's lawyer should discourage characteristic or idiomatic words of pain. An imaginative client may use analogies that can "catch on" with a jury. A description of a "hot knife being driven into my spine" will paint a picture more dramatically than will "a sharp pain in my back." The plaintiff who has lived with a pain for a considerable time may have many good analogies. When a colorful, descriptive phrase or word is used by the client during the course of the interview, it should be written down so that the plaintiff can be reminded later of these exact words.

Conveying the Message of Pain Through the Family

It is more effective to dramatize pain and suffering through the plaintiff's family or friends than through the plaintiff himself. If the plaintiff must carry the ball in presenting evidence as to his pain and suffering, the jury is less likely to be moved by the testimony. The reasons for this are apparent. First of all, the average person does not care for a complainer, and second, the plaintiff has more financial reason for protesting his pain. As a matter of fact, many jurors will admire a person who does not dwell on it. Samuel Johnson said: "The usual fortune of complaint is to excite contempt more than pity." For example, it will be more effective for the plaintiff's 10-year-old son to testify as follows:

Q. What, if anything, did you notice about your Daddy before June 13, 1965?

A. He used to play ball with me and he gave me piggyback rides. He was always happy and he used to talk to me a lot.

Q. And what, if anything, have you noticed about your Daddy since June 13, 1965?

A. He doesn't play ball with me anymore and he never gives me piggyback rides. He seems to be kind of mean to me now and he never seems to want to talk to me.

Q. What, if anything, have you noticed your Daddy doing?

A. Well, he lays on the couch a lot now, and when he's home, I see him taking lots of pills from a bottle and I see Mommy rubbing his back all the time.

This technique can be used with other members of the family. Each member of the family may have had his or her life changed to some extent because of the disability of the father. As can be seen from this approach, not only will the defendant be paying for the injury inflicted upon the man of the house, but the whole family is being brought into the act.

This technique can be used to correct other problems as well.

I recall a case I had in which the plaintiff was a woman who suffered a rather severe injury. She had an unpleasant personality because she was a "grumbler" and had a whiny voice. If I had asked her about her complaints of pain, she could have consumed an hour discussing all of her suffering and anguish. Fortunately, she had an engaging daughter who was capable of carrying the ball. I kept the direct examination of the plaintiff to a minimum, covering only the essential details. Then I urged her daughter to describe conditions before and after the accident. The result was an adequate verdict.

CONDUCT AND STYLE OF A LAWYER

Keep the Jury's Attention

Because of the importance of the role the lawyer plays in persuading the jury, this section would not be complete without some comments along these lines. Although the jury may have been told during *voir dire* that the trial of a lawsuit is not a personality contest and that its verdict should be based upon evidence, nonetheless a lawyer's personality and behavior will play a part in its decision because jurors are human beings.

During direct examination, the lawyer will recede into the background more than at any other time during the trial. If he is fortunate enough to have a most persuasive witness on the stand, he should direct all of the attention to that witness. He should make a conscious effort not to distract the jury's attention from the witness by rattling papers or engaging in any other distracting behavior. He should also be mindful of any efforts by his opponent to distract the jury's attention from an important witness. These distractions can be created deliberately, by his opponent or perhaps even inadvertently. If there is any disturbance, such as an unusual noise from the street, persons coming into the courtroom, or other distraction, the examiner should wait until they subside. When he is again confident that the witness has the attention of the jury, he can continue with the examination. I have known opponents who will purposely cause their chairs to squeak or who will tap loudly with a pencil on the table, pace up and down, or perform some other distracting act. One of the most common and effective forms of "play acting" is to deliberately look for a piece of paper in the file—a hurried, whispered conference with a colleague will set the stage while they are both rummaging desperately through a briefcase looking for the piece of paper. This type of action can capture the attention of the jury and it may be caught up in this game, wondering if the piece of paper will eventually be found. In the meantime, the direct examiner has been the victim of a theft. The jury's attention was elsewhere during the time he had a persuasive witness on the stand.

Keep the Faith

Even though he may not feel it, the lawyer should always show confidence in the case. By putting on a display of confidence and faith in the outcome, he is helping to persuade the jury.

> " 'Tis easy enough to be pleasant,
> When life flows along like a song;
> But the man worth while is the one who will smile,
> When everything goes dead wrong."—Ella Wilcox.

If the lawyer is skeptical of his case, the jury will sense it. This skepticism will also rub off on the witnesses. In fact, they are likely to sense his pessimism even more. The witnesses, as well as the client, look to the lawyer for leadership. A confident lawyer will find witnesses eager to follow his instructions. There can be only one "captain of the ship," and if the lawyer finds himself quarreling with his client or witnesses as to procedure or strategy the case will founder like a ship without its captain.

Don't Get Angry at the Witness

If you begin to show irritation with your client or witnesses in the presence of the jury, then you, as well as your witnesses, will be less effective in the battle of persuasion. When you have a client or witness on the stand who is violating some of the basic rules even though you have cautioned him about them, it is necessary to resist any display of anger or irritation. If you fail to project the image of a confident gentleman or "nice guy," it may appear to the jury that something has gone wrong with your case. It is impossible for a jury to be so objective that it will decide issues based only on evidence. The lawyer's attitude will certainly contribute to persuading the jury. When you recognize that your witness on the stand is a "talkative witness," a "ham," a "dull witness," or that he has any other undesirable characteristics, keep in mind that he is only a part of your case. Hopefully, there will be other, more persuasive evidence in some other phase of the proceeding. Don't highlight these unpleasant characteristics by showing irritation. Get the witness off the stand as quickly as possible, while continuing to project an image of an affable lawyer confident of a favorable result.

A problem that constantly confronts the lawyer on direct examination is the witness' continued violation of the hearsay rule. Witnesses are continually saying, "as we approached the intersection, she said to me ... and I said to her ... ," or "I said to the policeman ... and the policeman said to me ... ," or "in the emergency room, I said to her ... and she said to me ...." Many lawyers will constantly object to references to these conversations. In spite of the court's admonition and instruction to the witness that he cannot testify as to conversations, but only as to what he saw or heard, the witness will continue to make the same mistake. People just don't talk that way. Many find it difficult to conform to the rules. A trial judge who possesses poor judicial temperament may act outraged at the witness' mistakes in the presence of the jury. Such an attitude will reduce the import or value of the testimony, to say nothing of the fact that it shakes up the witness. If the trial lawyer becomes irritated and loses patience, the witness may become hopelessly confused because he is in unfamiliar surroundings with lawyers and a judge "barking" at him. The examiner must remain calm and attempt to soothe him by maintaining a pleasant attitude while patiently questioning him.

Let the Jury Hear

It seems almost too elementary to mention, but the examiner on direct examination should be standing in such a position that the jury is between the witness and him. In this way, each voice must travel across the entire jury before the other hears it. The examiner can then feel fairly certain that the questions and answers are being heard by the entire jury. In the movies or on television, one invariably finds the lawyer with his back to the jury, carrying on a private conversation with a witness in such a manner that it would be impossible for the jury to hear. In cross-examination, it will often be advantageous to be closer to the witness, as on page 120.

If the witness has a speech impediment or a heavy accent, care should be taken to insure that the jury hears and understands his testimony. It may be necessary to ask the witness to speak louder or to ask him to repeat the answer until the examiner is satisfied that he can move on to the next point. If the witness' command of the English language is so poor as to make it impossible to paint a picture in words through his testimony, then, by all means, an interpreter should be employed.

Not Too Much Objecting

Generally speaking, I think it is better for a lawyer to avoid making objections unless he feels that the question calls for an answer that is not only improper, but can damage his case. Even though the jury has been cautioned that part of the lawyer's job is to object when he feels that it is necessary, individual jurors quite often feel that this is an attempt to conceal facts. If a lawyer makes numerous objections over technical matters, the jurors may feel downright antagonistic because this practice will irritate them. If most of the objections are being overruled, the lawyer will put himself in an even worse light in the eyes of the jurors. Remember that the jurors are eager to hear all of the facts and will be annoyed if they feel that anything is deliberately being withheld from them. They genuinely want to find on the side of truth and justice. They feel that they are intelligent enough to discard that which is irrelevant or unimportant, so they will not look with favor upon efforts made by a lawyer to prevent them from getting all of the facts. Overly technical objections, in addition, can appear to be pompous and ridiculous. An example of this follows:

Q. Did you have an opportunity to observe the plaintiff's automobile as it approached the traffic light?

A. Yes, I watched it for about 200 feet before it got to the traffic light.

Q. Did it maintain approximately the same speed as you continued to watch it?

A. Yes.

Q. Do you have an opinion as to the speed it was traveling at that time?

Objection. There has not been a sufficient foundation for this witness to give his opinion.

Sustained.

At this point, the examining lawyer can assume an attitude of disgust as if to say: "It's a shame that this lawyer insists on wasting everyone's time with these silly objections." This can be doubly effective where the trial judge has shown irritation at the objections. At this point, the examining lawyer can then politely continue as follows, enunciating clearly to add emphasis:

Q. Now, Mr. Jones, have you had occasion to ride as a passenger in automobiles?

A. Yes.

Q. Did these automobiles have speedometers?

A. Yes.

Q. And as you were riding in these automobiles, did you have occasion to look at the speedometer?

A. Yes.

Q. Was this on more than one occasion?

A. Many times.

Q. All right, Mr. Jones, now going back to my original question, did you form an opinion as to the speed of the other automobile as it was approaching the traffic light?

A. Yes.

Q. And what was that speed?

A. About 40 M.P.H.

While this is an elementary illustration, certainly everyone would agree that the objecting lawyer could have helped his case in no way. It is quite possible that this, coupled with other such objections, would reduce his image in the eyes of the jury, thereby impairing the effectiveness of his persuasion.

Another example of overobjection that is committed quite frequently occurs in those jurisdictions that require that before a hospital bill can be admitted into evidence as an exhibit, there must be a foundation to establish that the amount of the bill is fair and reasonable for the services rendered. A physician or an employee of a hospital who is experienced in handling charges for services rendered by a hospital will almost always qualify to testify as to their reasonableness. The bill can be identified by the plaintiff only as to what it is, and cannot be received in evidence over the objection of the defense lawyer. But an objection from the defense lawyer at this point, which would prevent the jurors from knowing the amount of the hospital bill, would seem to them to be lunacy. How can they decide the amount of damages without this information? The plaintiff, of course, will have no difficulty in getting the bill into evidence when the doctor or hospital administrator testifies, and if there is an objection the jury will believe that the defense lawyer has made an unsuccessful attempt to block a perfectly proper item of evidence.

How About Your Appearance?

I do not think that the physical appearance of a lawyer has much influence in the persuasion of a jury if he projects sincerity and conducts himself as a gentleman. We have all heard of the sales manager who said: "Give me a young man who is a college graduate, 6'4", and I'll make a successful salesman out of him." It may be that his height will capture the attention of a customer. However, at the outset of a trial, there is no need to capture the attention of the jurors because they are extremely interested. Whether the lawyer continues to hold their attention will not depend on his physical characteristics. There may be a few jurors who harbor a dislike for persons who have certain physical characteristics, and it is even possible that their dislike will affect their judgment. However, this type of juror certainly is an insignificant minority. The majority of the jurors will not let another juror's prejudice influence their judgment in the face of convincing facts that warrant a verdict. If a lawyer has a physical handicap, I am convinced that it will work to his advantage if he also has a pleasant and gentlemanly approach. However, if the handicap has given him a sour or unhappy outlook on life, then he must control it or he will surely fail as a trial lawyer.

We all possess faults that can be detected. Sometimes these faults are obvious and annoying. A jury lawyer should always keep in mind that he cannot afford to have characteristics that annoy. When a lawyer has met with some success, he is likely not to concern himself with a quirk and it may become more pronounced with the passage of time. That quirk can become a real handicap, even though he may think of it as an asset. It was Heine who said: "We keep on deceiving ourselves in regard to our faults, until we at last come to look upon them as virtues."

At What Speed Should the Lawyer Travel?

When the trial lawyer has a good case, he should keep it moving at a good clip. This does not mean that he should hurry through the presentation of evidence at the risk of losing the jury. He should put on as much evidence each day as possible, resisting the inclination to string out the case—a practice prevalent among lawyers. The longer a trial takes, the more likely the jurors are to lose interest and let their minds wander. In addition, they may forget or lose sight of some of the significant points that have been made. It is best to have them decide the case as quickly as possible while the important points are still fresh in their minds. If a trial is permitted to continue over a weekend, they will probably be talking to their neighbors and friends; this will invariably result in a blending of other ideas and philosophies. It should be a general rule that whenever an extremely favorable point is made, or a telling blow is given to the other side, all systems should be "go" so that the case will be in the hands of the jury as soon afterwards as possible. When making a favorable point, travel slowly so that it will "stick." This is comparable to writing it on stone rather than in water.

PRESENTING THE EVIDENCE

Requirements for Admission

At some point, the lawyer must make a determination as to what proposed testimony or exhibits he will be permitted to present to the jury. He will also have to "play some of this by ear" as the trial proceeds. With this in mind, the basic concepts of the "Rules of Evidence" should be firmly fixed in his mind. This statement may frighten the reader or discourage him from taking on a jury trial. These basic concepts, however, are not difficult to understand and every lawyer knows them. He may not have analyzed them carefully, but with reasonable effort he can have a good working knowledge of them. The evidence should be broken down into its simplest form; everything that you offer must satisfy three requirements: (1) it must be material; (2) it must be relevant; and (3) it must be competent. If the evidence that you intend to offer does not satisfy all three of these requirements, it is not admissible. Let's analyze each of them separately.

Materiality.—The testimony that you are seeking from the witness on direct examination must be material. That is, it must relate to the issues of the case. An issue is created by the pleadings whenever an allegation made by the plaintiff is denied by the defendant. It is the defendant's prerogative to raise any issues he chooses. If an issue is raised by a denial, then any evidence brought out by the parties that relates to that issue is "material." If the Answer of the defendant admits or confesses an allegation in the Complaint, then the plaintiff need not and cannot present any evidence regarding that allegation; it is no longer material.

A case I defended, which was mentioned earlier, is an example of this. My client, a 17-year-old boy, while driving a car at a high rate of speed, ran down and seriously injured the plaintiff while she was in a crosswalk. He also failed to stop for a stop sign. During the trial, the plaintiff's attorney attempted to introduce evidence establishing that my client had been speeding, that he had gone through a stop sign, and that he had run down his client in a crosswalk. I had admitted these allegations in my Answer. Because these allegations were admitted, there was no issue as to fault. The plaintiff's attorney was precluded from putting in evidence on this point. Had I denied the allegations of wrongdoing, then it would have been not only proper, but necessary, that the plaintiff put these facts into evidence to prove the issues. When the jury retired to consider its verdict, its function was to assess the damages. Certainly, there can be no doubt that it would have been influenced in the assessment of damages had I not prevented the "poison" from getting into the evidence. From a strategic standpoint, the plaintiff's attorney probably would have obtained a better result if he had alleged willful and wanton misconduct on the part of the boy. I would then have been faced with the dilemma as a pleader. To confess that my client was acting in a willful and wanton manner would be tantamount to confessing that punitive damages were in order. Had we denied the allegations, my opponent could then have presented evidence to show what a "bad boy" I represented.

In conclusion, any evidence offered not plenary in nature that is at variance with the issues is immaterial and is, therefore, objectionable.

Relevancy.—The testimony sought to be elicited from the witness on direct examination must be relevant. This means that it must have some logical, probative weight tending to prove or disprove some fact in the case. If the lawyer has an occurrence witness on the stand, he is eliciting facts from the witness in an attempt to persuade the jury to his side of the case. The witness who has just testified to the facts of an automobile accident could be an Eagle Scout with 50 merit badges. On the other hand, the witness could be a man who has never held a job for more than two months in his life, and who, if he isn't at the race track, can usually be found intoxicated at the local pool hall. The testimony as to what each of these witnesses saw or heard is relevant as evidence tending to prove or disprove how the automobile collision took place. Any evidence establishing that one witness is an Eagle Scout and the other witness is a pool room bum does not help establish the manner in which the collision occurred.

If a young man out "joy riding" with his girlfriend has an automobile collision, it might be a reasonable assumption that he did not have both hands on the steering wheel. If a witness did not see the young man before the collision, it would hardly be proper for the witness to say he thought the driver had one arm around the girl. This testimony would be merely guess, speculation, and conjecture. To use another example, assume that the plaintiff made an allegation in his Complaint that, at the time of the collision, the defendant was speeding. If there are no witnesses who observed the automobile of the defendant shortly before the collision, then there is no evidence that the defendant was speeding at the time. Assume this defendant was given a speeding ticket ten minutes before the accident and that he subsequently pleaded guilty to this charge in traffic court. As inflammatory as this evidence would be, it does not tend to prove or disprove that he was speeding at the time of the collision. If this same defendant had been given six speeding tickets the year before the collision, then it would probably be safe to say that he has a reputation for speeding. In the trial of a civil case, however, evidence as to a person's reputation for being negligent is not relevant to a specific charge of negligence.

To further nail down this concept, let's use one more hypothetical situation. Assume that two men of the same age and physical description, while crossing the street, are struck by an automobile under identical circumstances and suffer identical injuries with exactly the same damages. Under the law, these two men should be treated the same. If justice is equal, then both men should receive identical awards if they are entitled to the verdict. Evidence tending to show that one man is nicer than the other man would not be relevant. If these two identical cases were tried before different juries, both juries would have the same duties. Their first duty would be to decide the liability issue, and assuming the plaintiff is entitled to a verdict, the second duty would be to assess compensatory damages without regard to any other factor. There is no doubt, however, that the amounts of the two awards would vary considerably if evidence established that one man spent his spare time helping old ladies across the street, while the other man delighted in frightening little children.

Unless the evidence presented has some probative value in establishing the truth of the fact that is in issue, then it cannot be relevant. It is uniformly accepted that background is not relevant. Relevancy is the opposite of guess, speculation, and conjecture. If an allegation is made that the defendant was speeding at the time of the automobile collision, then there would be no logical, probative weight tending to prove he was speeding *at the time* by establishing that he received a speeding ticket ten minutes before the accident and that he subsequently pleaded guilty to that violation. We can speculate that if he was speeding before the collision, he might well have been speeding at the time of the accident. It would not, however, be relevant as evidence having probative value as to wrongdoing *at the time* alleged in the Complaint. Another example of irrelevancy would be a show-ing through the witness that the defendant is a good, solid, substantial citizen who has been on the same job for a number of years, or to show on cross-examination that he is just the opposite.

Competency.—The testimony that you elicit from the witness must be competent. That is, it must not be barred by some rule of evidence such as the "Dead Man's Act," nor can it be privileged com-munications such as those between an attorney and his client or a clergyman and his parishioner. Other communications may be made privileged by statute. In some states, automobile accident reports by a motorist to the Secretary of State have been given such status.

Evidence illegally obtained—such as by wiretapping—is usually incompetent.

Hired Opinion to Persuade

More and more the trial lawyer is relying on opinion evidence as one of his tools to persuade the jury. The use of opinion evidence has come a long way since the turn of the century. Traditionally, juries were permitted to hear only what have been termed "facts." If there were any inferences to be drawn in the form of opinions based upon the facts, then there was no reason for anyone to testify as to his opinion because the jury could draw its own conclusions. If a given set of facts can give rise to an inference or can be the basis upon which a person can form an opinion, and if it is further accepted that it is possible to draw different inferences or form different opinions, then what justification is there for presenting a witness who will testify as to his opinion? It is that if this particular person possesses the ability to greatly move and persuade people, then the other party to the lawsuit is not necessarily getting the benefit of a jury's opinion arrived at through a detached, unemotional, and considered judgment. Instead, it may have been moved to an opposite conclusion, in spite of the facts, by a paid, professional witness. With this tradition firmly implanted in our jury system as given to us by our mother country, the courts have been reluctant to permit opinion evidence. The re-sistance against opinion evidence has been slowly chipped away over the years until today it is very much a part of our modern jury system.

Is It Opinion or Fact?

It isn't always easy to distinguish between a fact and what is called an "opinion." We may elicit testimony from a witness who describes a person as tall, heavyset, dark-complected, with long, dark hair and a high-pitched voice. Another witness might describe the same person as being of medium height and weight, with a ruddy complexion, a nondescript speaking voice, and medium-colored hair cut to an average length. Another way of describing this same person would be to say that he is about 5′11″ in height, weighs approximately 210 pounds, and is olive-complected, with dark hair about three inches long. All of this testimony would be permitted, and yet, aren't all of these things really opinions? Whether a person is tall, short, or medium in height, whether he is fat or thin, whether he is dark- or medium-complected are all subject to a difference of opinion. Clearly it would have to be a witness' opinion that the man was 5′11″ in height and that he weighed approximately 210 pounds. This type of opinion is permitted in evidence without question and classified as a "fact."

When a witness testifies to his estimate of speed, or that a person appeared to be in pain, intoxicated, angry, frightened, or dazed, or that the streets were slippery, or that the visibility was poor, and so forth, he is testifying as to opinions. They are classified as such and are permitted in evidence today. It may or may not be necessary to have a witness first establish a foundation or a reasonable basis upon which he arrived at the opinion. In order to arrive at an opinion, it was probably necessary to form opinions as to other details that would then give rise to another inference or opinion. For example, if it is required that the witness testify as to the facts upon which he arrived at the opinion that another person was intoxicated, he would probably reply as follows: "I detected a strong odor of alcohol on his breath; he was staggering; he had difficulty in talking—like a person with a 'thick' tongue; he had a glassy look in his eyes; he had a flushed appearance in his face, and so forth." Each of these so-called "facts" upon which he formed his opinion is really an opinion in itself.

The More Persuasive Opinion

It is certainly fair ground for the cross-examiner to inquire in great detail as to all of the things observed or heard by the witness that gave rise to his opinion. It can be established that the opinion is erroneous or doubtful if it can be shown it is based upon faulty premises or observations. It is, therefore, obvious that the lawyer is employing opinions in his battle to persuade the jury. The more persuasive the witness, the greater the likelihood that the jury will accept his conclusion or opinion. For example, let's take an automobile collision that occurred at an intersection controlled by traffic lights. One automobile had the green light and the other had the red light as they were proceeding through the intersection. Each driver was alone in his automobile. There were two occurrence witnesses, each of whom arrived at opposite conclusions as to which car had the green light. The jury must decide which version is correct. The lawyer fortunate enough to have the more persuasive witness will, of course, have a decided advantage over his opponent. Each of these trial lawyers must rely on the persuasive ability of his respective witness. Knowing this in advance of the trial, it would seem that the lawyer's job is quite clear. He must evaluate his witnesses, as described earlier. It may be that his efforts might best be served by "cleaning up" the witnesses. He should analyze the basis upon which his witnesses came to their opinions, such as their experience, their ability to observe, their close proximity to the drivers in order to have had an opportunity to smell alcohol on their breath, or the basis upon which they arrived at the conclusions that the streets were or were not slippery. By careful and patient preparation, he can "beef up his forces" for the battle of persuasion through the use of opinion evidence.

Rationale of Using Opinions to Persuade

Through the use of expert opinion evidence, the trial lawyer now has available extremely effective and persuasive opinion evidence. In our highly complex and mechanized modern-day society, the trial lawyer finds himself leaning heavily on the expert opinion for its persuasive value. The courts recognize that a jury composed of lay persons is not capable of coming to opinions or conclusions in difficult or highly technical areas. It may require great study to even begin to comprehend the subject matter. Clearly then, the jury must either accept or reject the opinion of an expert witness. The persuasive ability of a witness is of paramount importance, especially when we have experts on both sides coming up with exactly opposite conclusions. In selecting an expert witness, it would then seem that the astute trial lawyer—while he should be concerned with the witness' background in the field, such as his studies and experience—should be even more interested in the persuasive effect he will have on a jury.

When a defendant in his Answer denies the plaintiff's allegation of permanent injury, an issue has been created. Possibly it is the only issue that the jury will be asked to decide. Courts in various jurisdictions will attempt to distinguish issues upon which they will permit a witness to express an opinion. Attempts will be made to distinguish between the ultimate issue and subordinate issues. However, in spite of all the attempts by the courts to hold the line against permitting opinions to come into the evidence or perhaps to limit the extent of the opinion, the trend is quite clear that opinions play an ever greater role in the battle of persuasion. Where the only issue is the nature and extent of the injuries, the treating physician is universally permitted to testify as to the nature of his examination and the various laboratory tests that he employed, such as X rays, and that all of these findings led him to form an opinion as to the diagnosis. In addition to this, he is permitted to testify as to his opinion regarding the prognosis of the injured person. The physician in this instance is giving his opinion on the precise issue of the case—the ultimate issue, or any other name that the courts choose to use. In some jurisdictions, the courts have had to do some rationalizing and have set up, through a series of decisions, some artificial and sometimes clumsy requirements in order to obtain an opinion from an expert witness relating to one issue in the case. One of the better-known examples is the use of the hypothetical question. The examiner must ask the expert to assume some facts. The hypothetical facts, however, happen to be identical to the facts of the case. The jury must reflect upon the purpose of this bizarre method of securing opinion evidence.

Regardless of whether one agrees with the theory or expediency of this practice set up by our courts, the fact remains that it is a reality. Effective utilization of experts is necessary to obtain desired results. The lawyer has a responsibility to his client to persuade the jury to agree with his point of view through whatever legal, proper, and ethical tools are available.

Let's assume that the lawyer has brought in the most eminently qualified orthopedic surgeon in the community to give an opinion. The jury likes his looks, he testifies well, and, based on his qualifications, he must know what he's talking about. The opponent has also put on an expert witness who is equally well qualified who has testified as to an opinion completely opposite to that of his contemporary. His opinion might be that the degree of permanency is not as great or that the condition is not related to the automobile accident. In addition to this, the jury has heard the treating physician and perhaps some other doctors as well, and now they must go back into the jury room to "kick it around." Their task is to decide whether the condition the plaintiff is complaining of was caused by the accident, and if so, just how bad the injury is. Maybe it was caused by the accident and will always give him a lot of pain, just like that nice Doctor Brown said. On the other hand, Doctor Green was certainly convincing and he said that the problem would clear up in a short time. He also said that whatever the problem is, it wasn't caused by the accident.

The jury will make its decision and whatever conclusion it comes to will, in a large measure, be governed by the persuasive abilities of the expert witnesses. As can be seen, both trial lawyers should be most anxious to have the jury accept their man as the more honest and knowledgeable in his field. Since the client is paying for this opinion, the trial lawyer ought to see that he gets his money's worth by making certain that the jury is properly impressed. The American Medical Association, in recognizing various specialty boards, has made it possible for the public to feel fairly confident that a man is truly qualified as a specialist in his field. The significance of these specialty boards should be made clear to the jury if the expert is a member of one. Memberships in other medical societies, hospital connections, and articles published are important, but nothing so impresses a jury as medical professors who teach other doctors. In considering the use of an expert, one should also consider his physical appearance, demeanor, age, general attitude, and other characteristics that would reflect on the confidence that a jury would have in his opinion. The Greek philosophers tell us "Gray hair is a sign of age, not wisdom." Jurors seldom read Greek philosophy.

It should be kept in mind that the opening statement should pave the way for the jury to receive the expert. The defendant who arranged an examination of the plaintiff by his doctor should tell the jury about this wonderfully qualified doctor who, at his request, examined the plaintiff and that the doctor will testify that, in his opinion, the plaintiff has made a full recovery from the injuries or that the condition the plaintiff is complaining of is a congenital or arthritic condition of the spine.

Breaking it down to its simplest terms, the reason that we use experts is to attempt to persuade the jury in our favor regarding the ultimate issues that they must decide. In order for a person to give his opinion on an ultimate issue, the only requirement is that it be established that the witness is truly an expert in his field. The opposing attorney has a right to cross-examine the proposed expert as to his qualifications before he is permitted to give his opinion.

Never Stipulate to Impressive Qualifications

All jurisdictions recognize that it is proper to bring out a witness' education and background so that the jury will be in a position to give proper weight to his opinion. It is, therefore, necessary that the lawyer bring out the witness' qualifications in the best light possible to properly impress the jury with the value of that witness' opinion. It is not, of course, necessary to present evidence to establish that the witness is truly a qualified expert and, therefore, competent to give an opinion if the opponent stipulates that the witness is qualified. The stipulation will, of course, be most welcome if the expert has a rather unimpressive background and barely qualifies as an expert; however, if he is eminently qualified, with an impressive background and education, and is well recognized in his field, then such a stipulation would deprive the examining lawyer of obtaining the full benefit of the persuasive value of this man's opinion. In reply to an offer to stipulate, the examining lawyer should state that he is willing to stipulate to the witness' qualifications if the opposing counsel will agree that this witness is the best informed and most eminently qualified expert in the country. (The examining lawyer may find it useful to reduce the territorial limits in varying degrees, depending on the facts and circumstances.) The opponent will hardly dare to stipulate to this suggestion, especially if he is relying on his own expert to persuade the jury to the opposite conclusion. The direct examiner, at this point, can then continue to proceed in qualifying his witness.

I recall a case in which it was necessary to travel to another county to try a plaintiff's case that involved an orthopedic problem. At great expense and trouble I arranged to bring in a top, qualified orthopedic surgeon from Chicago, who, incidentally, traveled to the courthouse in a chauffeur-driven Rolls Royce. After being certain that the Rolls Royce and chauffeur were well concealed, I brought my prize into the courtroom. I was, of course, prepared to spend a great deal of time qualifying my witness so that the jury would fully understand what a "big shot" I had. The trial judge, who, of course, knew my opponent intimately, looked down from the bench and with a smile said: "I suppose we can have a stipulation here, counsel, to save the time of the court and jury. . . ." The judge forced me into quite a discussion in the presence of the jury to establish that we had a legal right to establish the doctor's qualifications. My opponent was, of course, quite willing to "expedite the trial for the benefit of the jury." Had the plaintiff been dissatisfied with the results of the verdict, it is quite possible that the judge's attitude would be reversible error in creating an inference that we were unduly wasting the court's time in not accepting the stipulation.

A Legitimate Expert?

In recent years, there has been a new breed of man known as the "accident reconstruction expert." This man, by reason of his training and experience, contends that he can deduce the manner in which an accident occurred by means of the physical evidence. The physical evidence usually consists of the damaged vehicles, skid marks or other marks on the pavement or shoulder of the road, or other physical signs. Since he is rare because of his unusual abilities, his fee for testifying in court is quite high. If he has an impressive educational background coupled with extensive experience, he can, of course, demand a higher fee. In large cases, he might even be imported from another part of the country, and this would amount to quite an investment for the party bringing him in. There is no question that if this person has impressive engineering degrees, is articulate, and makes a good appearance, he can be quite persuasive with a jury. Sometimes he is able to form an opinion as to how the accident occurred based upon very few facts—even if he is limited to photographs and a visit to the scene of the accident.

The problem is that for every "reconstruction expert" who will give an opinion as to the manner in which an accident occurred, there can always be found an equally qualified expert who will have a completely opposite opinion. In view of this, one might come to the conclusion that the opinions of these experts are the natural and probable result of their employment.

The author's opinion of this new occupation is not meant to reflect, however, upon the value of qualified opinion evidence with regard to many areas of technical problems confronting trial lawyers. In establishing the condition of brakes, tires, windshield wipers, or other such items, the courts should not be reluctant to admit this evidence, provided proper foundations are laid. Oftentimes tests made by a trained engineer will almost conclusively establish the truth. The Lawyers Co-operative Publishing Company has a useful book for lawyers to help them find the expert for their problem entitled *Lawyers Desk Reference.*

What Are Exhibits?

Part of the presentation of direct evidence will probably consist of exhibits. The effective presentation and use of exhibits can be an invaluable aid to the jurors and play a major role in persuading them. Exhibits can be found in almost every form. Just to mention a few, you may have photographs of the scene of the accident, of damage to automobiles, or of mechanical or physical objects, or perhaps an aerial photograph showing the approach of a highway to the point of impact, photographs of a leg cast or of the patient in traction or other evidence of the injury suffered by the plaintiff. You may have maps drawn to scale, plats, physical objects such as surgical tools, or other objects too numerous to mention. Other examples of exhibits are motion pictures, X-ray films, blow-ups (enlargements) of letters, medical reports, hospital records, or other types of documents that may or may not go into the jury room after being interpreted and displayed before the jury.

Exhibit Worth 1,000 Words

Not to be overlooked are sketches of an intersection or other objects drawn by the lawyer in the presence of the jury based upon testimony elicited from witnesses. Many persons have difficulty in forming an accurate picture in the mind's eye solely from the spoken word. Direction, distances, and objects placed into the scene of an accident or terrain are difficult to put into words—to say nothing of the varied pictures that will result in the minds of the jurors. The listener may think that he has formed an accurate picture based upon the spoken word, but each juror will have a little different picture in his mind. Some jurors may even have a picture that is completely erroneous.

Should the Injuries Be Displayed?

The injuries or the results of the injuries should be displayed if they are an element of damages the jury is asked to evaluate. In the past, there has been a tendency not to let the jury see the injury or its effect. It was felt that it might tend to inflame them and result in an assessment of damages over and above those that are legally compensable. By keeping the jury in ignorance in not showing them the scars or stump, we are forcing them to speculate as to the damages for disfigurement and permanency. This speculation could result in an unrealistic assessment of damages for either the plaintiff or the defendant. If a young girl has keloid scars resulting from burns on various parts of her body that will show when she is wearing a bathing suit, then the disfigurement should definitely be displayed to the jury, even though it is not apparent when she is wearing a dress. By not showing the keloid scars, it is possible that the jury will not realize the extent of the disfigurement that will always be a source of embarrassment to the young girl. Conversely, the scarring could be quite minimal and not showing it could result in an overassessment of damages. For the same reasons, there should be no reluctance to display before the jury any permanent limitation of motion in walking, moving an arm, turning the head, or any other disability in a joint or portion of the body. To prevent a demonstration of this nature to the jury is to withhold the very evidence that is needed to evaluate any alleged permanent disability. It must be remembered that any deliberate attempt on the part of the plaintiff to overplay the limitation while giving a demonstration to the jury will probably boomerang in the form of a low verdict. Some lawyers have a tendency to overestimate the gullibility of juries. But, in reality, the plaintiff, while making a demonstration, must be completely honest, since any apparent exaggeration will almost certainly be detected. The plaintiff's lawyer not only must caution the plaintiff of the dangers of overacting, but also should go through several rehearsals until he is completely satisfied that the client is going to help rather than hinder his cause.

How can a juror, without personal experience, possibly know the difficulties encountered in the normal routine of life by a man with an artificial leg? Either movies or demonstrations should be given of the labors involved in rolling to the edge of the bed in the morning, strapping on this device, taking a bath, putting on trousers, walking up or down stairs, getting in and out of an automobile, getting in and out of a chair, getting up from and down to the floor, and treating the irritated, sore, and bleeding stump.

The defense lawyer, on the other hand, is entitled to have the jury see the aftereffects of what was described as a large, gaping wound that required several hundred stitches to close when there is little, if any, visible sign of the injury left. There should not be a distorted vision in the minds of the jurors as to what the plaintiff must look like in a bathing suit if in reality the cosmetic results were excellent. When a plaintiff has implied that an ugly scar remains following an injury and this is contrary to the facts, the defense lawyer has an excellent opportunity to work this to his advantage in holding down the damages. The technique is to get the plaintiff as far out on a limb as possible in exaggerating the appearance of the scar, and then ask him to display the scar to the jury. If the jury has to strain to detect anything at all, then the plaintiff's description as to pain and suffering and other matters in issue will be greatly discounted. This can, of course, be done only if the injured portion of the body is so located that to display it would not ordinarily cause embarrassment. If the jury feels that the plaintiff is justified in declining on grounds of embarrassment, then the defense lawyer will appear sarcastic and unfeeling.

Visual aids or demonstrative evidence in the form of medical charts, portions of a skeleton, photographs, or other similar material should be routinely used by both the plaintiff and the defendant. Photographs of the plaintiff taken shortly after the injury will resolve any doubts in the minds of the jurors. The plaintiff, after all, is the one making these claims, and nothing helps so much as a photograph of a puffed-up, discolored face with black eyes swollen shut to establish that he really was injured. With a plaintiff looking perfectly normal in court, it will be impossible for the jurors to visualize accurately what he underwent—to say nothing of possible downright skepticism on their part as to whether he was really injured at all. Photographs—marked with dates on which they were taken to show the length of time treatment was necessary—demonstrating a body cast, leg traction, or any other hardships undergone should be preserved. The investment in preserving this evidence will be returned manyfold to the plaintiff. Without this evidence, the jury cannot possibly know the discomfort and suffering endured by a severely injured plaintiff. Having the benefit of photographs, unfortunately for the plaintiff, is the exception because often the lawyer is called in after the opportunity for obtaining this evidence is gone. Fortunate is the seriously injured accident victim who is represented early by competent counsel because he then has greatly improved the likelihood of obtaining his full measure of damages.

Photographs that Clarify and Show Perspective

Slip and fall cases that occur in large retail chain stores are among the more difficult cases for a plaintiff to win. The successful plaintiff must manage to hurdle two obstacles to obtain a verdict. The first hurdle is the requirement that he show that the defendant had actual or constructive notice of the defective condition; the second is the requirement that plaintiff was exercising ordinary care for his own safety at the time of the occurrence. Where a plaintiff slips on a vegetable leaf or the proverbial banana skin in a store, it is not sufficient that he prove that this hazard was, in fact, the cause of the fall. He must prove that the defendant store had actual knowledge of these circumstances through its employees or agents and that, notwithstanding this knowledge, it failed to remove the skin or leaf for the protection of the plaintiff. If he cannot prove this, he must prove in the alternative that the object was there long enough for the defendant, had it made a reasonable inspection through its employees or agents, to have discovered it. Human nature being what it is, I doubt whether a plaintiff's lawyer has ever had an employee of such a corporation eagerly answer that he knew it was there, but that he just never got around to picking it up. If the plaintiff's lawyer is lucky enough that the object involved is a milk crate that was sitting in the aisle, then it is quite clear that the defendant corporation must have had actual or constructive notice of such an obvious roadblock. In this situation, however, the defendant can throw up the second hurdle by offering the defense that the plaintiff, had he been exercising ordinary care, would have been watching where he was walking.

This second hurdle is cleared quite easily by establishing that the defendant was deliberately directing the plaintiff's attention to everything but the floor on which he was walking. All of the counters have attractive displays calculated to attract the customer's attention—to induce him to buy the merchandise offered. In addition to the displays, there are other attention-diverters such as promotional material, indicating various merchandise on sale or conveying other messages. To top matters off, the floor is usually an uninteresting, neutral color to prevent it from capturing the customer's attention. Enlarged photographs depicting the area should help persuade the jury that the ordinary man is almost prevented from watching where he is walking.

As to the first hurdle, it will always be a problem for the plaintiff to establish notice, actual or constructive. One ingenious Illinois case held that the fact that a lettuce leaf was dirty indicated that it had been on the floor for a sufficient length of time for the defendant to have constructive notice of its presence. Perhaps some day the law will find an equitable solution to this perplexing problem. Certainly, the defendant cannot be held responsible for a lettuce leaf that was dropped to the floor by another customer a few seconds before the plaintiff slipped on it. Then again, it is unfair to require a plaintiff to establish that it had been on the floor for a fairly long period of time when there usually isn't any way on God's green earth to prove it.

A lawyer I know does defense work for an insurance company that insures hotels against public liability. This company carries as a risk one of the large Chicago hotels that has a sunken dining room; it is necessary to walk down a short flight of stairs to reach the level of the dining room floor. The stairs are covered with expensive carpeting maintained in excellent condition. Frequently hotel guests stumble and fall on the stairs, and the ultimate result is a lawsuit. As a matter of routine, a photograph is identified by a defense witness as a true and correct portrayal of the carpeted stairs as they existed at the time of the fall. The photograph clearly establishes that the stairway and carpet are in an excellent state of repair, and further evidence establishes that the lighting situation is always excellent. Inasmuch as evidence of previous falls is inadmissible, a jury will invariably find the defendant hotel "not guilty." What doesn't show in the photograph, however, is that the tread of each step is only seven inches wide; this makes it a rather hazardous stairway to negotiate, as the normal tread is about ten inches wide. A photograph showing a person stepping on the tread makes it immediately obvious that this is a narrow tread. When a plaintiff's lawyer introduces this type of picture, the jury invariably finds for the plaintiff. If pictures are used for the purpose of establishing a defect in design, oftentimes they are practically useless without a familiar object in the picture to give it perspective.

Order in Which Witnesses Appear

The order of appearance of witnesses is within the sole discretion of the trial lawyer. Often there will be discussion as to the permissibility of the plaintiff's putting a doctor on the stand "out of order." I do not know where this prohibition began against putting a treating doctor on the stand before the plaintiff has testified, but certainly it was not in a court of review. The only answer seems to lie in the maxim—"ancient custom has the force of law." The only practical problem arises when a lawyer offers an expert witness who must base his opinion on hypothetical facts. Assurance to the trial court that this evidence will, in fact, be presented will usually be sufficient to permit the expert's opinion to be given in advance of the proposed evidence.

The ideal situation is to present the strongest witnesses first and last. This is to make a favorable, strong first impression and then slam the lid down tight with the last witness. The plaintiff will ordinarily fare better if he gets the liability issue out of the way first. If the jurors are to think in terms of a high verdict, they must not be troubled with doubts as to fault. Many trial lawyers have had experience with "compromised" verdicts where the amount of money given by the jury does not seem adequate for the damages sustained. Sometimes the sheer magnitude of the damages themselves can override a weak liability case. If the evidence bearing on liability is extremely favorable to the plaintiff, he should immediately punch hard on that point, so that the jurors can occupy themselves completely with the damage evidence. If the defendant has a strong witness whose testimony is in complete conflict with the plaintiff's case, he should be used by the defendant at the first opportunity. A prompt counterpunch can send the plaintiff reeling and he may never recover.

I've Got Movies of Your Guy

A defense lawyer should carefully reconsider before he discloses damaging evidence that he possesses. Movies taken of the plaintiff while he is doing physically active sports or work around the house when he is supposed to have been a convalescent are only valuable if their existence is unknown to the plaintiff's attorney. The defense attorney, in an effort to avoid a trial, may be tempted to "let the cat out of the bag." In the *Defense Law Journal*, Volume 4, p. 147 (1958), a defense lawyer recited his experiences as follows:

"He was defending a case where the plaintiff claimed total and permanent disability as a result of a back injury. When the case was called for trial, he told the plaintiff lawyer, 'Tom, let me tell you something,' he said 'I have motion pictures of your man weeding his garden, hoeing in his garden, climbing a step ladder and putting on storm windows and even shoveling snow.' The plaintiff lawyer said absolutely nothing. He got up before the jury to make his opening statement and after describing the horrible injuries that this man suffered, said something like this: 'Members of the jury, when this man was injured he went to the railroad company doctors. They examined him, told him that if he would exercise his back, he would recover more rapidly. They told him to do everything he could do to get his back exercised and tone up the muscles that had been injured. He followed the doctor's advice. He did everything. He went out and weeded in his garden with, of course, such strenuously painful results that they put him in bed in agony with agonizing pain for a couple of weeks. When he could arise from his bed of pain, he went again to follow the railroad company doctor's advice. He hoed in his garden with the same terrible result. Feeling that he might be able to exercise his back violently, he attempted to put on some storm windows where it was not necessary for him to bend over as much as he had in the other tasks. Ladies and gentlemen, this man even went so far as to try to shovel snow with his back so terribly injured that every moment was one of agonizing pain.' When he had finished, the plaintiff's attorney walked over to the other attorney and said, 'Now, my friend, what the Hell are you going to do with your motion pictures?' "

For the defense attorney to display the movies during his case in chief now not only would confirm the plaintiff's testimony, but would establish the defendants as a bunch of snoops, sneaking around with a camera. A feeling could come over the jury that the defendants would go to any extremes to avoid paying their just obligations to the plaintiff.

For years, there have been stories floating around as to how enterprising claims investigators can "get the goods" on the malingering plaintiff. One story has it that an inventive investigator was assigned the task of obtaining evidence to show that a plaintiff was exaggerating the immobility of his back from an alleged injury. Keeping this man under surveillance, he observed that the plaintiff always walked with a slow gait and meticulously avoided any bending or anything more than very limited movements of the back. Observing him one day watering the front lawn while carefully guarding his back, the investigator seized upon an idea. He rented a small truck, setting himself up inside with a movie camera that he could aim through an opening in the side, and arranged to have the truck parked in front of the house. With a co-conspirator in the person of a small but fast boy, he was now ready for action. The boy walked up to the man, grabbed the hose out of his hand and deliberately gave the man a thorough but unwanted shower. Some interesting movies were taken of the plaintiff leaping over the bushes like a gazelle and chasing the boy up the street. Another more common and less contrived production is to let the air out of a tire on a car belonging to the plaintiff. Movies taken of a man bending over to change a tire may serve to contradict testimony as to his degree of immobility.

It should be kept in mind that these tactics can be extremely hazardous to a defendant's case. The jurors may not care for what appears to them to be an almost flippant attitude concerning the plaintiff's injury. The more acceptable and recommended rebuttal evidence of this nature would be in the form of movies or pictures of a suspect carrying heavy groceries, performing strenuous work around the house, or bowling or engaging in some other active physical sport. These movies or pictures should not be used unless the plaintiff has gone far enough out on a limb that he cannot get back. He must be committed on either direct examination or cross-examination to the effect that he has been unable to participate in the very things that the pictures or movies will establish that he has been doing. It is then that a defense lawyer can, with the approval of the jury, saw off the limb so as to bring the plaintiff and his entire case crashing down.

Look Out for Hospital Records

The plaintiff's attorney must be extremely careful that there is not something in writing in the hospital records that can be used by the defendant as a club over the head of the plaintiff. Even more caution must be exercised in those states following the federal procedure that permits hospital records into evidence on the theory that they are kept in the regular course of business. An intern or treating doctor in obtaining the history from an accident victim is not concerned with preciseness as to the manner in which the accident occurred. A line or two such as, ". . . Patient states he was running for bus when he fell on the street . . ." can be catastrophic when in conflict with plaintiff's testimony. The plaintiff after he has testified to carefully walking toward the bus when a defective condition of the street caused him to fall can be completely "blown out of the water" by a few careless strokes of the doctor's pen. The technique of the cross-examiner in highlighting this discrepancy is as follows:

Q. Part of good medical practice with the treating doctor is to take a history from the patient; is that correct, Doctor?

A. Yes.

Q. A part of that history is the manner in which the patient says he was injured?

A. Yes.

Q. So, whatever information the doctor gets is from the patient himself if he is able to talk?

A. Yes.

Q. Was the plaintiff in this case able to talk to you?

A. Yes.

Q. Did he have any difficulty in talking?

A. No.

Q. So far as you are able to determine, he could properly hear you?

A. Yes.

Q. And, for that matter, you could clearly hear everything the patient told you?

A. Yes.

Q. Is it part of good medical practice to write down what the patient tells you when he describes how he was injured?

A. Yes.

Q. In this case, Doctor, did you take a history from the plaintiff as to how he was injured?

A. Yes.

Q. And, likewise, did you write it down?

A. Yes.

Q. Did you write it down immediately following the conversation with the plaintiff?

A. Yes.

Q. Now, I show you what has been previously identified as part of the hospital records and ask you if you can recognize the handwriting on page 14 of the hospital records.

A. Yes.

Q. Whose handwriting is that, Doctor?

A. It's mine.

Q. Then, will you read for the court and the jury exactly what you wrote immediately following a conversation with the plaintiff.

A. Patient states he fell on the street while running for bus.

The same problem exists with regard to histories concerning previous physical conditions. There is no excuse for a plaintiff to testify on the witness stand that he never had a pain in his back before the injury when there is a notation in the hospital records entered by an intern that he had pain in the back for some years previous to his admission into the hospital. The trial lawyer must know of its existence, confront his client with this fact, and demand an explanation. Either the plaintiff is lying or the statement is inaccurate because of a mistake. When one is aware of the problem in advance, steps can be taken to meet it.

It is difficult to understand how hospital records have been held to be "entries kept in the regular course of business." Hospital records are replete with opinions and conclusions oftentimes written by interns and residents no longer available for cross-examination. Either the plaintiff or the defendant can be unduly prejudiced by having an erroneous opinion go into evidence if they are unable to cross-examine the person making the entry. Perhaps his opinion was based upon a faulty premise.

I recall a plaintiff's case I was trying in an Illinois state court (Illinois does not permit hospital records to be admitted into evidence). The plaintiff, a pedestrian, was struck by an automobile and taken to the hospital as an emergency patient. During the course of treatment at the hospital, a resident made an entry in the records that he had examined the plaintiff for signs of an inguinal hernia and found none. The principal treating doctor, who testified at the trial, did not see the plaintiff until after his discharge from the hospital. The first examination made by the witness disclosed a left inguinal hernia. Based upon the patient's history that he had never had a previous hernia problem, it was the doctor's opinion that the condition was traumatic in origin and, therefore, related to the accident. The defense attorney located the resident, who was then associated with a hospital in another part of the country. At great expense, he arranged to bring him in to testify as to the negative findings. Cross-examination revealed that the hernia examination was made while the patient was lying flat on his back in bed. The witness had to admit that the proper method of making hernia examinations is for the patient to stand and cause pressure to be brought in the area by coughing and that quite often a hernia does not demonstrate itself even with a great deal of pressure brought to bear in an attempt to force it out. He had to honestly admit that it is quite possible that the examination that he performed could easily have missed a hernia. As can be seen from this example, it would have been most unfair to the plaintiff to let a notation in the hospital records go to the jury without testing by cross-examination the premise upon which the opinion was based. Vigilance must be exercised to avoid untested opinions' going to the jury. H. W. Shaw was credited with: "Error will slip through a crack, while truth will stick in a doorway."

Don't Gild the Lily

When you have made a point sufficiently clear by using one or more witnesses, you are probably better off to let it go at that. Just because you have another witness to add more evidence on the point that you have already established, don't feel that you must use him. Remember that you vouch for every witness you put on the witness stand. The more witnesses you use, the greater the risk of inconsistencies creeping in that can create doubt in the minds of the jurors that would not otherwise have been there. This will be especially true if the witness has a personality defect. Keep in mind that the fewer witnesses you present, the less exposure you will have. The opponent will be denied a larger target for "shooting holes" in the case.

The exceptions to this rule are situations involving occurrence witnesses. The jurors want to hear from all known occurrence witnesses when liability is a question that they are expected to decide. Failure to produce a known occurrence witness without explaining his absence will cast a shadow of suspicion on your case. Not only will his absence trouble the jury, but it will give the opposing lawyer a strong argument in pointing out that the opposition did not give them the benefit of all of the evidence; and further, that it would be reasonable to infer that had the missing occurrence witness been produced, the testimony would have been unfavorable. Even a sleeping passenger in an automobile should be produced. It is not sufficient for the lawyer or a party to the lawsuit to state that passenger Jones was asleep at the time of the accident and, for that reason, does not know any of the facts of the collision. Witness Jones should be produced and asked one or two questions so that the jury hears it directly from Jones and not from someone else.

A practical problem arises in the situation where the lawyer has three occurrence witnesses—one or two of whom may have a serious personality defect. The temptation is to use one good, strong witness to nail down the liability issue and avoid the risks involved in using a dull witness who may leave holes in the case after the cross-examination is completed. Despite what he would like to do, he must use them all. The technique in handling this problem is to put the strong witness on first and get the complete story from him. Then put the dull witness on and preface your questions with a statement something like this:

". . . Now, Mrs. Brown, the other passenger in the car, Fred, has already testified fully as to how the accident happened. Rather than go into all of those details again, let me just ask you these questions. What, if anything, did you notice about the weather conditions at the time of the collision?"

Follow this up with a few inconsequential questions and then let her go. The jury will appreciate that you did not belabor the point and may even get the impression that she did testify to the facts. You can't be criticized by your opponent, because you did, after all, produce all of the occurrence witnesses. There can be no inferences drawn that the witness would have testified unfavorably to your side of the case. After all, your opponent can question her in more detail. Therefore, you have produced all of the evidence available on the liability issue and can argue that point to the jury. What about the other lawyer? What have you done to him? You have left him a very limited field in which to cross-examine, and he must call Mrs. Brown as his witness if he intends to go beyond the scope of your examination. What would otherwise have been a very dangerous and perhaps vulnerable witness has been nicely taken care of and you have effectively limited your exposure.

The same rule applies to any other fact issue in the case. If it is necessary to produce two investigating police officers, then do so, but select the more persuasive of the two to carry the ball, thereby avoiding any doubt that would be created by the absence of one.

Using the Innocent Codefendant

When the plaintiff is involved in a collision of three or more cars, with the facts in dispute, it is wise to join all of the drivers as defendants. This is true even though the plaintiff's lawyer feels confident the evidence will establish liability against one driver and the other drivers will clearly be found "not guilty" by the jury.

Many plaintiff's lawyers have lived to regret the dismissal of a defendant by executing for a nominal amount of money a "covenant not to sue." There are five reasons for employing this strategy:

(1) Any driver joined as a defendant will have to be present for the trial or run the risk of losing by default. Therefore, there is little danger that he will be unavailable because, for instance, he has moved out of the state.

(2) Any driver called as a witness by the plaintiff to prove his case will be adverse; therefore, he will be easier to examine. Also, the plaintiff does not vouch for his testimony.

(3) There will be no expense involved to have the benefit of his testimony—no subpoena fees or obligation to reimburse him for time lost from work.

(4) He will be anxious to help establish liability and will be insurance against a double cross, such as may occur if he is not a party to the lawsuit—especially dangerous if the statute of limitations has expired.

(5) There is no danger that a jury might go haywire and find the named defendants "not guilty" because of a conclusion that the real culprit was not named.

Before a plaintiff "lets out" a defendant on a "covenant not to sue," he should consider carefully the possible consequences.

Stealing the Defendant's Witnesses

The plaintiff has a definite advantage in those jurisdictions permitting him to call the defendant as his witness as though under cross-examination. This privilege can extend to employees of the defendant or other persons having an interest in the outcome of the lawsuit. The plaintiff should take advantage of this tool frequently for several reasons, the most important reason being that the jury has been instructed during *voir dire* examination that there are two sides to every story. Most jurors conscientiously want to hear the defendant's side of the story and will lean over backwards to be fair. Sometimes they lean so far that they actually become unfair to the plaintiff. If the defendant is called to the stand and asked a few questions, they may get the impression that they have heard both sides of the story by the time the plaintiff rests. Whether the defendant is used as a first, middle, or last witness during the case in chief will depend on many variables.

When there are two or more defendants, the plaintiff may be wiser not to call either defendant unless they are at odds with each other. It should be kept in mind that the other defendant will have a right to cross-examine if the defendants are fighting together, and the testimony might hurt you badly during your case in chief. The additional unfavorable points brought out by the other lawyer will put the plaintiff's lawyer in a bad light because it will appear that he was unfair in not bringing out all of the facts.

I Was at Your House Last Night

Whenever the trial lawyer goes to the home of a witness for the purpose of interviewing him, this fact should be brought out by the attorney on direct examination. The chances are that not one juror has ever had the experience of a lawyer's coming to his home at night to interview him regarding an accident he witnessed. The incident may seem so unorthodox as to shock them if the opposing lawyer first brings out this fact on cross-examination. Like Caesar's wife, the trial lawyer must be above suspicion if he is to get the benefit of any doubts on disputed issues. It should be treated in a natural, matter-of-fact manner, similar to the following:

Q. Mr. Brown, did you ever talk to me about this case before?
A. Yes.

Q. As a matter of fact, I went to your house last night to discuss it with you; isn't that correct?
A. Yes.

Q. Have you been served a subpoena to appear here today to testify?
A. Yes.

Q. Have you been paid or has there been any promise to pay you any money at all in connection with this case?
A. No, only $20 I was given when the subpoena was handed to me.

Q. That is the subpoena fee given to you as required by law? (If there is any objection made, then the opposing lawyer should be called upon to make a stipulation that this is the proper fee to be given a witness when a subpoena is served as required by the law.)

What About Evidence Depositions?

In presenting his case in chief, the trial lawyer will sometimes find it necessary to use evidence depositions to prove his case. Several points should be kept in mind to avoid common traps. The taking of testimony during this deposition is nothing less than the trial itself. It can be distinguished only in that a jury does not see the witness and the court does not make spontaneous rulings to the objections or other matters of law. Because of the informal atmosphere surrounding the deposition, the deponents as well as the lawyers have a tendency to be careless. When an objection is made, the lawyer conducting the examination should be particularly careful in order to avoid a situation wherein the objection will later be sustained and he will be left "high and dry."

If an objection is made that a question is leading and later sustained by the trial judge, the unfortunate lawyer may find that essential evidence cannot be heard by the jury because of a careless examination. The usual procedure is that the lawyer offering the evidence deposition at the time of trial will place a colleague or someone from his office on the witness stand to read the answers. It should be kept in mind that the true demeanor of the witness will never be known to the jury. If the witness is alert and gives prompt answers in a loud, clear voice or if he is the "shifty-eyed" type and takes a long time to answer questions in a thin, unconvincing voice, it will never be of consequence to the jury. A lawyer who has a strong, convincing witness should never be content with a deposition in lieu of his testimony in person. His appearance and the manner in which he testifies are more important than the testimony itself. Therefore, no substitutes should be accepted unless there is no alternative. If the witness has undesirable characteristics, however, the imaginative lawyer can give some thought to the advisability of a deposition.

It should also be kept in mind that whoever is playing the part of the witness on the stand will, most assuredly, be identified with that witness. True, he is nothing more than an actor, but human beings tend to associate a voice with a person; so be certain that the "actor" projects a favorable image. Paradoxically, a deponent possessing numerous undesirable characteristics might come across strong through an "actor" with a personable and convincing demeanor.

It Was My Fault and I'm Sorry

The rarest thing, next to hen's teeth, is the defendant who says, ". . . it was my fault. . . ." It is the very nature of human beings to justify their wrongdoing or to blame the other guy. This attitude is really incongruous when one considers that most people will forgive the offender when he "confesses his sins." When the defense lawyer finds that he is defending a hopeless liability case, he should prevent the defendant from attempting to justify what the jury will surely feel was negligent conduct. After all, facts are stubborn things. The best examples of this situation are the common rear-end cases. When the defendant says, ". . . I applied my brakes but must have skidded on some oil on the street . . .," or ". . . my brakes just suddenly went out . . .," the chances are that the jury will not believe this explanation. If, instead, he testifies, ". . . I misjudged my speed and could not stop in time . . .," or some other such admission that he was guilty of an error in judgment, the jury will admire him for his frankness and honesty. Because they admire him, they will want to reward him and the only method of doing it will be by the size of the verdict.

"To confess a fault freely is the next best thing to being innocent of it."—Syrus.

Examine the Exhibits Carefully

Make certain that there isn't any poison in the exhibits that you are about to place into evidence. For example, if income tax returns are to be offered, care should be taken that there isn't something in them that will offend any of the jurors. Perhaps the client has no charitable donations listed; this may reflect badly on him in the eyes of jurors who regularly donate to their favorite charities. There may be a large capital gain reported that could influence the jury into awarding lesser damages because, they feel, the plaintiff really doesn't need money anyway. A hospital bill or other item of damage might indicate that it was paid in whole or in part by an insurance company; this would almost certainly affect the amount of the verdict.

When putting on a witness who is there for the purpose of laying a foundation for the admission of exhibits or to interpret them, the lawyer should make certain that the witness has all of the exhibits in his possession. When a doctor takes the stand, he should have not only all of the records of this patient, but all of the X rays as well. If the doctor does not bring with him all of the X rays concerning that plaintiff, the opposition is given ammunition to use in closing arguments by raising an inference as to why all of the X ray films were not brought to court. Even though all of the X ray films are not interpreted by the doctor, they should at least be in court to forestall any argument by the other lawyer concerning their absence.

The Other Guy Got a Traffic Ticket

When the opponent gets a traffic ticket, appears in court and enters a plea of "guilty," this fact should be made known to the jury. There are many persons who feel that the one who receives a traffic ticket is the one at fault. They will be instructed otherwise, but the traffic ticket weighs heavily against the one receiving it. Evidence of the traffic ticket, of course, would not be relevant, but the plea of "guilty" lets it come in as an admission against interest. The cross-examiner bringing this information out should not overplay the fact that the other party made a plea of "guilty." Probably most of the members of the jury have at one time or another received a traffic ticket for some type of violation. Even though they felt they were not guilty, they made a plea of "guilty" in order to avoid spending an entire day in court to have their case heard. They can readily sympathize with a person who is invited to plead guilty by an over-worked traffic court. Any belaboring of the fact that the party pleaded "guilty," by way of either unduly tedious questioning or argument, may bring forth a feeling of sympathy for the other party. A strong selling job to the effect that he must have been guilty or he never would have pleaded guilty can detract from the significance of the traffic ticket itself.

How About Judicial Notice?

In presenting the case in chief, it is quite often practical and necessary to have the court take judicial notice of certain facts. For some reason or other, trial judges are fearful and downright reluctant to take judicial notice of facts that are quite obvious. Often it saves a good deal of time and money to short-cut the expense of bringing in formal proof. It might be helpful to state for the record outside of the presence of the jury, ". . . the Courts are presumed not to be more ignorant than the ordinary man. . . ."

Is Rebuttal Evidence Necessary?

If any witness testifies to a damaging admission allegedly made by a party to a lawsuit, it becomes essential that that party take the witness stand and deny it. Failure to do this will create an impression that there must be something to it. The same rule will apply to any important witness if he is contradicted on an important point.

IV. Cross-Examination

What Is Cross-Examination?

WHAT THE CROSS-EXAMINER is attempting to obtain is nothing more than the facts. Cross-examination takes place even in our daily conversation. You are cross-examining a friend when you ask, "What did you do last evening?" "Where did you have dinner last night?" "Did you read the article last night about the big tornado?" "How is business?" "Are you planning on having lunch at the Bar Association?" We have no reason to doubt what our friend tells us, and we are getting at the facts. The fact that a witness is being cross-examined does not mean that the cross-examiner is dragging something out of the witness against his will. It may well be that the witness desires to be as accurate as possible and the cross-examination is merely instrumental in bringing out the unalloyed facts.

Whether the cross-examiner has willing or unwilling witnesses, his purpose is still the same. The trial lawyer, in his everlasting quest for truth, becomes its great admirer. When what he elicits is not the truth, it may be that the witness deliberately intends to create impressions opposite to the real facts or that he is genuinely mistaken

114

for one reason or another. Therefore, cross-examination is just as necessary a tool with the lying witness as it is with the mistaken witness.

Right to Cross-Examine

The right to cross-examine is regarded as one of the most valuable of all our rights. The right of an accused to face his accusers and to test the accuracy of their accusations by cross-examination is basic in our adversary system.

It is only fair that direct testimony walk the plank if for no other reason than to discourage prevarication and exaggeration. Cross-examination will test the accuracy of direct testimony in many areas. In questioning an occurrence witness, the cross-examiner may test the witness' ability to remember details—such as the distance that separated the witness from the occurrence or the lighting conditions that prevailed at the time—or may establish the improbability of the occurrence's happening in the manner in which the witness testified, the lapse of time between the occurrence and the time of his testimony, the variance between his testimony at the trial and a statement or deposition given on a previous occasion, his friendship with the party for whom he is testifying or a prejudice against the other party, a reputation for being untruthful, a financial interest in the outcome, an honest mistake as to the facts as testified to, a hasty conclusion not based upon considered judgment, or a variety of other possibilities. Cross-examination may also test the opinion of the expert witness in a number of ways and may demonstrate that the probative value of his opinion is much less than the opponent would have the jury believe.

Knowledge of Human Behavior Necessary

A lawyer should have some understanding of logic as well as of anticipated behavior of persons in a multitude of situations. Some individuals have a remarkable facility for predicting the reaction that a person will have in a given set of circumstances, while some are so insensitive to the reactions of others that one marvels at how they can be so blind or "thick" as not to foresee what will cause another person to be angry, happy, pleased, flattered, surprised, shocked, believing or disbelieving. Disraeli said: "Knowledge of mankind is a knowledge of their passions." All of us can predict with varying degrees of accuracy how others will react. Even a five-year-old child knows that if he uses his coloring set to draw on the living room wall, this action is likely to provoke anger on the part of his mother. To admire a woman's new hat or to call a person "stupid" will create reactions that are easily predictable.

We have all had the experience of asking a person a question that we were certain he heard and understood, only to have him request that the question be repeated. We repeated the question, a little annoyed at having to do so, and, without analyzing it, sensed that there was an ulterior motive for his request. For example, assume that you asked your law clerk to deliver some important documents to another lawyer's office, and the following morning you asked: "Did you remember to deliver those papers to Mr. Brown's office yesterday?" Assuming that the question was asked in a clear, audible voice, easily heard and understood by the law clerk but in spite of this he requests that you repeat the question and he answers with a familiar "Huh?," "Pardon me?," or "What?," you can be quite sure that there are only two possible reasons why he did not give a direct answer to your simple question. One is that he is reluctant to answer the question and is hoping to divert his questioner so that an answer need never be given, and two, he is stalling for time to think of an answer to excuse or justify his forgotten assignment. If the person in this situation is known to "fib," the questioner will have strong reason to believe that the forthcoming answer may be less than accurate. Another example of this might be a stern father who has laid down an 11:00 P. M. curfew for his teen-aged daughter and has forbidden her to associate with one Jimmy Brown. In the morning when he asks her the time of her arrival the preceding evening and whom she was with, if the daughter asks him to repeat the question the father can be quite sure that she fits into one or both of these patterns.

Such symptoms in a witness should alert the cross-examiner to the fact that there is vulnerability in this area. A change in the witness' manner of testifying when asked a simple question will, by itself, create an aura of insincerity; so more questions should be asked in that area. Even if nothing remarkable is brought out, it will help reduce the effectiveness of the witness, as the jury will sense a lack of conviction or possibly a deliberate attempt to distort the facts.

Interest in People Essential

Regardless of how much effort, time and study a lawyer has put into his technique, he is constantly discovering new tactics or points. There are as many possible variations in cross-examination as there are persons in the world. To be an effective cross-examiner, the trial lawyer should know something of the backgrounds of various ethnic groups so that he can understand what motivates individuals in forming opinions common to their group. This will help him gain insight into the reaction to be expected from a witness as well as the effect it will have on the jury. He must be prepared to devote whatever time and energy are necessary in order to become sufficiently knowledgeable in a given subject to effectively cross-examine a witness—whether he be a lay witness or an expert witness.

Every lawyer is the architect of his own success. The techniques of making his point will be developed with effort, whether it be establishing the fact that the witness is mistaken, that he is lying or that he is exaggerating. Every now and then a new lawyer comes along who quickly joins the ranks of those who are feared because of their adeptness at cross-examination. Perhaps they are gifted or perhaps it is exigency. Whatever the reason, invariably their skill is the result of hard work.

> ". . . Yond Cassius has a lean and
> hungry look;
> He thinks too much: such
> men are dangerous."—

> Shakespeare, *Julius Caesar,* Act I, Scene 2.

Objectives of Cross-Examination

Before beginning the cross-examination the lawyer should have his objectives clearly in mind. There should be a purpose for making the cross-examination and a general plan as to its procedure. For our purposes we shall outline the possible objectives of cross-examination. The goal to be reached will be one or more of the following:

(1) To establish that the witness is lying on one or more material points;

(2) To show that the witness is prejudiced—this will establish a motive for coloring testimony in accordance with his prejudice;

(3) To show that his testimony is improbable;

(4) To force the witness to admit certain facts;

(5) To supplement testimony that the witness has already given;

(6) To weaken the testimony of the witness by showing his opinion is questionable because of his inability to observe, to hear a conversation, or to see because of poor lighting conditions, or by showing other facts to reduce the value of his opinion;

(7) To show that an expert witness or even a lay witness who has testified to an opinion is not competent or qualified because he lacks the necessary training or experience (the purpose is to negate or reduce the probative value of his opinion);

(8) To impeach a witness by showing that he has given a contrary statement at another time;

(9) To show that a witness has been convicted of an infamous crime in order to cast doubt on his credibility;

(10) To obtain necessary evidence to establish the case through examination of an adverse witness during the case in chief.

If one has the objective or objectives clearly in mind before he sets out on his cross-examination, he will almost certainly conduct a more effective examination. The technique or art of accomplishing these objectives will vary from lawyer to lawyer, but every cross-examiner is attempting to do one or more of the foregoing whether or not he is conscious of it.

The Deposition Game

With the discovery procedures available to lawyers today, it is rare that a trial lawyer does not have the benefit of the discovery deposition of the other party. The trend of "discovering" what the other fellow's case is all about is rapidly expanding throughout the country. Because of this trend, litigation lawyers now find themselves devoting most of their time to preparing for trial. With interrogatories directed to the opposing party compelling him to disclose the names of witnesses, copies of photographs, previous injuries, details as to income, and so forth, there is little room for surprise during the course of the trial. Because this information is so readily available, to say nothing of the fact that witnesses are committed under oath in great detail as to the occurrence, it is now possible for all of us to be successful cross-examiners. It is difficult to conceive of a question that a cross-examiner could ask to which he wouldn't already know the answer if he had taken full advantage of the discovery procedures available to him.

The trial lawyer of yesterday was handicapped by the maxim that advised against asking a question where he didn't know the answer. Certainly, there were answers that would be helpful to his side of the case, but then he couldn't be too sure of how to "fish out" these answers without being hit by lightning. Perhaps Mark Twain had something when he said: "All you need in this life is ignorance and confidence, and then success is sure." Modern discovery procedures will lengthen the life of a trial lawyer, but will not serve as a substitute for careful preparation.

The technique of cross-examining a party litigant today is, therefore, much different from that of prediscovery days. The trial lawyer has the opposing party committed to virtually every facet of the case. The defense lawyer knows exactly what the plaintiff can testify to with regard to the most minute details of the occurrence such as speeds at various distances from the point of impact; observations of the other automobile, together with opinions formed at various stages of approaching the point of impact; any actions that the plaintiff took, and when he took them, to prevent the collision; the various areas of the plaintiff's body where he suffered pain; the degree of pain and its duration, together with the treatment the plaintiff underwent; and a multitude of other things. There is no reason why a complete and effective cross-examination cannot be prepared without fear of unexpected, damaging answers.

The cross-examination conducted under today's rules may even take on the complexion of a game to see who remembers the contents of the deposition better—the trial lawyer or the witness. The trial lawyer has the advantage in that he has played the game before and is, therefore, a bonzer marksman. The witness must remember all of the answers that he has given, whereas the questioner is interested only in a limited bailiwick and can direct his questioning in those areas. Any deviation from the answers given previously in the deposition provides ammunition for the cross-examiner. An average deposition can be abstracted on one or two pages of paper with the page number on each line in the left-hand margin for quick reference by the cross-examiner. By abstracting the deposition, the cross-examiner will frequently have an opportunity to show that the witness has just testified in court incompatibly with his testimony previously taken at a deposition. Techniques of impeachment are discussed on page 137.

CONDUCT AND STYLE OF THE TRIAL LAWYER

Fear Is an Ally

Cross-examination is the part of a lawsuit that the public has been exposed to second only to closing arguments. This exposure through the movies and television gives many witnesses a feeling that through some particular training, the lawyer is able to "dig out" information from a witness or extract a disclosure from him that he does not want to furnish—perhaps even get him to say something contrary to what he meant to say. This is the monstrous phase of the lawsuit that the witness fears the most. However that may be, from the preceding discussion and examples it can readily be seen that a witness has nothing to fear if he is accurate and conforms to the conventional. The cross-examiner is looking for an opening that will give him an opportunity to get in and produce damage. This feeling of apprehension on the part of the witness is helpful to the lawyer, as fear will impede the ability to effectively counterfeit the facts.

The Gladiator Must Be Fair

The cross-examiner should never patently attempt to confuse a witness, as the jurors will be quick to sense this and penalize the lawyer for his pettifogging tactics. The jurors naturally feel that the lawyer has a decided advantage because of his background and training in this pursuit of verbal interchange. Thus, the advocate begins the contest with a handicap, since the jurors tend to identify with the witness, who, like themselves, is usually unsophisticated in the mysterious *modus operandi* of a trial. Because a courtroom is an arena in the battle of persuasion, the lawyers are viewed by lay people as skilled gladiators who have a marked advantage over all nonlawyers; thus, no juror is ever likely to identify with the lawyer. Even if a juror happens to be the wife of a lawyer, she is unlikely to identify with the advocate. The courtroom, with its awe and dignity, is foreign to all but the trial lawyer and those who work there. The trial lawyer should, therefore, not forget for a moment that the sympathy lies completely with the witness. In cross-examination the lawyer will be carefully scrutinized for fairness and honesty. For example, when a cross-examiner has an obviously "dull witness" who has testified incorrectly as the result of a glaring mistake that obviously can be corrected, the lawyer can enhance his position with the jury by pointing it out and helping the witness.

Too many lawyers will try to make capital out of an obvious mistake and then vigorously object when their opponent on redirect examination attempts to clarify the issue and correct the mistake that was apparent to everyone. To a jury, these are obvious, unfair tactics. Jurors are conscientious and sincerely want to decide the case correctly; therefore, they are anxious to hear the unvarnished facts. They view these tactics as "hanky-panky." Any dishonesty displayed by misquoting or misleading the witness will reflect on the character of the lawyer. It is important that the lawyer's fairness and honesty be unquestioned by the jurors so that they will rely on him during closing arguments. If they feel he is tricky, the effectiveness of his closing arguments will be much the less for it. The jurors may admire a lawyer for his brilliant mind if he displays brilliance in other ways; but if they feel the lawyer is duplicitous, he will have little persuasive power with them.

Eye to Eye

Unlike direct examination, it is important in cross-examination that the questioner attract and hold the eye of the witness. The witness should be made fully aware that the lawyer has a stare fixed on him and is studying his every expression and slightest movement. He is then less likely to be tempted into exaggerations or inaccuracies helpful to the other side. The witness should be made to feel much like the person who finds himself on someone else's property—being studied by the family's large watchdog, ready to pounce at the slightest suspicious move. If the cross-examination is conducted a great distance from the witness (as direct examination usually is conducted in order to insure that all jurors hear the testimony), the effectiveness and control over the witness will suffer. If the witness has a normal speaking voice or is speaking loudly enough, then you can move in closer without the danger that his testimony will be lost to the jury. If he has a quiet speaking voice, you will have to increase the distance between you and the witness to fit the need. The normal reaction of most persons is to unconsciously raise or lower the voice according to the circumstances. If the witness has an unusually soft voice, perhaps the examiner can stand in such a way that the witness, in facing him, must also face the jury so that the voice is projected in the direction of the jury.

A close study of the witness is important. A nervous gesture to the back of the head, a movement in the chair, a glance at the other lawyer, and other such signs tell the cross-examiner he is in a sensitive area. In direct examination, however, the examiner is not looking for weaknesses or sensitive areas; he is then more concerned with having his witness feel comfortable so that he will project a more natural image, characteristic of one who has a comfortably clear conscience. It may be necessary for the cross-examiner to frequently remind the witness to keep his voice up so that he can maintain his advantageous position close to the witness. But these efforts are justified, since if the witness begins to telegraph the fact that he is uncomfortable, the cross-examiner will then be close enough to observe and exploit the opening.

Roll with the Punch

There will always be those unpleasant situations where the cross-examiner will get an unexpected and damaging answer. When he gets "hit on the head" with this type of answer, he must not flinch or appear concerned even though the answer may appear to be fatal. If he maintains his composure and lets no concern or anxiety show in his face, the cross-examiner removes a good deal of the sting by seemingly not attaching significance to it. When these "bombshells" hit, and they will hit from time to time even with the best cross-examiners, the jurors immediately turn to the lawyer to observe his reaction. A loss of composure at this point could increase the potency of the answer, perhaps making it fatal. I have been present when the lawyer in these unpleasant circumstances did not even hesitate and, without a change of pace, proceeded with the cross-examination.

Don't Beat a Dead Horse

When a cross-examiner has a witness on the run and is making many good points that are damaging to the opposition, it is important that he know when to stop. Every cross-examination needs a culmination where the cap is put on at just the right point. When the witness is down and no longer running, to continue to beat him will probably reduce the effectiveness of the prior cross-examination. Even the most despicable witness will begin to gain some sympathy from the jury if the lawyer continues to administer the beating after the witness is completely down and out.

When Should Mud Be Thrown?

Discretion is vital as to wielding an attack on the character or reputation of a witness. This can be the sword of Damocles, as jurors may deeply resent such an action. Where a witness has been convicted of a felony many years before and has "paid his debt to society," it is probably best to leave this information alone. This is especially so if the witness has lived an exemplary life or is known in the community as a respected citizen. On the other hand, if a witness has a record of various convictions or has a bad reputation and this can be established by competent evidence, there should be no hesitation to use this weapon. It is unlikely that a lawyer presenting a witness to establish a point would fail to bring out on direct examination the unpleasant fact of a long criminal record. However, if his unsavory past first comes to light during cross-examination, then whatever value this witness may have had will be materially reduced, if not destroyed. This "bad feeling" that the jury will have about that witness may spill over and contaminate the entire case. The only conclusion the jurors could come to, at best, would be that the lawyer is deceitful. Why else would he present a witness answering that description to establish through testimony the truth on a given point and then neglect to inform them about his background?

If the cross-examiner has information on a female witness that would imply or even establish that she has a questionable moral background, it is probably wise to forget it. There may be instances where it could conceivably not backfire, but I think, by and large, that jurors are sufficiently sophisticated to deeply resent such tactics by a lawyer. To deliberately embarrass a woman in the presence of so many people could create such ill feeling that the jury could only look for an excuse to "get back" at the offending lawyer.

Let the Jury Keep Up

When you are making a point, speak slowly. Your pace must not be more rapid than the average mind can follow. If a good point comes and goes too quickly in rapid questioning and answering, the significance of it will be lost to the jury. The lawyer must realize that he is more accustomed to the art or game of thought perception from words than are the jurors. He has trained his mind over the years to grasp the significant facts through a maze of unimportant detail. The jurors, on the other hand, do not necessarily have the ability to go immediately to the heart of a problem. Damaging answers severely injuring the opponent's case may float away like so many ripples on the water. The trial lawyer who is well prepared may know his case so well that he feels a point made by his cross-examination was so obvious that no one could escape noting its commanding import. But the cross-examiner must constantly ask himself: "What effect does all this have on the jury?" "Are the significant points crystal clear?" He should not shrug it off with a feeling that any doubts can be cleared up in his closing argument.

Ironically enough, however, because the opponent is likewise trained in the art of quickly grasping significant facts, the examiner will often feel that the rapid-fire cross-examination inflicted more damage than it really did. This is the principal reason why the jury so often does not get a chance to decide the issues.

Making Speeches While Objecting

A lawyer should be conservative in his objections when the opponent is cross-examining a witness, as it is easy for the jurors to get the feeling that the lawyer is afraid the testimony is hurting him and that he is trying to keep the facts from the jury. All trial lawyers have suffered torment when their opponent is effectively cross-examining a witness. The torment is at its worst when the witness does not realize that he is being led into a trap that is quite apparent to his lawyer, and the trap is about to be sprung. It is at this point that the unfortunate lawyer would like nothing better than to have a conference with the witness in order to prepare him for this line of cross-examination. Unable to do that, he may find himself, in sheer desperation, making frivolous objections that are overruled by the trial judge that, in turn, amplify the damage.

It is at this point that some lawyers, often successfully, have faked an objection for the purpose of trying to suggest the answer to the witness or "wise him up." If the witness grasps the point, it may prevent him from falling into the trap that is being laid by the cross-examiner. An example of this is a situation where the witness is asked whether he has ever talked to anyone about the case and he replies, "No." The cross-examiner is using this old, stock method of casting doubt on the witness' credibility and can follow this up with a few questions to demonstrate how absurd the answer is.

Q. Have you ever talked to anybody about this case?
A. No.
Q. Have you ever talked to a lawyer about the facts of this case?
A. No.

Objection. I'm going to object to this line of cross-examination because the questions are tricky and not clear to the witness. It's
perfectly obvious that the witness has talked to me in my office
and has talked to his relatives and friends about the case, but only
in relation to what he actually witnessed.

As can be seen from this type of objection, it is completely frivolous and without legal merit. The objecting lawyer has made a
"speech" and has suggested to the witness the position he should take
in response to this line of questioning. Actually, all of this could
have been avoided had the objecting lawyer taken only 30 seconds to
explain to this witness that this question might be asked and that
he should not panic and feel that he must take a ridiculous and false
position. The jurors will probably realize what the objecting lawyer
has done, and, of course, he runs the risk of a reprimand by the
judge in the presence of the jury.

Endure the Torment

There will be many occasions when a trial lawyer will have to
endure a devastating cross-examination of one of his important witnesses. Its effect on the jurors will vary according to the reaction
displayed by the distressed lawyer. When the jurors hear damaging
testimony, invariably they will glance at the other lawyer to observe
his reaction. If they detect alarm or concern, the damaging testimony
will carry greater weight when they are considering their verdict.

I know of no remedy for these unpleasant moments that all trial
lawyers must endure. If the damaging testimony is unexpected, so
much the worse. But the trial lawyer can only remind himself that
he did not make the facts or the witnesses, and regardless of the
outcome, he must be satisfied that he presented the facts as best
he could.

On those agreeable occasions when you find the shoe is on the
other foot and things are definitely going your way because of the
devastating cross-examination you are administering, be prepared to
stop the other lawyer from delivering a speech under the pretense
of making an objection, as discussed above. You should in turn make
an objection, and point out what the objecting lawyer is attempting to do.
A statement by the trial judge that the opponent made an improper
objection by attempting to suggest an answer to the witness can
cause this strategy to completely boomerang on the objecting lawyer.

Usually Some Cross-Examination Is Desirable

There are rare occasions when it is best to decline any cross-
examination of a witness. Some lawyers subscribe to the theory that
the jurors will feel there is nothing in the testimony just given by

the witness that the lawyer fears if he declines cross-examination. However, I feel this situation is rare and usually find a point or two that can be made that will be helpful. If the direct testimony has been damaging and not one single question has been asked of the witness, the jurors may get the impression that the lawyer completely accepts it.

The lawyer must disagree without being disagreeable. Even though the facts may entitle the opposition to a verdict, those facts should not go uncontested. For example, an occurrence witness who was a passenger in the other automobile may have been a completely honest, accurate, objective, and articulate witness. Perhaps the witness was used only to establish one important point. There is probably nothing much that can be done directly to break this witness down on that point. If the point is important and the cross-examiner has a witness whose testimony conflicts, to decline any cross-examination at all could be interpreted as an unchallenging acceptance of that testimony. The lawyer should not appear to accept it; he should at least give the jurors something to think about. For example:

Q. You came here today of your own free will to testify?
A. Yes.
Q. You were not brought here under subpoena?
A. No.
Q. And Mary Jones is a friend of yours?
A. Yes.
Q. And you would like to see her prevail in this lawsuit?
A. Yes.

If nothing else, the cross-examiner has pursued one of the objectives mentioned above. True, it may be only a small point, but at least he is giving the jurors a little something to think about. They have been reminded that the witness is, after all, a friend, and it is conceivable that a friend might stretch a point for a friend. More important, the cross-examiner does not appear to blindly accept the testimony, and he even has a little something for his argument.

There Are Times When No Cross-Examination Is Wise

You might well resist the temptation to cross-examine when your opponent has put on a witness who, in your opinion, obviously is honest and trying to be accurate but is completely inarticulate and has painted a confusing picture for the jury. By questioning this witness, you may clarify points that, fortunately for your case, were confusing to the jury or you may open up an area that would be proper for redirect examination and thereby permit your opponent to clarify these points. This may be an excellent time to decline any questioning at all if the examination was clumsy and ineffective. While ordinarily I like to ask every witness at least a few harmless questions, this unexpected break may be so important that not even the smallest risk should be taken that would permit this witness to clarify any points at all. What Talleyrand said of the Bourbon dynasty is apropos of the jury: "They have learned nothing and forgotten nothing."

TECHNIQUE

Indirectly Depreciating the Witness

It is often said of cross-examination that a question should never be asked unless the examiner knows the answer. This statement has so often been repeated that it has become a maxim for cross-examiners. A lawyer who does not know his case before he proceeds to examine a witness can be said to have both feet firmly planted in the air.

While basically the principle is sound, I think too many trial lawyers have taken it as an inviolable rule in all circumstances and have, consequently, neglected to cross-examine witnesses in instances where damage to the opposition could have resulted. Certainly a witness that your opponent puts on who has one or more of the undesirable characteristics discussed above can be exploited. If a witness is grossly exaggerating or is antagonistic or demonstrates some other undesirable characteristic, the cross-examiner should keep the witness on the stand long enough for the jury to develop a dislike for him. In a case that is hopeless, what does the cross-examiner have to lose in fishing around? There is always the remote possibility that he may stumble onto something significant, and it may be the breaking point in the case. Because of the pretrial preparation that goes into a case today, a lawyer does not find himself skating on thin ice with cross-examination as did his predecessors. This is not meant to endorse a reckless policy, since it would not take long for his opponents to recognize this characteristic in the cross-examiner and lay traps for him.

Avoid Copious Notes

Refrain from using a long, tedious cross-examination. To repeat all of the direct examination or to spend much time on trivialities will bore the jury to such an extent that significant points may be lost. I think it is better to go immediately to the heart of the matter and then cover whatever smaller points may support the major point. Save something important so that you finish on a climactic point. I have seen many trial lawyers make notes of almost the complete direct testimony, study them from beginning to end and then on cross-examination duplicate practically all of the points made by the witness on direct examination. This type of cross-examination does not fall under any of the objectives mentioned on page 117. It serves no purpose to repeat the direct testimony already given by the witness; the re-echo may even inflate its value. Also, the rewording may clarify possible ambiguities—to your disadvantage. If notes are to be made at all, there should be only a brief point or two made on any of the objectives previously outlined. Inconsistencies, improbabilities, exaggerations, or other points that should be tested can usually be brought to mind by just a word. The lawyer who is busy checking his notes before asking questions loses the benefit of observing any "signs" given by the witness. After completing an objective, the lawyer can, if necessary, refer to his notes to remind himself of another objective and then pursue that to a conclusion before proceeding to the next point.

How About Sarcasm?

Some lawyers may, on occasion, enjoy a measure of success in cross-examination by employing a sarcastic attitude and a vicious, explosive tone of voice. This may so rattle a witness that he will be stampeded into blurting out the truth in spite of himself, even though he may have been prepared to conceal or distort some facts in his testimony. This is an unusual tactic and is not ordinarily recommended. An exception, however, is the witness with a weak personality who is obviously lying. But if a lawyer uses this strategy he should conduct himself with politeness and courteousness in every other respect throughout the trial. There are only a few other occasions when a lawyer can be rough with a witness with the approval of the jury, such as when the witness is contemptuous or grossly exaggerating out of prejudice. If the truth does emerge after a sarcastic and hard cross-examination, the jurors will align with the lawyer. This feeling of concurrence will be increased if he apologizes for his conduct in his summation, reminding them that it was in the interest of truth and justice that such questioning occurred.

Even though this technique can be successful with the right witness, the safest method is to always be a gentleman. The undesirable traits of the witness will be highlighted if the lawyer contrasts himself by being fair and courteous. "Sharp wits, like sharp knives, do often cut their owner's fingers."—Arrowsmith.

Hot on the Trail

Often the "talkative witness," under cross-examination, will "throw a bone" to the cross-examiner during an unresponsive, narrative type of answer. Many lawyers will immediately chase after the "bone" like a hound dog after a fox. There may be occasions when it is desirable to do this, but by and large I think it is better to accomplish your current objective before proceeding to another. But the mere fact that the cross-examiner does not know where this new chase will ultimately end does not mean that he should invariably abandon the idea of a new pursuit. Many promising chases develop from unresponsive answers. Every fact that is learned can become a key to other facts. The witness who testifies to a gross exaggeration or an obvious mistake in what he observed minimizes the effectiveness of the balance of his testimony. The cross-examiner should always be prepared to look for these little "extras" that are passed out as free gifts from time to time. Even a careful, well-prepared, responsive witness may occasionally provide an opening for such a chase. This type of opening should always be viewed with suspicion, however, because it could be a well-laid trap.

A classic example of this "trap" is this experience of a friend of mine, who was caught rather badly. After the cross-examination of an occurrence witness to an automobile accident had gone along fairly well, my friend, who represented one Mr. Murphy, closed off as follows:

Q. Now, Mr. Fleming, have you testified as to all of the conversations and things that you noticed?
A. Yes—well, practically everything.
Q. Then there are some details that you have not testified to?
A. Well, only that Mr. Murphy had a strong odor of alcohol on his breath.

Never let yourself become careless with a witness because you are convinced that he is a fool and you "can handle him." That is when the examiner becomes the fool.

Slow in Answering

The witness who takes a considerable length of time in answering questions leaves an indelible impression in the minds of the jurors. This type of witness may well answer the description of "the thinking man," as mentioned on page 75. When you find a witness taking a long time to answer a question, you can be quite sure that the jurors are considering the possibility either that the witness is unsure of what he is testifying to or that he may even be lying. At this point, don't prod the witness to give answers; you can even tacitly encourage him to take his time and answer the questions carefully by not pushing him. To emphasize the ridiculous amount of time elapsing between the question and the answer, you can even sit down, if you are not already seated, and look at your watch. When as much as 30 or 45 seconds have elapsed for "thinking time," the value of this witness for the opposition is lost.

Step by Step

It is necessary at times to get a witness who is partial to the other side to agree with you on a point that is helpful to your side. This is one of the ten objectives covered on page 117. To simply ask this witness to agree with you on an important point will probably result in a refusal or a great amount of hedging. For this reason, in order to force him to agree on a fact or point, it may be necessary to lead him step by step until there is only one inescapable conclusion. For example, if you asked an occurrence witness partial to the opposition to agree that your client's automobile was traveling at a reasonable rate of speed as it approached the point of impact, he would deny it. But he will have to agree if he is led step by step so that he must come to only one conclusion or appear to be ridiculous in his contrary opinion. Assume a witness has testified that your client was traveling 70 M.P.H. just before impact. The cross-examination might be as follows:

Q. This collision occurred at about two o'clock in the afternoon; is that correct?

A. Yes.

Q. Was it a clear day?

A. Yes.

Q. That is, the sun was shining and it was not overcast?

A. Yes.

Q. It had not rained that day or the preceding day?

A. That is correct.

Q. Then the road surface was dry?

A. Yes.

Q. Then there wasn't any condition on the road surface that would make driving hazardous?

A. That is correct.

Q. And at this particular area, it is relatively flat; is that correct?

A. Yes.

Q. That is, there are no curves in the road or rises to interfere with vision?

A. Yes, that is correct.

Q. And you testified that in your opinion Mr. Jones was traveling at about 70 M.P.H.; is that correct?

A. Yes.

Q. And are you familiar with the posted speed limit for the highway on which Mr. Jones was traveling?

A. Yes.

Q. What is that speed limit?

A. 70 M.P.H.

Q. And, as a matter of fact, he was not exceeding the speed limit; is that correct?

A. Yes.

Q. Then, based on all of these observations, it is your opinion, I take it, that Mr. Jones was traveling in a reasonable manner.

(At this point, you have made it difficult for him not to agree. To disagree at this point would show partiality.)

Never Ask "Why?"

The cross-examiner should never give a witness a chance to explain his answer by asking the question, "Why?" This is especially true with expert witnesses whose business it is to disagree. This type of question permits them to go into long, narrative answers on subjects that they know a great deal more about than the examiner. The narrative type of answer can sound like a classroom lecture. An impressive, well-informed, articulate witness may so impress a jury as to carry it away so that the cross-examiner can never recapture it.

The very reason that cross-examination is such an effective tool in the hands of a lawyer is that he can choose the area of inquiry— the ground rules are all in his favor. If a series of questions can each be answered by a simple "Yes" or "No," a witness can be required to make such answers; these will serve as admissions or a basis upon which to establish the improbabilities of the witness' direct testimony.

To use a hopeless case as an example, assume the following facts in representing a defendant: Two automobiles collided at an intersection where one street is regulated by a stop sign, while the other street is a through street; the defendant, who had the stop sign, struck the side of the plaintiff's car while it was traveling through the intersection. To paraphrase the testimony, the defendant states that he brought his car to a stop, looked both ways, decided he had time to proceed through the intersection and started up, striking the side of the plaintiff's automobile, which, he says, must have been coming at a fast rate of speed; the plaintiff testifies he was traveling at a reasonable speed and did not notice the defendant until he was struck in the side. Assume, further, that the plaintiff is an articulate person with an above-average ability to persuade a jury. The proper way to cross-examine this plaintiff is to give him no opportunity to explain or give narrative answers. Questions calling for explanations might be as follows:

Q. Now, if the visibility was good and nothing interfered with your vision, why was it that you didn't see Mr. White's car until it hit you?

A. It just never occurred to me that a car coming from Green Street with the stop sign would drive right into my side. I was going along at a reasonable speed in a wide, open intersection, and there just isn't a reason in the world why Mr. White should not have waited for me until I passed through the intersection.

Q. But, if you were paying attention, how is it that you didn't see Mr. White's car until the accident?

A. The only explanation must be that I didn't expect a car and never really noticed it until he suddenly drove into my side.

Now compare the following examination:

Q. You have driven down Main Street in the past?

A. Yes.

Q. As a matter of fact, you have driven down Main Street quite a number of times in the past; isn't that correct?

A. Yes.

Q. You were, therefore, quite familiar with the intersection of Main Street and Green Street?

A. Yes.

Q. Then I'm sure you were aware that the street you were on was a through street?

A. Yes.

Q. And you knew that Green Street had a stop sign?

A. Yes.

Q. You had driven on Green Street in the past?

A. Yes.

Q. This accident occurred at about 11:00 in the morning?

A. Yes.

Q. This was a clear, bright day; wasn't it?

A. Yes.

Q. There wasn't anything to obscure visibility at that time?

A. No.

Q. And as you drove on Main Street that day, there was nothing to prevent you from seeing cars traveling in either direction on Green Street?

A. Correct.

Q. That is, you could see cars moving from your left to your right or from your right to your left; isn't that true?

A. Yes.

Q. I believe you testified that you approached Green Street at about 45 M.P.H?

A. Yes.

Q. The posted speed there is 50 M.P.H.?

A. Yes.

Q. Then you weren't speeding at the time?

A. No.

Q. You were paying attention to your driving?

A. Yes.

Q. There wasn't anything to distract you from your driving?

A. No.

Q. You can see a considerable distance on Green Street both to the left and right as it approaches Main Street; is that correct?

A. That is true.

Q. When you were some distance from the intersection, there was nothing to interfere with your vision in seeing Mr. White's car, was there?

A. No.

Q. And as you continued to approach Green Street, was there anything to interfere with your vision in seeing Mr. White's car?

A. No.

Q. And as you began to enter the intersection of Green Street, was there anything to interfere with your vision in seeing Mr. White's car?

A. No.

Q. And as you entered the intersection, I take it there was still nothing to interfere with your vision in seeing Mr. White's car?

A. Yes.

Q. And after you were driving in the intersection, I take it there still was nothing to interfere with your vision in seeing the other car?

A. That is correct.

Q. And then there was an accident . . . .

A. Yes.

Q. And I believe you testified that you did not see Mr. White's car until the accident?

A. Yes.

Q. You wouldn't know whether Mr. White stopped at the stop sign, would you?

A. No.

Q. Or how long he waited at the stop sign before proceeding?

A. No.

Q. And the reason you wouldn't know whether he stopped is that you never even took the simple precaution of looking out for other cars as you drove into that intersection.

Notice that the foregoing questions can each be answered by a simple "yes" or "no"; any attempt on the part of the witness to elaborate or justify his actions should be blocked. He has no choice but to admit that all of these things are true; do not leave any room for escape. It was once said, "The mouse that hath but one hole is quickly taken." The defense lawyer will probably not get the verdict, but at least what might have appeared to be all black or all white has been shaded to some extent. The jury will have no great desire to play fairy godmother to a plaintiff who did not even bother to look.

The lawyer is now provided with material for his summation:

"How can the plaintiff contend he was exercising ordinary care before and at the time of the occurrence? There was nothing to interfere with his vision. It was a bright, clear day. All he had to do was look—just look. John's white car did not drop out of the sky. If only the plaintiff had taken the one, simple precaution of looking, none of us would be here today.

"Under the law, and it is this jury's sworn duty to follow the law, the plaintiff cannot collect ten cents unless he proves that before and at the time of the accident he was exercising ordinary care for his own safety. . . ."

What About Intuition?

Do some trial lawyers possess a sixth sense, like a homing pigeon, that enables them, on rare occasions, to "zero in" on some obscured but important fact? It may appear to others that the cross-examiner possesses this power, and he, himself, may even occasionally feel that he does. Perhaps the case appeared to be hopeless; necessity knows no law. However, whatever success he has had in this line was more likely due to thorough preparation and a skill developed through hard work. It may be that some cross-examiners feel they are clairvoyant, but if they really analyzed their success, they would probably have to agree that they merely followed the common-sense rules of the trade. It is simply a matter of taking a calculated risk. Like any gambling game, there are times when the odds are in a person's favor, but the trick is to know when the right moment arrives. The decision to take a "shot in the dark" will depend on many factors. For example, assume that a lawyer is defending a hopeless liability case involving back injuries to the plaintiff and that the plaintiff has been using crutches since his discharge from the hospital. He is using them in the courtroom and everyone is acutely aware of them. The lawyer, in cross-examining the orthopedic surgeon, seemingly takes a wild gamble when he asks:

Q. Doctor, is there any reason why the plaintiff cannot throw away those crutches he is using?

Even if the doctor answers that there is no reason, there would be lawyers who would say this was a foolhardy gamble and hardly worth the risk. However, let us analyze the possible circumstances that might have justified this gamble. For example:

(1) If the plaintiff's lawyer on direct examination did not ask the doctor how much longer the plaintiff might have to use crutches, the mere fact that this information was not brought out would make it conspicuous by its absence. The reason for the omission might be that during the pretrial interview the physician told the plaintiff's lawyer that, in his opinion, the crutches were no longer necessary; or, on the other hand, the plaintiff's lawyer might have set a "trap" for the defense lawyer, and the answer would have been a devastating, "Mr. Jones will have to use those crutches for the rest of his life."

(2) The defense lawyer might have consulted with another orthopedic surgeon, who advised him that, in his opinion, the crutches were not necessary. If this was a valid opinion, then there is a good possibility the plaintiff's doctor would have to agree with that point of view.

(3) The defense lawyer might have personal knowledge from past experience that the doctor appearing for the plaintiff has strong convictions opposing the use of artificial walking aids when the weight-bearing bones are sufficiently strong to perform their function.

(4) The defense lawyer might have knowledge of a rumor, but no evidence, that the plaintiff had been seen walking without the aid of crutches.

As can be seen from some of the foregoing examples, the dramatic question asked of the doctor was a calculated risk. In this particular case since the defense lawyer received a favorable answer, the jury may well suspect the plaintiff of malingering, and the defense lawyer has been supplied with an effective argument in his efforts to plant some seeds of prejudice against the plaintiff.

Another occasion for using this seemingly dangerous and reckless form of examination is when the cross-examiner has a strong "feeling" that the witness is lying—not only that he is lying, but that he is uncomfortable with the lie. For example, if the cross-examiner has this feeling about an occurrence witness who testified on direct examination as to the many details preceding an automobile collision he can quickly lead him into a trap as follows:

Q. You had no reason to look toward the intersection before the accident occurred, did you?

A. No.

Q. As a matter of fact, you were not looking toward the intersection before the accident occurred, were you?

A. No.

Q. Your attention was attracted to the intersection by the crash; isn't that correct?

A. Yes.

Q. And, of course, you saw what happened after the automobiles collided?

A. Yes.

Q. As a matter of fact, you never saw the actual collision, did you?

In the foregoing example, the cross-examiner should closely observe the witness so as to have the benefit of detecting any signs of nervousness—he may almost be able to feel the witness' discomfort. Then the final question should produce a better-than-even chance that the witness will admit he did not actually see the accident. With righteous indignation in his voice, the cross-examiner can now make a motion that all of this testimony be stricken and that the jury be instructed to disregard it—all of which was made possible by what some would call a "sixth sense."

Stay in Command

When the witness is not responsive to the questions, the examiner should immediately take measures to correct the situation. He must be in complete control at all times. If the questions call for a simple "yes" or "no," but the witness insists upon qualifying the answers with speeches, the examiner should request the trial judge to instruct the witness to be responsive and to insist upon responsive answers from the witness. Most trial judges will make it quite clear to the witness that his answer is unresponsive and will admonish him to answer the question. If the witness continues to violate the trial judge's instructions, he may lose his effectiveness with the jury because of his apparent disrespect for the Court.

If, on the other hand, the cross-examiner has a weak trial judge, then a variety of techniques can be employed. One of the better-known techniques is to say: "Mr. Jones, your lawyer will have every opportunity to clarify any points that you feel need clarifying when he questions you again on redirect examination. Now, please answer my questions for me." Another procedure is to ask the court reporter to read back the last question so as to emphasize the difference between the question asked and the answer given. If the answer is again unresponsive, then the cross-examiner can again ask the court reporter to read back the same question. In this way, the fact that the answers are in no way related to the questions is highlighted.

The "Evasive Witness"

The evasive witness is the most vulnerable in cross-examination. He hesitates to give a responsive answer when he knows the answer is harmful. He will do this on even relatively minor concessions that should be made to the cross-examiner. Because of his lack of experience in the courtroom, he is not aware that he emphasizes the very things that he attempts to play down. For example:

Q. At the time you repaired the brakes on this automobile, how long had you been working in the brake department of the Acme Auto Service Company?

A. I had been with the Acme Auto Service Company for 12 years.

(The examiner should again ask the identical question very slowly to emphasize it.)

Q. At the time you repaired the brakes on this automobile, how long had you been working in the brake department of the Acme Auto Service Company?

A. Two days.

Another method of accomplishing the same objective is to ask the court reporter to read the question back. This is a change of pace, as the question is read back in a different voice; this further emphasizes the question that was asked. When the witness realizes that you are insisting on an answer to the question and sheepishly gives it, his lack of forthrightness is most apparent. Strangely enough, this type of witness will quite often continue to play into the cross-examiner's hands by supplying more of these opportunities. Oftentimes he will deliberately testify in variance to his deposition wherein he is committed to a contrary position. Then, of course, his value is practically destroyed by showing not only that he is not straightforward, but that he is actually lying to the jury.

What About the Child Witness?

One of the most difficult witnesses to cross-examine is a child. Because adults naturally have a protective feeling towards children, the child has an advantage over any other witness. A child can easily be led by suggestion and will readily agree with an adult out of habit. Jurors know this, and any hint that the cross-examiner is employing this tactic will provoke their indignation. Where a young child is cross-examined, the examiner should be extremely considerate and more than fair in order to win the approval of the jury. Whatever the point the examiner has in mind, he should make it as quickly as possible. If he feels, for example, that the child is lying on an important point, he can be almost certain that it is because an adult told him to do so. But bringing a child into a conspiracy is very risky because the child is unpredictable and can break the conspiracy wide open. He has not learned to lie with the efficiency of an adult. If his father (or mother or even the lawyer) has told the child to say something contrary to what he knows is true, he is quite apt to say: "My daddy told me to say that."

It is tragic and sad when children are told to lie. The grown-up game of deceit is quite different from the stories children invent in their active imaginations. Although a lawyer may be forced into establishing that a child is lying, he will invariably find it a disagreeable task. But be that as it may, the primary duty of the trial lawyer is to establish the truth in order that justice be served. Even at the risk of losing the approval of the jury, the cross-examiner must try to uncover the truth. The techniques for doing this will depend on too many variables to establish a rule.

Impeaching the Witness

A definite style and technique should be adopted by every trial lawyer in using a deposition to impeach a witness. With trial practice as it is today, most trial lawyers obtain an oral deposition of the other party to the lawsuit to use as a basis for their cross-examination. These depositions quite often are taken of important witnesses as well. A summary of the deposition should be made in advance of the trial. It can be in the form of an abstract on one or two pages, with page numbers of the deposition in the margin for quick reference. By referring to this summary of the testimony elicited during the deposition, the cross-examiner can quickly determine whether there is a variance between the testimony in court and the testimony taken at the deposition. If the lawyer finds a discrepancy significant enough to impeach, he has quick reference to the page of the transcript of the deposition on which the inconsistency appears. The following is one of the techniques used to impeach a witness:

Q. You testified in court today that when you first saw Mr. White's automobile, it was traveling about 40 M.P.H.

A. That's correct.

Q. Now, Mr. Smith, do you recall giving your deposition about six months ago?

A. Yes.

Q. That deposition was taken in your lawyer's office, was it not?

A. Yes.

Q. I was there at that time and asked you some questions, did I not?

A. Yes.

Q. And your lawyer was present the entire time I was asking you those questions?

A. Yes.

Q. There was a court stenographer present at that time, just as there is one here in court today?

A. Yes.

Q. And that court stenographer was taking down all of the questions I asked of you and all of the answers that you gave?

A. Yes.

Q. Before you testified, were you sworn to tell the truth?

A. Yes.

Q. Before I proceeded to ask you any questions, I asked you to listen carefully to my questions and told you I would be happy to repeat any questions you did not understand; is that correct?

A. That is correct.

Q. Do you remember this question being asked of you and this answer being given by you?

    "*Q.* Can you estimate the speed of Mr. White's automobile when you first saw it?

    "*A.* Yes. It was traveling about 25 M.P.H."

Q. Do you recall that question being asked of you and that answer being given by you while you were under oath?

A. Yes.

At this point, the witness has been impeached. There are several possible questions to ask next in following up the impeachment in order to highlight the inconsistencies. Some of the more commonly used are as follows:

Q. Were you lying then or are you lying now?

Q. At the time you gave your deposition, less time had gone by and you undoubtedly remembered the facts more clearly at that time; is that not so?

Q. Mr. Smith, would you like to change your testimony at this time?

I feel it is usually preferable to say nothing at all. If the point has been properly made by the cross-examiner, it is not necessary to give the witness a slap in the face. I do not feel such a slap adds any emphasis to the point already made, and it is always possible that the jurors may sympathize with the witness and dislike the examiner for what they may feel is an unnecessary affront.

If the witness denies that he testified as indicated in the deposition, then the cross-examiner must bring in the court reporter who took the deposition. I think this adds even greater emphasis to the inconsistencies, as now the witness cannot claim that he was mistaken; he has taken a stand on this point and it was resolved against him through an impartial witness.

Don't Telegraph Your Punch

It may be necessary for the cross-examiner to conceal the purpose of his questions, especially with a partisan witness. Of course, it isn't always easy to do this, but at least a partial concealment is often essential.

I am reminded of a case that I defended in which the extent of plaintiff's injuries sounded stupendous. A treating doctor testified as to all of plaintiff's injuries and the treatment she received while under his care in the hospital immediately following an automobile accident. He described a large, gaping wound on her forehead that exposed the raw skull. In addition to this, she had fractures of both hips, four fractured ribs, a compression fracture of a vertebra, bleeding into the lung, and other soft tissue injuries about her body. He also testified that shortly after she was brought into the hospital, he noticed a shortness of breath that he diagnosed as a heart malfunction. Following this, he ordered a cardiogram; this was followed up by another cardiogram a few days later. The conclusions from the cardiograms and other findings indicated to him that the woman had suffered a heart attack, and that this heart attack was related to the automobile accident. He went on to testify that because of this, there was some damage to the wall of the heart that would be of a permanent nature. He did not prescribe anything for the heart condition other than bed rest, which, by necessity, was provided for her other injuries as well. His previous medical reports made no mention of the heart problem, and the hospital records that contained the history, findings, and treatment in his own handwriting did not cover this particular point. However, in his preliminary diagnosis in the hospital records, he mentioned a shortness of breath that he diagnosed as a heart condition and ordered that cardiograms be taken. There were no other follow-up notes covering the heart condition. It was my opinion that the heart condition was more of an afterthought and was not really considered significant until he testified in court. I wanted him to admit that at no time did he consider the heart condition a problem and that if she did have a heart condition, it was a preexisting condition.

Q. Doctor Travis, you are on the staff of Sherman Hospital; is that right?

A. Yes, sir.

Q. Is that how you happened to become the treating doctor of the plaintiff?

A. Yes, I was called to the emergency room. I was on duty that day.

Q. And so, of course, you treated her while she stayed in Sherman Hospital?

A. Yes, sir.

Q. And in addition to your treating her, I believe you mentioned that you had an orthopedic surgeon also taking care of her hips, didn't you?

A. Yes, sir.

Q. As the treating doctor, you treated her principally for the large, open wound on her forehead; is that correct?

A. Yes, principally.

Q. And, of course, this treatment took place on the day of the accident, did it not, Doctor?

A. Yes.

Q. And in repairing the wound, you sutured it with about 60 to 80 stitches; is that what you said?

A. Yes, between 60 and 80. I didn't count them.

Q. And do you recall whether you had X rays taken before you did the suturing?

A. After, I think, because . . . .

Q. You felt you should administer to the wounds first?

A. The bleeding, yes.

Q. And did you get a good result, Doctor?

A. Well, I think I did. I suppose it's for others to say. I am very happy with the result.

Q. And at the risk of being immodest, do you feel that you obtained a pretty good result?

A. I feel I obtained as good a result as was possible.

Q. I see.

A. I am not trying to boast.

Q. And you took the stitches out later? Was that a few days later, Doctor?

A. Yes, I customarily take the sutures out on the third or fourth day—I do this on all facial wounds.

Q. Then in the event there are no complications—they would come out about three or four days after the suturing?

A. Yes, sir.

Q. And were there any complications on this repair job, Doctor?

A. No, there were no unexpected complications.

Q. Then she had a complete and uneventful recovery, so far as this wound is concerned?

A. Yes, sir.

Q. Is there any permanent damage as a result of that wound?

A. Damage? No. The scar is there.

Q. The scar—but otherwise she made a complete recovery; is that correct?

A. Yes.

Q. And you had some X rays taken of the skull, and those were all negative?

A. Yes.

Q. Is that as far as any head injuries are concerned?

A. Yes, sir.

Q. That would be the extent of it?

A. That is the extent of it.

Q. And no further treatment has been necessary since you took the sutures out?

A. Not on the head.

Q. Now, in the . . . did Doctor Schmidt . . . did he treat her for the fractured ribs?

A. No.

Q. That would fall under your . . . .

A. Yes, that would be . . . yes.

Q. And these ribs that were fractured—there were four of them, were there not, Doctor?

A. Yes.

Q. And did nature heal them? Did they knit all right?

A. Yes.

Q. You didn't have to reduce them in any way, did you, Doctor?

A. No.

Q. And reducing means putting them together? They were already together, weren't they?

A. Yes.

Q. So the ribs healed without your having to do anything to them; isn't that right?

A. Essentially, that's correct.

Q. And did they heal properly?

A. Yes, they healed satisfactorily.

Q. So there is no permanent damage to these ribs then, is there?

A. Nothing permanent.

Q. And she made a complete recovery within the usual, expected time?

A. Yes, sir.

Q. And part of the treatment—or while you were treating her—I believe you said that you noticed that she was having some difficulty in breathing, so you prescribed a couple of pillows under her head; did you, Doctor?

A. Yes.

Q. When you prescribe a couple of pillows under the head, what is that for?

A. Well, people who have broken ribs, or any other condition that involves the breathing, breathe better when they are propped up. It takes the pressure of the diaphragm away from the bottom of the lungs.

Q. And in treating heart patients, is there any significance in putting a couple of pillows under the head?

A. Just for relief of symptoms.

Q. It does relieve the symptoms?

A. Yes, some, usually.

Q. Then it is quite typical, isn't it, Doctor, for a patient with a heart condition to use a couple of pillows under the head?

A. Yes, I would say so.

Q. And in the course of your taking the history from this woman, did she tell you that she had been using pillows under her head for some time before the accident?

A. I would have to refer to the record.

Q. Please do that.

A. She sleeps . . . yes, sir. Yes, sir.

Q. Did she tell you that she sleeps with a couple of pillows under her head?

A. Yes.

Q. And she told you that? That she had been doing this before the accident?

A. Yes.

Q. And what is arteriosclerosis, Doctor?

A. Well, it's commonly referred to as hardening of the arteries. It is caused by deposits of cholesterol crystals within the inner linings of the arteries; these deposits of cholesterol get firmer and more consolidated as time goes on, so that the arteries lose their normal elasticity and become more rigid.

Q. And they also restrict the flow of blood in the artery, itself, do they not, Doctor?

A. With progressive disease, yes.

Q. And does she have a progressive disease, Doctor?

A. Well, she has arteriosclerosis, but you can't . . . . It's difficult to determine how much more progressive it will get. It may remain static for the rest of her life, or it may get progressive; in each individual it is different.

Q. Well, she had this arteriosclerosis before the accident, didn't she, Doctor?

A. Oh, yes.

Q. And it would be reasonable to assume that the flow of blood, the passage of the blood through the arteries themselves would be restricted, would it not?

A. Yes, in her particular condition, I think it would.

Q. And this, of course, creates more burden on the heart. The heart has to work a little harder; isn't that right?

A. That's correct.

Q. Now, as part of good hospital practice, the treating doctor makes entries in the hospital records concerning his examination, his findings, and his diagnosis; isn't that correct, Doctor?

A. Yes.

Q. And you did that in this case, did you not?

A. Yes.

Q. And on your final diagnosis, Doctor, you would incorporate all of those findings that you made and complete your diagnosis at the time of discharge, would you not?

A. Well, we usually pick the important things. I mean, if you mentioned every little thing, the hospital chart would get quite redundant, you see.

Q. You pick the important things in your diagnosis, then?

A. Yes, the important things.

Q. And that would be your final diagnosis?

A. Yes.

Q. Well, will you look at your final diagnosis, Doctor, and tell us whether you made any diagnosis concerning the heart?

A. No, I did not. I'm sorry. I have to correct myself. You said the final diagnosis? No, I did not.

Q. Your final diagnosis, Doctor, mentions chronic bronchitis, does it not?

A. Chronic bronchiectasis.

Q. Would that be bronchitis, Doctor?

A. Well, it's a little more involved than bronchitis. Bronchiectasis not only is a bronchitis wherein you have an inflammation of the inner lining of the breathing tubes—the bronchial tubes—but also involves weakness in the linings of the bronchial tubes, so that you get pouchings in the tubes. The tubes, instead of being straight tubes with no bumps in them, no pouchings, become tortuous tubes with many outpouchings, due to weaknesses in the wall.

Q. And this is a condition that she had before the accident?

A. Yes, it was preexistent.

Q. For a patient who has this condition, there would be a life expectancy considerably less than there would be for a patient without this condition, would there not?

A. Yes, sir.

Mr. Scott: Objection.

The Court: Doctor, in the future may I ask you to hesitate a little before you answer, so that the attorney can propose an objection. The answer will stand; the objection will be overruled.

Mr. Morrill: Q. The fractures to the hips, of course, were taken care of by Doctor Schmidt?

A. Yes, Doctor Schmidt.

Q. And you weren't present when he did that, were you?

A. No, I wasn't.

Q. And Doctor Schmidt reduced the hip fractures; is that correct? When I say reduce, I mean bring them together and hold them together for nature to take over and knit; isn't that right?

A. Yes.

Q. And Doctor Schmidt obtained a good result, did he not?

Mr. Scott: Objection.

Mr. Morrill: Q. If you know.

The Court: Sustained. Do you know?

The Witness: Well, no, I can't say positively.

The Court: The objection will be sustained.

Mr. Morrill: Q. You don't know what . . . you wouldn't be able to tell us whether Doctor . . . from your own knowledge, whether Doctor Schmidt did obtain a good result from his operation?

Mr. Scott: Your Honor, the reason I am objecting is that they objected to my going into Doctor Schmidt's operation with this doctor, and now they are trying to get a result without my going into Doctor Schmidt's operation.

The Court: The objection will be sustained.

Mr. Morrill: Q. You have . . . when was the last time that you saw this patient, Doctor?

A. Professionally?

Q. Yes.

A. On October 20, 1965.

Q. And that would be about the time she was being discharged from the hospital, would it not?

A. Yes.

Q. And you haven't seen her since then?

A. Other than today?

Q. Yes.

A. Oh, no. I have seen her. She was subsequently . . .

Q. Oh, you testified she was in the hospital again after that, and you saw her, but you didn't treat her?

A. Not professionally.

Q. Now, there was also mention made of a compression fracture of the ninth thoracic vertebra. You can see that, can you, Doctor, on the X ray film that you interpreted for us?

A. Yes, sir.

Q. Now, could I ask you, Doctor, to step down again for just a few minutes, and look at these X ray films again?

(Whereupon the witness left the stand.)

Q. When you interpreted that X ray for us, Doctor, I believe you said you could see some bleeding into the lung. Did I understand you correctly?

A. Yes, you did. You see a density in the right side. It is difficult to see, but we interpret it as possible bleeding, or not actively bleeding—the presence of blood there.

Q. What is a hemothorax, Doctor?

A. A hemothorax is a mass of blood within the pleural space of the lung. That is, the space between the lung and the inside, and the chest wall and the inner chest wall on the outside.

Q. As you interpret that X ray, is it your opinion that there is bleeding in the lung, Doctor? Do I understand it correctly? Or is it possible?

A. Within the substance, within a small segment of the lung.

Q. Can you see that on that X ray?

A. Well, we interpret this density here as being that.

Q. Do you interpret it as that? Is that what you said? *Your* interpretation, Doctor?

A. Yes, my interpretation. And also the interpretation of the X ray doctor who read them.

Q. Doctor Elly?

A. Doctor Elly.

Q. Is that his interpretation?

A. Yes.

Q. As you understand it?

A. I think that was his interpretation. I didn't attach much significance to it.

Q. You didn't? Did this . . . was there another . . . did you order another X ray taken shortly after this to determine whether the bleeding had stopped, or was there any problem?

A. Well, I didn't feel that there was active bleeding going on here.

Q. So it wasn't necessary to have any further X ray studies made?

A. No, that's right.

Q. And whatever this condition was, in your opinion, did it clear up very shortly thereafter?

A. Yes, I think so.

Q. And it was an uneventful recovery in this area?

A. Yes.

Q. Is it on that same film, Doctor, that you can see a compression fracture of the ninth thoracic vertebra, or is it on the other X ray that you interpreted for us?

A. I can see it here.

Q. You arrive at that interpretation by the fact that the vertebra appears to be a little smaller than the other vertebra, is that right?

A. Yes, here it is. Here is the lower and here is the upper. See how narrow that is compared to the others?

Q. What treatment did you give the patient for this, Doctor?

A. Here again the patient . . . no particular treatment was necessary here.

Q. In other words, you didn't have to do anything for this condition, am I correct?

A. If this were the only thing that she had, then we would first of all have her on bed rest for a while and put a brace on her back, but she was on bed rest, and therefore no further treatment was necessary.

Q. So whatever this condition was, the bed rest was the extent of your treatment?

A. Yes.

Q. And, were any further X ray studies made in the hospital for this fracture, Doctor?

A. Of this particular fracture?

Q. Yes.

A. No, there were no further X rays made of that particular fracture. No.

Q. And then the next time we picked up this fracture is two years later on this side view of the thoracic?

A. Yes.

Q. And who took the side view of that thoracic?

A. This was all at Sherman Hospital. Doctor Schmidt ordered it.

Q. And it shows a . . . healing process there, Doctor; can you see any?

A. Well, the compression fracture is static there. The compression is there.

Q. Can you see any calcium deposits indicated?

A. I see an increased density, so it is as healed as it is going to be.

Q. No treatment has ever been necessary for that condition, then?

A. No.

Q. Thank you, Doctor. Resume the stand, if you will.

(Whereupon the witness resumed the stand.)

Q. Do you know whether the patient ever used a cane before the accident?

A. I don't know.

Q. And she made a complete recovery from all the conditions that you treated her for, Doctor, didn't she?

A. Yes, yes. All that I treated her for.

Q. Yes?

A. And that is eliminating the hips.

Q. And the hips, of course, would be Doctor Schmidt's concern?

A. Doctor Schmidt, right.

Q. So, with the exception of the hips, she has made a complete recovery from everything you treated her for?

A. Yes.

Mr. Morrill: Thank you very much.

In order for the witness to answer these questions, it was necessary for him to refer to the hospital records. I feel that referring to the hospital records and then answering the questions gave the testimony a definite aura of accuracy.

Misrepresentation by the Defendant as to Insurance

In the game of deceiving the jury as to the existence of liability insurance, what should the plaintiff's lawyer's course of action be when the defense lawyer states that the defendant will have to pay the judgment himself? If the defendant is a married man with six children who earns $100 a week, this statement will undoubtedly go a long way toward creating a Tom Thumb-sized verdict. The plaintiff's lawyer can, of course, spring to his feet and object, and the objection will be sustained by the trial judge.

The question is: How will the jurors interpret the objection and the ruling from the court sustaining it? More than likely, they will feel that the defense lawyer's message should not have been communicated to them and that they have an obligation to render a verdict in an amount commensurate with the damages regardless of the defendant's ability to pay the judgment. But in spite of all this fine sentiment, in actual practice the jurors probably will have compassion for the defendant and "go easy on him." Although most states will grant a new trial where the plaintiff's lawyer deliberately informs the jury of the existence of liability insurance, they will not always do so in situations where the defense lawyer deliberately misrepresents the facts to the jury. Therefore, a motion for a mistrial by the plaintiff's lawyer, subsequently denied by the trial judge, may or may not be sufficient for the plaintiff to obtain a new trial should the verdict be low. Since this is true, I think the only safe course for the plaintiff's lawyer to take is to make an objection something as follows:

"If the law seals my lips from informing the jury as to the real facts, certainly it is not fair that the lawyer for the defense should have the right to deliberately misrepresent the facts to the jury."

How Many Feet per Second?

A lawyer should be familiar with the rule that a car travels in feet per second approximately one and one-half times its speed in miles per hour. In other words, if a car is traveling 50 M.P.H., it is traveling at the rate of 75 feet per second. Speeds and distances are frequently important in the trial of automobile accident cases. Witnesses often testify as to how far away the other vehicle was when it was first seen and the approximate speed of each vehicle. The accuracy of their testimony, or the inaccuracy, can effectively be pointed out through the use of this mathematical formula.

To use an example, assume a plaintiff drove his automobile into an open, unguarded intersection. When the plaintiff's car was almost through the intersection, the right rear of his automobile was struck by another automobile approaching from his right. From this set of facts, the physical evidence clearly establishes that the plaintiff was the first into the intersection, as he was almost through the intersection, while the other car was just beginning to enter the intersection, when the impact took place. There would certainly be a presumption that the plaintiff's automobile had the right of way and that the defendant was the offender, as he should have had his car sufficiently under control to permit the plaintiff to continue safely through the intersection. Typical testimony of the plaintiff might be as follows:

"I slowed down as I began to approach the intersection and looked both ways and did not see any cars coming from either direction. As

I began to enter the intersection, I again looked and did see a car approaching from the right and would estimate that at the time he was about halfway down the block, or 300 feet away. When I saw him, I was traveling about 20 M.P.H. I continued on through the intersection. When I first saw him, I could not estimate his speed, but felt that he was far enough away that I could safely pass through the intersection. When I got into the lane of traffic that the other car was traveling in, I saw him again. He was coming at a great rate of speed and there was nothing I could do to avoid the impact. From the time I first saw him up to the time he hit me, I traveled about 40 feet."

His testimony probably sounds so familiar as to seem a stereotyped version of an intersection collision. The cross-examining lawyer can write down on a blackboard:

(1) First saw the other car when it was about 300 feet away.

(2) Was traveling 20 M.P.H. when first saw other car.

(3) Traveled about 40 feet from time he first saw other car until time of impact.

It can now be effectively demonstrated to the jury that it would be impossible for the accident to have happened the way the plaintiff testified. The plaintiff, in traveling 20 M.P.H., was traveling 30 feet per second, which means that he was one and one-third seconds away when he first saw the other car. The other car, in order to close the gap to collision, would have had to travel 300 feet in one and one-third seconds, which would mean that he was traveling at the rate of 150 M.P.H. The length of the skid marks laid down by the automobiles, together with photographs indicating property damage, would, of course, be useful to bolster the case.

Assume a witness testifies that when he was about 75 feet from an intersection, the traffic light turned from red to green; that when it changed color, he was traveling about 50 M.P.H.; that as he continued to the intersection, he kept watching a car coming from the left, which was traveling about the same speed; that when it got to about 50 feet from the intersection, it started to speed up and while he watched it, it appeared to continue to speed up; that he kept watching it and then became convinced that it was speeding up and he started to apply his brakes, blow his horn, and so forth. By using this mathematical formula, it can be seen that many things happened during that period of one and one-half seconds, which was the entire time that he had the other car within his vision.

In addition to the feet-per-second the automobile was traveling, the lawyer should be familiar with the braking distances required for stopping a car at various speeds. There are variables within this rule that depend upon the road surface, weather conditions, type of tires, weight of the automobile, condition of the brakes, whether the road level is inclining or declining, and other such factors. Because of this, it cannot be argued as a mathematical formula, but introduction of expert evidence should be considered if an effective closing argument can be made to contradict the testimony of opposing witnesses. Familiarity with the average braking distances and reaction time can be valuable in cross-examining a witness who professes to be an expert, such as the investigating traffic officer. The Secretary of State usually prepares a chart of these figures for inclusion in the instruction booklet for applicants seeking a driver's license. The chart used in Illinois follows:

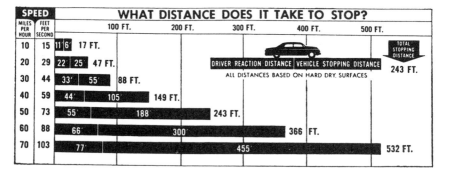

SPEED		WHAT DISTANCE DOES IT TAKE TO STOP?				
MILES PER HOUR	FEET PER SECOND	100 FT.	200 FT.	300 FT.	400 FT.	500 FT.
10	15	11' 6' 17 FT.				TOTAL STOPPING DISTANCE
20	29	22' 25' 47 FT.		DRIVER REACTION DISTANCE VEHICLE STOPPING DISTANCE	243 FT.	
30	44	33' 55' 88 FT.		ALL DISTANCES BASED ON HARD DRY SURFACES		
40	59	44' 105' 149 FT.				
50	73	55' 188 243 FT.				
60	88	66' 300' 366 FT.				
70	103	77' 455			532 FT.	

Preserve the Damaging Answer

When a witness, on cross-examination, blurts out a ridiculous answer or one damaging to the opponent's case, take extreme care not to let the opportunity fade away. The witness himself, to say nothing of the other lawyer, may immediately realize the foolishness of the words he has just uttered, and he may want to modify or completely change the import of the statement. The cross-examiner can reduce, if not eliminate, the possibility of such an escape by writing verbatim on a blackboard the answer just given. If he is not certain of the exact words, he can ask the court reporter to read back the last answer so that the jury will know he is being completely accurate and that the words written down are not his, but those of the witness. It will then be extremely difficult for the witness to change his words or alter their meaning because they are written down for everyone to see.

The spoken word comes out as sound waves; they fade away and disappear. Most people are accustomed to giving new versions of what they have already said, and if the two versions are completely contrary, they will justify the change by stating that "this is what I meant to say. . . ." The answer written on the board will probably serve to forestall any changes and will also continue to illustrate the damaging testimony as long as it remains before the jurors; it will be burned into their minds if the blackboard is left in their presence for the balance of the trial, on through closing arguments. This method will be extremely helpful in cross-examining those witnesses who have a facility for hedging or changing their testimony without seeming to do so.

Dramatizing It

On rare occasions, a lawyer may be given an advantage by his opponent's failure to bring out the fact that the other party to the lawsuit is blind in one eye or suffers from some other infirmity. If a driver has a handicap that may affect his driving ability, the jurors may think that there has been a deliberate attempt to conceal that fact if it is not brought out on direct examination. We may meet many persons in our lifetime who have lost the sight of an eye, and we may not even be aware of it. However, the trial lawyer cannot overlook such a fact; if he is not aware of it or if he purposely fails to bring it out, the jurors will strongly suspect that an attempt was made to conceal it from them. The cross-examiner should graphically reveal the infirmity if it has been overlooked so that a strong impression is created in the minds of the jurors. For example, a plaintiff pedestrian who was blind in the left eye was struck by an automobile that approached from his left while he was crossing a street. The plaintiff's lawyer had failed to reveal the existence of the infirmity to the jury and the cross-examination went as follows:

Q. Mr. Black, will you take this book and hold it over your left eye and tell me how many fingers I'm holding up on my right hand?
A. Three.
Q. All right, Mr. Black, while I'm standing back here in the same position about 20 feet from you, take that book and hold it over your right eye and tell me how many fingers I'm holding up on my right hand.
A. I don't know.
Q. All right, Mr. Black, I'll move in closer to approximately 10 feet. Now tell me how many fingers I'm holding up with my right hand.
A. I don't know.
Q. Well now, Mr. Black, I'll move in to approximately five feet; can you tell me how many fingers I'm holding up now?
A. No.
Q. Mr. Black, can you see my hand?
A. No.

Q. Mr. Black, can you see me at all?

A. No.

Q. Can you see anything with your left eye?

A. No.

Q. Mr. Black, are you blind in your left eye?

A. Yes.

Q. Were you blind in your left eye when you started to cross that street?

A. Yes.

Q. In fact, were you blind in your left eye for a considerable time before you were injured?

A. Yes.

Q. Did you forget to tell us that you were blind in your left eye?

A. I wasn't asked.

Q. I have no further questions.

As you can see from the above example, demonstrating that the plaintiff was blind in the important left eye dramatizes that fact much more than merely asking him whether he was blind in that eye.

Transcribe Testimony When Possible

A trial lawyer is always amazed, when he reads a transcript of his cross-examination, to see how he failed to exploit some of the answers given by a witness. This is especially true when the cross-examination is lengthy. It is well worth the investment to have the court reporter transcribe the direct examination and the cross-examination of an important witness whenever the opportunity arises.

In an ordinary trial, the witness comes and goes without a sufficient interval of time to have the record transcribed. However, in any situation where the testimony of a key witness is continued until the following day, the opposing lawyer should definitely have that testimony transcribed. It is of significant value if he can get not only all of the direct testimony, but also a major portion of the earlier cross-examination to use as the basis for his cross-examination the following day. It is rare, indeed, that a witness giving lengthy testimony does not become careless because he is tired or overconfident; any slip can be used as a basis for casting doubt on his testimony. Having the record written up not only will help in preparing further cross-examination, but also will serve to show that the witness' testimony is different from that of the previous day. It will make a strong impression in the minds of the jurors if a lawyer can argue that this witness is so careless with the facts that he changes his testimony from day to day.

Because of the advantage a cross-examiner has if he has part of the testimony written up, some thought should be given to preventing the opposition from also having this advantage. If possible, put an important witness who has lengthy testimony on the stand early enough in the day so that it will be unlikely that he will be returned the following day to a better prepared cross-examiner.

You Are Awfully Expensive, Doctor

The cost of medical testimony is often expensive. This fact is frequently made known to the jurors by one of the lawyers for whatever value he can derive from it. The purpose in bringing this out is to shock the jurors and perhaps cast doubt on the impartiality of the witness. It may, at first blush, seem outrageous to the average juror who earns an average salary that a doctor will charge from $150 to $250 for less than one hour in court. If this revelation is left unchallenged and justification for the doctor's charges is not shown, the opposing lawyer will be supplied with a weapon in the form of "this $250-an-hour doctor they brought into court...." The obvious implication is that for that kind of money, you can get anyone to say almost anything.

If the doctor has testified for the same lawyer in the past, perhaps numerous times, it may appear that not only is the doctor well paid for his services, but the lawyer is well satisfied with the services rendered. Aside from whether these implications may or may not have merit, there are techniques to bring out the information, as well as techniques to justify it. All of this inquiry is proper since the cross-examiner is entitled to show any partiality on the part of a witness that may affect the probative value of his testimony. An example of a plaintiff's cross-examination of a doctor follows:

Q. Are you being paid for this testimony today?

A. I will render a bill for the time spent away from my office.

Q. In any event, however, you're going to make a charge for being here in court today?

A. Yes.

Q. How much are you going to charge?

A. It all depends on how long I will be here.

Q. Well, assume that we stop right now, Doctor; how much will your charge be?

A. $250.

Q. To whom do you present your bill?

A. To Attorney Black.

Q. Have you testified for Mr. Black before?

A. Yes.

Q. Did he pay you on the previous occasions?

A. Yes.

Q. Do you always get money regardless of the outcome of the law-suit?

A. Yes.

Q. Do you get paid before you come to court or after you have appeared in court?

A. I submit my bill afterward.

Q. Do you charge $250 for a house call, Doctor?

Objection.

Sustained.

To let this testimony go without an explanation or justification of the charges would render the value of the testimony of the doctor questionable, at best. A suggested reexamination justifying the charges follows:

Q. As a doctor, you render various charges for your services.

A. Yes.

Q. The amount of these charges will vary from doctor to doctor?

A. Yes.

Q. The amount of the charges would depend upon many facts, including such things as the amount of education and training a doctor has. Is that correct?

A. Yes.

Q. And, as you indicated previously, you are a specialist in your field, Doctor?

A. Yes.

Q. As a matter of fact, you indicated you are the head of the department at your hospital?

A. That is correct.

Q. Doctor, if you leave now, how much time will you have consumed away from your practice?

A. Well, counting my traveling time to and from the court, together with my time in court, it will be approximately two hours.

Q. Will the charges that you render today be comparable to the charges that you render in the operating room?

A. Yes.

Q. To your own knowledge, are your charges comparable to those of any other specialists of your standing?

A. Yes.

Q. This would be true, Doctor, in the operating room or in the court-room?

A. Yes.

The defense lawyer, in using a high-priced doctor, might anticipate this type of cross-examination and protect himself by cross-examining the plaintiff's doctors about the amount of their charges. It is rare that a doctor in a large city will charge less than $150, so a specialist charging an additional $100 is not startling. In large cities, a few professional testifiers will often be found who will not hesitate to be less than honest regarding the amount of their charges. I recall a case a few years ago in which I represented a party who sustained a back injury. The defendant brought in a well-known orthopedic surgeon to testify as a means of minimizing the degree of permanency. Routinely, the question was asked as to the amount of the doctor's charges and the reply was $75, instead of the customarily higher fee. This opened the door for cross-examination on the subject of much higher fees received by this doctor on previous occasions. The jury could not have been satisfied with the doctor's explanations which, I am sure, affected the probative value of his opinion.

Getting the Plaintiff to Rotate His Head

One of the methods that a defense lawyer can use to demonstrate to a jury that the plaintiff is "putting on" about the pain in his neck is to ask him to rotate his head. It must be remembered that the plaintiff is at a disadvantage on the witness stand, since he is out of his element, in addition to the fact that he is nervous about the whole thing, anyway. While testifying as to the limitation of motion in his neck since the accident, it is easy for him to hold his head in a rigid position. It's amazing, however, to see how often a witness forgets about his limitation of motion when the cross-examination seems to imply that his vision is not very good. After a series of questions about the witness' vision with and without glasses and as to whether he was wearing glasses at the time of the accident, he is usually ready for the bait. At this point, he is anxious to prove how well he can see. By asking the witness to look over his right shoulder in back of him to see if he can see the picture, flag, or clock, and then over his left shoulder to see some other object, you will have him demonstrating in the presence of the jury how well he can rotate his head. This demonstration will often cause the jurors to smile or even laugh audibly. The entire complexion of the case can turn in a matter of seconds when the jurors suddenly get the impression that the plaintiff is greatly exaggerating his injury.

"So, You Were Talking to the Other Lawyer"

If your opponent neglected to bring out the fact during direct examination that he had a nice little visit with a so-called "independent witness," then he has given you the opportunity to bring it out for the first time on cross-examination. You can begin by asking the witness whether he has ever talked to the other lawyer, as discussed earlier. If he denies that he talked to the other lawyer at any time before he testified, you can proceed to completely discredit him. If, on the other hand, he admits that he did talk to the other lawyer, then you can bring out where these conversations took place. Your opponent may have been to his house the evening before, or perhaps they had a visit at the lawyer's office during the lunch hour. If the witness unhesitatingly volunteers the facts without attempting to evade the question, then the cross-examiner should move to another area. But if, on the other hand, the witness is evasive, then a certain amount of doubt can be cast upon his testimony. For example, if the cross-examiner knows that the witness spent some time in his opponent's office during the lunch recess and he can sense that the witness is reluctant to admit it, then adroit questioning can make it appear that the witness is deliberately attempting to conceal this fact. An example of this type of examination follows:

Q. By the way, Mr. Brown, where did you have lunch today?
A. At Clark's Restaurant.
Q. Where did you go then?
A. I went to the drugstore to buy some cigarettes.
Q. Where did you go then?
A. Well, I guess I walked back to the courthouse.

(The next question can be emphasized by a change in the speed or tone of voice.)

Q. As a matter of fact, Mr. Brown, isn't it a fact that you went over to the office of the lawyer who represents the defendant?
A. Yes.
Q. Did you talk about this case?
A. Yes.
Q. And you talked about the testimony that you were going to give here under oath today?
A. Yes.
Q. Who was present during this conversation?
A. Well, just myself and the lawyer and Mr. Black.
Q. When you refer to Mr. Black, you are talking about the defendant in this case?
A. Yes.
Q. Mr. Brown, were you paid any money or was there any promise to pay you any money?
A. No.
Q. Are you quite certain of that?
A. Well, only the amount of money that I lost as a result of taking the day off from work.

Any number of avenues can be explored for dealing with an "evasive witness," and the foregoing is an example of one of the possibilities.

Witnesses Who Refuse to Concede the Obvious

As previously mentioned, a witness will be more convincing if he has an aura of impartiality about him. This will be especially true with expert witnesses and more particularly so with medical doctors. There are a few doctors, even well-qualified ones, who feel that it is necessary to "take sides." Their entire attitude projects partiality and even an antagonism toward the cross-examiner. Such an attitude will reduce this witness' value because the jurors expect fairness and impartiality. After all, the medical doctor should not have any interest in the outcome of the lawsuit—he should be there only to give them the facts.

In defending a medical malpractice case, I had a perfect example of such a doctor who appeared as the medical expert for the plaintiff. The witness was certified to the American Board of Orthopedic Surgery, a fellow in the American College of Surgeons, and a professor of orthopedic surgery; in addition, he had other impressive qualifications. The plaintiff had injured his hand in a power saw accident. He was taken to the defendant hospital for emergency care and came under the care of the defendant doctor whom I represented. It was the contention of the plaintiff that the surgery and care he received resulted in the permanent loss of the use of his hand.

As the cross-examination of the plaintiff's doctor proceeded, it became quite obvious that he was extremely partisan. He played into our hands by constantly refusing to be responsive to my questions. In addition, he became argumentative with me and refused to admit to certain points which should have been readily conceded. (If one must concede a point, he must do it gracefully and quickly to maintain an air of fairness.) It was Publius Mimus who once said, "He gives twice who gives quickly." The examination was as follows:

Q. Now, the tendons themselves are very strong, supple parts of our body that do not contract or expand; is that correct?

A. That is true; the tendons do not contract unless they have been injured.

Q. And we could liken these tendons, could we not, Doctor, to cords with a pulley on the other end pulling the cords; would that be a good analogy?

A. It is an analogy.

Q. All right. Whether or not it is a good analogy, you won't concede that, Doctor. Now, all living tissue requires oxygen and blood; does it not, Doctor?

A. Yes, sir.

Q. And tendons would be living tissue that would require oxygen and blood; is that correct?

A. That is correct.

Q. And as a matter of fact, the tendons have very little of their own blood supply; is that correct?

A. That is true.

Q. One or two small veins?

A. No, they have arteries also.

Q. They do have arteries?

A. Otherwise they could never survive, Mr. Morrill, unless they had arteries.

Q. We are referring to these tendons now, Doctor.

A. I'm talking about tendons.

Q. All right; and to aid the nourishment of these tendons there is a link-like web of blood vessels known as a vinculum?

A. Vinculum.

Q. What is the purpose of it?

A. It helps to keep the tendon in place, but its major purpose is to form a web through which the blood may travel to the tendon—arteries as well as veins.

Q. All right, and do the tendons also draw nourishment from the peritenon?

A. To some degree.

Q. Now, this is a sheath that covers these tendons; is it not?

A. Yes.

Q. And the purpose of that sheath is to provide an easy, smooth, gliding motion for the tendons when the muscle in the forearm contracts to contract the phalanges; is that correct?

A. Well, it is to establish a tube through which this system works.

Q. Well, would my description be inaccurate, Doctor?

A. Your description is inadequate.

Q. I see. So you say in addition to what I have stated, it provides a tube whereby the tendons travel inside the tube?

A. That is true.

Q. And the tube itself in the inner surface of that sheath or tube would be a slippery, moist tissue, would it not?

A. That is true.

Q. Now, the tunnels that you have indicated, Doctor, are usually confined to the proximal phalanx, and I assume it is correct on the middle phalanx as I've drawn them. What is the purpose of these tunnels?

A. Are you talking about tunnels or annular ligaments?

Q. Well, annular ligaments.

A. It is not the tunnels I was referring to.

Q. Are they sometimes referred to as tunnels?

A. Not by me they are not.

Q. I see, all right. For lay people, we might sometimes refer to them as "tunnels," Doctor?

A. I don't know what you are referring to.

Q. All right. What is the purpose of the annular ligament?

A. The purpose of the annular ligament is to keep the tendons against the bone so they may work at the joint level. When we were talking about tunnels before, this is not—and I make this point to distinguish it from the tunnel about which we were talking about through which the tendons go . . .

Q. In other words, you would call the sheath the tunnel; is that what you are saying?

A. That is true, yes.

Q. I see. All right. The sheath itself without the aid of the tough fibrous ligament would have a tendency to bowstring when the hand contracts, would it not?

A. The tendons would have a tendency to bowstring.

Q. Wouldn't they take the sheaths with them, Doctor?

A. They would.

Q. This would be known as the metacarpophalangeal annular ligament?

A. That is right.

Q. The fact that they call it metacarpophalangeal ligament would seem to imply that it would be associated also with the metacarpal bone, would it not?

A. It may mean also that it works with the metacarpophalangeal joint to bend it; this keeps the tendons against that joint.

Q. All right. So we have a picture of the anatomy of the tendons. When I flex my hand—my left hand—what I'm doing now, am I not, Doctor, is causing the muscle located in my forearm, high up in the forearm, to contract so that it pulls on these two cordlike tissues of my body that we call "tendons," and it pulls the distal and proximal phalanges so that my hand comes into a closed position; is that correct, Doctor? (Demonstrating.)

A. That is correct.

Q. Now, when I want to extend my hand, I must relax this muscle so that I can contract this, the muscle that would control this cordlike tendon so that I can now extend my fingers; is that correct? (Demonstrating.)

A. That is correct.

Q. Incidentally, Doctor, the proximal phalanges—these are helped by the intrinsic muscles for flexion; is that correct?

A. To a certain degree, that is true—yes.

Q. And when you first saw the plaintiff, I believe you said that the intrinsic muscles could close the hand; is that right?

A. No, no, I never said that.

Q. Was there any motion at all in the proximal phalanges?

A. Yes, there was motion in the proximal phalanges.

Q. What was that motion?

A. Extension.

Q. And once having extended, could the proximal phalanges then contract or flex? That is, by the independent will of the plaintiff, Mr. Borden?

A. I would have to state, that question . . .

Q. If you can answer my question, Doctor . . .

A. No, I can't answer it.

Q. What is the answer?

A. I said I cannot answer your question, sir . . .

Q. You cannot answer, all right.

A. . . . the way it is worded.

Q. Well, the intrinsic muscles play an important part in the movement of the fingers, do they not?

A. Yes, they do.

Q. They give us the ability to use fine, precision-type contact with our fingers; is that right?

A. That is one of their functions.

Q. Do they help in spreading the fingers apart?

A. Yes, they do.

Q. Were these intrinsic muscles damaged as a result of the injury to Mr. Borden?

A. I would say that very likely an injury such as his would result in some damage to the intrinsics.

Q. As a secondary injury or a direct injury to the intrinsics?

A. Direct injury.

Q. From the saw itself?

A. That is right.

Q. The saw blade?

A. Yes.

Q. Are you familiar with an expression, "the golden period," Doctor? Have you ever heard that expression?

A. Of life, you mean?

Q. With regard to surgery?

A. Specifically what do you mean?

Q. Are you familiar with the expression?

A. I'm more familiar with it literally as well as scientifically, than I am with many expressions.

Q. When the skin is opened up in any part of the body—but we will confine ourselves to the hand—foreign bacteria enter the living tissue; is that correct?

A. That is correct.

Q. And once the skin has opened up and bacteria do invade the living tissue, they begin to multiply. These bacteria multiply rather rapidly by new generations, do they not?

A. They may or may not.

Q. Well, Doctor, would it be fair to assume the likelihood that bacteria once invading an open wound would multiply. Would that be a fair assumption?

A. It would indeed not be a fair assumption.

Q. Am I to understand that once the saw blade had opened up this deep laceration, it is likely that foreign bacteria obviously entered? Would you concede that the bacteria did enter with the saw blade?

A. It is very possible bacteria could enter.

Q. It is very possible. Do you feel—would you put it this way, Doctor: Is it likely that foreign bacteria entered the hand?

A. I think it is likely.

Q. Would you say it is probable?

A. I don't know whether I would say that.

Q. Would you say it is more probable that they did not enter?

A. I don't know whether I would say that either. I would say it is likely.

Q. Now let us assume that foreign bacteria have entered the body. Now, once having entered the body, bacteria tend to reproduce rapidly; is that correct?

A. It is a very unscientific statement.

Q. Well, the enzymes are released from bacteria and the oxygen— isn't that what happens, Doctor, to create an infection?

A. No, that is not true.

Q. Well, what is it that causes an infection?

A. The infection happens to be related to the virulence, to the potency of the bacteria and the number of bacteria that enter into a wound. It also has a great deal to do with any dead tissue that is lying around it. It also has to do with the patient's ability as a host, his ability to resist disease. You have bacteria in your mouth—that is loaded with bacteria—yet you do not have a disease because, I imagine, you have great resistance to disease, Mr. Morrill.

Q. Thank you. Then, as I understand your answer, Doctor—and I'm not sure that I do—the likelihood of bacteria multiplying rapidly, once they have been introduced into the body, is not great, in your opinion; is that right? Do I understand your opinion?

A. Would you read back his question?

(Read by reporter: "Thank you. Then, as I understand your answer, and I'm not sure that I do, Doctor, the likelihood of bacteria multiplying rapidly, once they have been introduced into the body, is not great, in your opinion; is that right? Do I understand your opinion?")

Mr. Weiss: For the record, let me object. This question and this line of questioning are not relevant to the issue here, so far as I can see, if the Court please.

The Court: Well, I suppose this is preliminary to further inquiry. Your objection is noted and will be overruled at this time.

The Witness: A. I would have to answer that question by saying it depends on what body and what conditions you are talking about. You are asking me to generalize and I do not intend to generalize because it is impossible to generalize in a specific occurrence.

Mr. Morrill: Q. Well, Doctor, I believe you took a history from this plaintiff, did you not?

A. Yes, sir.

Q. And the history indicated the nature of the wound?

A. Yes.

Q. Based upon the history you received, would you feel that foreign bacteria had entered the body?

A. Yes, sir.

Q. And would you feel that it was likely that the bacteria multiplied?

A. This is a variable.

Q. You have no opinion?

A. I have a very definite opinion if you want to hear it.

Q. What is it?

A. I have had many experiences along these lines, and I have never had one infection from a buzz saw injury when there was proper surgery.

Q. Well, now, Doctor, we can have infections created even under the most ideal situations, can we not?

A. That is true.

Q. That has happened to you, has it not, Doctor?

A. Yes.

Q. So whether an infection ultimately develops has nothing to do with the degree of skill or care given a patient; is that right or wrong?

A. I would say it is wrong because it is not qualified.

Q. All right. How would you qualify that?

A. I would say that if a doctor uses proper techniques and proper skills, and utilizes a conservative approach to his surgery, it is unlikely that any infection will develop. If he violates any of these qualifications or conditions, I think the incidence of infection will rise.

Q. All right. Isn't it true, Doctor, that once bacteria have entered the body for a period of from four to ten hours, they have a greater foothold, and that any surgery attempted during that period or later would be less desirable than an operation almost immediately after the injury?

A. That is true.

Q. As a matter of fact, it would be most unorthodox for a doctor to attempt an operation where a crushing injury such as this had occurred if more than ten hours had elapsed; would that be correct?

A. You would have to define your term "surgery"; what do you mean by "surgery"?

Q. Any attempt to repair, Doctor?

A. I have made it plain that one should seek a clean wound. You did not get a clean wound in this case, and that is because there was too much surgery done at one time under conditions that were scarcely ideal. If you had stayed within the bounds of good surgical technique, you would have gotten a clean wound and made very little attempt to repair the deep structures, remove dead tissue, and close the bleeding points, as well as . . .

Mr. Morrill: If the Court please . . .

Mr. Weiss: Let him finish his answer and then make your objection.

The Witness: . . . as well as repair the skin.

Mr. Morrill: If the Court please, at this point I will ask that the witness' answer be stricken as not responsive.

Mr. Weiss: And I will vehemently object. He asked the question and he got the answer—a medical answer.

The Court: Read the question again, please, Mr. Reporter.

(Read by reporter: "Any attempt to repair, Doctor?")

The Court: Now read the answer, please.

(Read by reporter: "I have made it plain that one should seek a clean wound. You did not get a clean wound in this case, and that is because there was too much surgery done at one time under conditions that were scarcely ideal. If you had stayed within the bounds of good surgical technique, you would have gotten a clean wound and made very little attempt to repair the deep structures, remove dead tissue, and close the bleeding points, as well as . . .")

The Court: The answer is stricken. The question may be read to the witness again.

(Read by reporter: "Any attempt to repair, Doctor?")

The Witness: A. Extensive surgery would be contraindicated.

Mr. Morrill: Q. What degree of surgery?

A. Attempt at repair of tendons would be contraindicated.

Q. Any attempt at repair at all; would that be correct?

A. At ten hours.

Q. The only possible surgery would be merely suturing the surface skin; would that be correct?

A. That is incorrect.

Q. All right, what other surgery would there be that would be orthodox?

A. You would have to debride any necrotic tissue, close areas that were dead spaces, as at bleeding points, and remove skin edges which were frayed or devitalized.

Q. Okay, debride the tissue surrounding the wound and close it; would that be correct?

Mr. Weiss: He has already answered; now you are changing his answer and asking him the question again.

The Court: Well, he has answered that.

Mr. Weiss: Sure.

Mr. Morrill: Q. Incidentally, when a wound of that size requires that dead tissue be removed, on the basis of the history that you received, Doctor, what would you estimate would have to be the width of the debridement? With a reasonable, orthodox kind of work?

A. I don't understand your question.

Q. Well, you have testified that dead tissue would have to be removed around the wound; is that correct?

A. Within the wound and around the wound.

Q. All right. Now what width would that require, in your opinion?

A. I would have no idea what width this means. I would do what is necessary to do the job.

Q. You have testified that you have repaired buzz saw injuries before, Doctor. Based upon your experience, do you have an opinion as to the reasonable width required to properly repair the wound?

A. It depends on the type of wound and the location. It depends on how deep the saw went. It depends on the angle at which the saw went.

Q. I'm asking about this particular case.

A. I would say I cannot answer your question, Mr. Morrill, because it is not qualified; it is not conditioned.

Q. It is conditioned or not conditioned on what?

A. Your qualifications are—you do not make it a specific question. I'm sorry but I'm not trained to answer in generalities. My mind is—does not function that way; it has to have qualifications.

Q. I understand, Doctor, that you took a history from the patient, that you have examined the operating records of Community General Hospital, and that you have opened the hand up. Now, on the basis of the observation, the perusal of the hospital records, the history that you took, the knowledge of where this saw —this buzz saw—entered the body, do you feel that this is not enough information for you to decide what the average requirement would be, what the average requirement necessary would be to properly cleanse that wound and remove the dead tissue?

A. Yes.

Q. All right. It is true, is it not, Doctor, that many surgeons feel that any attempt at repair four to ten hours after the foreign body was introduced into the hand or into the body would almost invariably result in infection?

Mr. Weiss: Would you repeat that question? I'm sorry, I lost part of it.

Mr. Morrill: If the doctor does not understand the question . . .

Mr. Weiss: I don't. May *I* hear the question so I know what is going into this case?

The Court: You may hear it read back.

(Read by reporter: "All right. It is true, is it not, Doctor, that many surgeons feel that any attempt at repair four to ten hours after

the foreign body was introduced into the hand or into the body would almost invariably result in infection?")

The Witness: A. I would say not invariably; that is limiting it too much. Generally, yes. Invariably, no.

Mr. Morrill: Q. So that would be improper, Doctor, or unorthodox for a surgeon to attempt to repair this injury after four to ten hours?

A. To repair the tendons, I say, would be improper technique, correct.

Q. And once again, Doctor, referring to the "golden period" that I mentioned—does this refresh your memory as to ever having heard that term before?

A. I have heard it both in the literary field and in the scientific field, Mr. Morrill.

Q. I see. With regard to surgeons, have you heard that the "golden period" for operations is within a very short time after the injury occurred and the foreign body was introduced into the body?

A. I've heard the term applied to that.

Q. And as a matter of fact, suturing the tendons after that lapse of time would have a tendency to worsen the result, would it not?

A. Yes, sir.

Q. And we can even say that, on the basis of some history, we would even have to reduce that time, would we not? For example, if this wound had been opened with a meat handler, would you reduce the number of hours where you would feel it would be safe to attempt to repair that hand?

A. I certainly would.

Q. Or a human bite?

A. Yes, sir.

Q. You don't know, as a matter of fact, Doctor, what caused infection —what caused this infection to develop later?

A. I could not say specifically what caused it.

Q. This could happen, as we said, in the most ideal situations?

A. It is possible.

Q. And it has happened to you in the most ideal conditions, the most ideal situations?

A. Yes, it has.

Q. Now I believe, Doctor, that you testified that the reason for the patient's inability to flex his fingers is scar tissue; is that correct?

A. No, I did not say that.

Q. I see. It was my impression, Doctor, that you had said that scar tissue had developed and had surrounded and had become attached to surrounding tissue, and because of that, the man is unable to flex his phalanx; am I correct in that, Doctor?

A. I would state that I said that the tendons are bound down in the total mass of scar tissue. This extends from bone on up to skin, and there is no ability of the tendon to slide or to glide.

Q. Then this would be from scar tissue?

A. It is scar tissue that plays the role of binding it down.

Q. All right. Then can we say that the presence of scar tissue is the reason that these fingers do not flex?

A. It plays a great role in it.

Q. Without the scar tissue, would the man in all likelihood be able to flex the fingers?

A. I doubt it.

Q. Were the tendons attached, Doctor, when you opened the hand the first time?

A. Attached to what?

Q. To each other?

A. Were they in continuity?

Q. Doctor, I think my words are easy enough to answer. Were the tendons attached to each other or were they separated or was there an open space . . .

A. Each tendon was separated from the other except for scar tissue intervening.

Q. Were they all separated, Doctor?

A. Pardon?

Q. Were all the tendons separated?

A. All the flexor tendons separated?

Q. Yes.

A. They were all engulfed in scar tissue.

Q. My question, Doctor, was: Were all the tendons separated?

A. All the tendons were not separated. There are many other tendons involved, and therefore I do not think that one can answer your question.

Q. Shall we be more specific, Doctor?

A. I wish you would be; that is what I'm trying to get you to be.

Q. To be quite specific, were the profundus tendon and the sublimis tendon on all three fingers attached or were they separated?

A. They were bound down together.

Q. When you say "bound down together," what do you mean? Were they attached or were they not?

A. They were attached to scar tissue.

Q. Were they also attached to each other?

A. The profundus was attached to the sublimis; yes.

Q. Now when you opened that hand for the first time, Doctor, did you see—I believe you testified that you saw some sutures; is that correct?

A. Yes, sir.

Q. I believe you said they were 002, 20; what was it?

A. I didn't testify to that.

Q. What did you testify to?

A. I said they were heavier than those I ordinarily use.

Q. Do you know what size they were?

A. No, I don't.

Q. Were these sutures attached to all the tendons?

A. I did not see them attached to all tendons that . . .

Q. That were repaired. Well, how many were attached?

A. I don't remember.

Q. Did you make a note of it?

A. A mental note, not a physical note.

Q. What did your mental note tell you?

A. Exactly what I said to you.

Q. What is that?

A. I don't remember.

Q. Now, in successful operations with regard to injuries to the hand involving lacerations of the tendons, severance of tendons, the thing that the skilled hand surgeon or any surgeon looks for is to avoid scar tissue primarily; would I be correct in that, Doctor?

A. That is correct.

Q. Now, any trauma to living tissue is going to produce scar tissue; is that correct?

A. Yes, sir.

Q. So with scar tissue being the major problem with the surgeon, who knows that there will always be scar tissue with trauma, the surgeon then deals in the unknown with regard to the individual patient, does he not? Is that correct?

A. I don't understand the line of sequence you are following.

Q. All right, let me put it more simply, Doctor. All people vary in the amount of scar tissue their bodies create after injury; is that correct?

A. Some people vary.

Q. Some people vary. Some—can we put it this way, Doctor— some people have a tendency to create more scar tissue than others?

A. That is correct; that I will accept.

Q. This man has a tendency to create a lot of scar tissue, doesn't he, Doctor—the plaintiff in this case?

A. I don't know whether I could say that or not. I would have to see him under better circumstances than I have. He has very little scar tissue in his right foot.

Q. Doctor, on the basis of your operations and the scar tissue that followed those operations, would you say that a great deal of scar tissue resulted?

A. I would say he has very little scar tissue in that right foot, which is the ideal, uncomplicated surgical result where there had never been surgery before. He did not have scar tissue here; therefore, I conclude that this man . . .

Q. Doctor . . .

A. May I finish, Your Honor?

The Court: You may finish.

The Witness: Therefore, I conclude that this man does not have a propensity toward scar tissue.

Mr. Morrill: Q. Confining yourself to the hand, Doctor—there was, as a matter of fact, a great deal of scar tissue that resulted subsequent to your operation; isn't that correct?

A. That is true.

Q. This is scar tissue that did not exist, it did not exist before your operation; isn't that correct?

A. Scar tissue existed before the operation.

Q. The scar tissue that was created after your operation—this was additional scar tissue?

A. It may have been additional; yes, sir.

Q. All right; and this was scar tissue that was brought about by your operations, was it not?

A. I would say surgery produced some scar tissue, yes.

Q. Well, as a matter of fact, could we say a great deal of scar tissue?

A. I don't know; would you say that?

Q. I'm asking you, Doctor.

A. I would say he has a great deal of scar tissue, but I would not say that surgery produced a great deal of scar tissue.

Q. May we say this, Doctor: That after the operation that you performed, a great deal of scar tissue did, as a matter of fact, result; is that correct?

A. Scar tissue was present, yes.

Q. . . . which was not present before your operation?

A. More scar tissue was present after the second operation than existed before the second operation.

Q. Well, you removed the scar tissue that existed before your operation; did you not?

A. I removed some scar tissue; yes, sir.

Q. And when you removed that scar tissue and you transplanted the tendons from the foot, more scar tissue was then created, was it not?

A. Yes, sir.

Q. And a great deal was created, was it not?

A. He has considerable scar tissue.

Q. Now, the nature of the injuries which plaintiff sustained in this case have created a great many problems through the years, have they not, in regaining the use of the hand after repair of the tendons?

A. That is true.

Q. As a matter of fact, there have been experiments with plastic tubes, for example, have there not, in lieu of sheaths, but those were not successful, were they?

A. In general not successful, yes.

Q. Do you know of any that were successful?

A. Yes.

Q. In that portion of the hand?

A. Yes.

Q. Did you personally conduct any operations in which plastic tubes were successful?

A. I have never done it.

Q. Have you ever attempted it, Doctor?

A. No, I never shall, either.

Q. There have been metal tubes they have attempted to use in lieu of sheaths, too, I believe?

A. That is correct.

Q. Have those been unsatisfactory?

A. Yes, in general.

Q. They have attempted to use veins from the body?

A. That is true.

Q. And those have been unsatisfactory?

A. That is true.

Q. So as of the present time, there is no way for a sheath to be substituted for—there isn't any way to substitute for the loss of a sheath; is that correct?

A. We don't replace a sheath when we do a flexor graft.

Q. My question was easy enough to answer, was it not, Doctor?

A. What is your question again, please?

Mr. Morrill: Read the question back, please.

(Read by reporter: "So as of the present time, there is no way for a sheath to be substituted for—there isn't any way to substitute for the loss of a sheath; is that correct?")

Mr. Weiss: He has answered the question, if the Court please.

Mr. Morrill: I don't believe there was an answer.

The Court: He may answer.

The Witness: Would you read it?

The Court: Certainly. Read it again.

(Read by reporter: "So as of the present time, there is no way for a sheath to be substituted for—there isn't any way to substitute for the loss of a sheath; is that correct?")

The Witness: A. Yes.

Mr. Morrill: Q. And that is the most profound loss to the proper movement and flexion of a hand; is it not, Doctor?

A. I don't think it is.

Q. Well, the purpose of the sheath, Doctor, is to provide an easy, gliding motion for the tendons to perform their function, is it not?

A. It is to help preserve that motion; it isn't the total picture.

Q. Well, certainly we were all born with sheaths in our hands for that purpose, were we not?

A. Well, you were born with sheaths to help flexion.

Q. And medical science has not found a better substitute, has it?

A. I have operated on many patients in whom I have removed the sheath and the patient has full flexion. This is done in "tendolysis" every day of the week. This is freeing up the tendon; you excise the sheath, which is, in fact, what I would have done had I seen the patient initially; I would have taken out the sheath.

Q. But subsequently you did not take the sheath out, did you?

A. The sheath had been damaged; it was taken out when the flexor tendons were removed at the time of my initial surgery.

Q. The sheath was removed before you got to the man; is that what you are saying, Doctor?

A. No, I'm not saying that.

Q. I don't follow you. You said the sheath was damaged and it was removed?

A. The sheath was damaged by the initial injury. Subsequently infection occurred; it was bound down to the flexor tendons. At the time of my operation I removed all the flexor tendons that were bound down and scarred. This included the sheath.

Q. You removed the sheath?

A. That is correct.

Q. The sheath at that time was destroyed and useless; is that correct?

A. That is correct.

Q. You wouldn't take out a healthy, living sheath, I assume, Doctor?

A. Routinely, no.

Q. Now you said that it was bound down because of infection. The reason, Doctor, that we had scar tissue was because of infection; is that correct?

A. That is an inadequate answer.

Q. Well, that was your statement, Doctor. Was one of the primary reasons that we had scar tissue because an infection had developed subsequent to this repair?

A. That is one of the reasons why there was scar tissue.

Q. And this is the type of thing, once again, that can develop under the most ideal situation?

A. What is?

Q. Infection, Doctor.

A. Infection can arise under ideal conditions.

Q. And is it true, Doctor, that with the greatest surgical technique in the repair of this type of injury extremely poor results can be achieved. A failure can occur; is that true?

A. That is true.

Q. And this is a variable depending on many factors; is that not true?

A. I think that is true.

Q. One of those factors would be a person's tendency to form tremendous scar tissue; would that be true?

A. That is true.

Q. Doctor, when you transferred the tendons from the foot into the hand, did you take some of the surrounding living tissue—did you also transplant some of that?

A. Are you referring to the peritenon?

Q. Yes.

A. Yes.

Q. What was the purpose of that, Doctor?

A. It improves the gliding mechanism of the tendon.

Q. And you got a poor result on that, did you not, Doctor?

A. I would say a reasonable result within marked limitations with a severe injury of the hand.

Q. Well, ultimately the result was rather poor, was it not, Doctor?

A. I would say that is true.

Q. In fact, it was a failure, was it not?

A. No, I would not say that.

Q. Well, the last operation . . .

Mr. Weiss: Objection for the record. We are not trying this doctor in this case; he is not a defendant here. I don't see how this is proper cross-examination, if Your Honor please.

The Court: Objection overruled.

Mr. Morrill: Q. The last operation you performed was rather a drastic measure, was it not?

A. I wouldn't refer to it as that.

Q. Well, am I correct, Doctor, that the last operation was the scarring of the joints so that the joints would freeze or become immobile?

A. I think you are incorrect in what you said.

Q. Well, isn't that known as an arthrodesis?

A. Pardon?

Q. What is that called—what is the last operation called that you performed?

A. I'd say reconstruction of his hand; that is what I would call it.

Q. All right, would there be another term for the scarring of the joints?

A. There may be some other terms that you would apply. I don't know what you mean by "scarring of the joints."

Q. Well, what does the word arthrodesis mean, Doctor?

A. Pardon?

Q. Arthrodesis?

A. Arthrodesis—that means a fusion of a joint.

Q. Well, Doctor, wasn't this a fusion of the joint?

A. Yes, it was.

Q. And that is what you did, was it not?

A. That is what I said I did.

Q. I didn't catch it, Doctor. You wouldn't call that a rather severe type of operation?

A. I don't call any operation "severe."

Q. Now, as I get the picture, Doctor, when you saw the man, his fingers were in a position something like this (demonstrating); is that right—when you first saw the man?

A. That is true.

Q. And after the results of two operations you performed, the man's hand was in this position; is that correct? (Demonstrating.)

A. That is basically it.

Q. And for the record, I'm indicating in the first position the hand to be fully flexed; and in the second position—within how many degrees of the palm would you estimate it, Doctor?

A. May I correct your terminology? You said "fully flexed"—I'm certain you meant fully extended.

Q. Fully extended, yes, thank you.

A. You are welcome.

Q. And then my second position would be—what percentage from the palm would you say my fingers are?

A. I would say a half-inch to three-quarters of an inch from the palm.

Q. Now, the man can at will close these fingers to the palm; is that right?

A. That is true.

Q. Doctor, when you opened his hand up, could you determine whether the metacarpophalangeal tunnel, as I call it, was injured?

A. You will have to explain what you mean by "tunnel."

Q. The area that I drew on the blackboard for you, Doctor.

A. You mean the annular ligament?

Q. That is what I have reference to.

A. The annular ligament was bound down in the scar tissue.

Q. Well, wasn't the scar tissue proximal to the area that you had me draw on the blackboard (demonstrating); wasn't the wound over in this area, Doctor?

A. There was a portion of the wound there, but the edema and swelling—hemorrhage—had extended distally. We preserved some of the annular ligament when we set our graft through it, but we excised a good deal of it.

Q. You say it was injured and bound down when you opened the hand; isn't that what you said, Doctor?

A. Injured and bound down, yes.

Q. Was it injured by the saw blade?

A. This I couldn't say—whether it was caused by the saw blade or whether it was caused by the infection.

Q. At any rate, once the injury has occurred, that is irrevocable, is it not, Doctor—permanent and irrevocable?

A. What is?

Q. The tunnel, Doctor, that we are talking about.

A. The tunnel is irrevocable? I don't understand that.

Q. Well, Doctor, once having injured it—if you prefer to use the word "annular ligament" instead of "tunnel"—once the annular ligament is injured, that is permanent and irrevocable, is it not?

A. I still don't follow your question.

Q. Well, Doctor . . .

The Court: I think—I don't want to paraphrase, but he means whether that injury can be overcome or whether it is permanent—the injury he has made reference to—can it be repaired—can it be put back into use?

The Witness: Does he mean overcoming the adhesions formed from it or does it have bacteria present in it that would require excision?

The Court: Once it has been injured, whatever its function is, can it function again or is function irrevocably destroyed?

The Witness: It may be possible to use it again.

The Court: Does this answer your question?

Mr. Morrill: Yes, it does. Thank you, Judge.

Q. Did you attempt to repair the annular ligament, Doctor?

A. We used the annular ligament in the repair, yes.

Q. You attempted to repair it? Is that what you said?

A. No, I didn't say that.

Q. You didn't answer my question; did you attempt to repair the annular ligament?

A. What do you mean by "repair," then?

Q. Well, Doctor, you have said that it was damaged and injured; is that correct?

A. I don't believe I said that.

Q. Well, I believe the record speaks for itself, Doctor.

A. I'm willing to sit on it.

Q. Once the sheath surrounding the profundus and sublimis had been damaged and injured, Doctor, can that be repaired?

A. The sheath had to be removed at the time of surgery.

Q. Can the sheath be repaired, Doctor?

A. In any type of injury?

Q. In this type of injury to the hand?

A. No.

Mr. Morrill: All right.

The Court: Off the record now.

(Off-the-record discussion had.)

The Court: We will adjourn until 10:00 tomorrow morning.

(Whereupon these proceedings in this cause were adjourned until 10:00 A.M. on the following day.)

Charles M. Hogan, M.D., having been previously called as a witness on behalf of the plaintiff herein, having been previously duly sworn, resumed the witness stand, was further examined and testified as follows:

The Court: For the record, you are Charles M. Hogan, M.D., who was on the stand yesterday when we adjourned?

The Witness: Yes, Your Honor.

The Court: All right, you may proceed, Mr. Morrill, with your cross-examination.

Mr. Morrill: Thank you, Your Honor.

Q. Now, Doctor, not to belabor the issue as Mr. Weiss has presented it, I believe you established that one of the primary causes for a restriction of motion as was encountered here is scar tissue?

Mr. Weiss: I'm not sure that is a question, counsel, I don't want to object . . .

Mr. Morrill: Q. Is that correct?

Mr. Weiss: I think you are asking him if he said that.

The Witness: A. That is correct.

Mr. Weiss: All right.

Mr. Morrill: Q. Now, the first operation that you performed was on May 8, 1961?

A. That is correct, counselor.

Q. Now, that operation consisted of the transplant of the tendons, did it not?

A. In part, yes, sir.

Q. And it was your opinion at that time that you had a reasonable chance of some improvement as a result of your operation; am I correct?

A. That is correct.

Q. Now, subsequent to that operation, a great deal of scar tissue resulted, did it not?

A. I think that would have to be elaborated upon in order to give you a thorough answer.

Q. Well, Doctor, is the question possible to answer by a yes or no?

A. As far as I'm concerned, it is impossible to answer yes or no.

Q. Let me ask you this, Doctor: The second operation that you performed—that was April 13, 1962; is that correct?

A. That is correct.

Q. As I understand it, the purpose of that operation was to free up these tendon cords that were bound down by scar formation?

A. The purpose was to get more motion in the hands in whatever way was possible.

Q. In that second operation did you remove scar tissue?

A. Yes.

Q. Was that scar tissue caused by your operation of May 8, 1961?

A. I would say in part surgery enhanced the scar tissue that was there previously.

Q. Well, would you say that substantially all of the scar tissue that you removed during the second operation was caused by your operation?

A. I would say definitely that is incorrect.

Q. Well, Doctor, do you remember giving your deposition in my office on April 20, 1965?

A. I don't remember the date.

Q. You do recall being in my office for a deposition?

A. That is correct.

Q. Would that be the approximate date, in your opinion?

A. Approximately.

Q. And you swore—you were sworn to tell the truth at that time, of course?

A. Yes, sir.

Q. And there was a reporter taking everything down that you said and everything that I said; is that correct?

A. That is correct.

Q. Do you recall these questions that I asked and these answers given by you, page 39?

"*Q.* On April 13, 1962?

"*A.* Yes, sir, surgery was performed.

"*Q.* And what did that consist of?

"*A.* It consisted of freeing up of the flexor tendons and also removal of scar tissue in the region of the flexor tendons and arthrodesis of the proximal interphalangeal joints of the 3rd, 4th, and 5th fingers.

"*Q.* What method did you employ to free up the tendons?

"*A.* By sharp dissection.

"*Q.* Explain that.

"*A.* They were cut away by means of scalpel. Scar tissue was cut away from the tendons.

"*Q.* Was this scar tissue that was present before the first operation?

"*A.* No. I would say the scar tissue had occurred since the first operation."

Do you remember those questions and the answers given by you, Doctor?

Mr. Weiss: Objection for the record, if the Court please, to the use of that deposition in any respect. Examination and signature were not waived and there is nothing of record to indicate it was ever submitted to this witness for his examination and signature pursuant to the Rules of the Supreme Court of this state.

The Court: Objection overruled. He may answer.

The Witness: What?

The Court: The question was: Were you asked those questions and did you give those answers on the date indicated in that deposition?

The Witness: A. Yes, sir.

Mr. Morrill: Q. I assume those answers were correct at that time, Doctor?

A. I would say they were substantially correct.

Q. Then again on the bottom of page 44, was this question asked of you and did you make these answers:

"*Q.* Well, in your case, apparently scar tissue appeared following the first surgery that you performed?

"*A.* Yes, it did.

"*Q.* And in that period of time following your surgery, when did you first notice that scar tissue?

"*A.* I would say I probably noticed a month to six weeks after surgery that he was developing a serious amount of scarring in the operative area."

Do you recall those questions and those answers given by you?

Mr. Weiss: Same objection for the record, Your Honor.

The Court: Same ruling.

The Witness: A. I recall them.

Mr. Morrill: Q. Now, Doctor, in the first operation that you performed, as I understand it, the purpose of it was to create a flexion movement in the hand; is that correct?

A. In the fingers.

Q. In the fingers?

A. Yes.

Q. Were you satisfied with the results of your corrective surgery on the first occasion?

A. I was partially satisfied.

Q. Well, Doctor, after your surgery—the first surgery of May 8, 1961—to what degree could the patient extend his fingers at that time?

A. I don't recall.

Q. Do you have any idea?

A. No, I have no idea.

Q. Well, did you notice that after the first operation the hand was involuntarily contracting into the palm?

A. Yes, I did.

Q. Do you know to what degree this occurred over a period of time?

A. No, I do not.

Q. Did it get progressively worse?

A. Over what period of time?

Q. Following the first operation?

A. He had no flexion prior to the original surgery by me. After . . .

Q. I'm talking about . . .

A. May I finish, please?

Q. Please do so.

The Court: You may.

The Witness: *A.* (Continuing) After the surgery by me, he had ability to flex his fingers—from no flexion to flexion.

Mr. Morrill: *Q.* Would it be complete flexion?

A. No, it wasn't complete.

Q. Do you have any idea as to what degree he had after your operation?

A. Degree of flexion?

Q. Degree of flexion and extension?

A. No, I don't have it specifically at my fingertips now.

Q. Well, as you treated him, did you see the man after the first operation in your office?

A. I think I told you in my deposition that I did.

Q. Did you have occasion to note in your records the degree of involuntary flexion that was occurring at that time?

A. In substantial terms, yes.

Q. Well, do your records, Doctor, indicate what degree—have you made any notes as to what degree of flexion was involuntarily occurring during the time that you were postoperatively caring for this man?

A. I would say the records, as you know from the deposition . . .

Q. Doctor, is my question capable of being answered?

A. May I finish my answer?

Q. If the Court please . . .

The Court: I don't think you started out very directly in answering the question. Supposing we strike everything that followed there except the question, and the reporter will read the question and physically strike from the record the remainder so he won't encumber the record, everything out except the question.

(Read by reporter: "Well, do your records, Doctor, indicate what degree—have you made any notes as to what degree of flexion was involuntarily occurring during the time that you were postoperatively caring for this man?")

The Witness: *A.* I don't see in my records any note of degree.

Mr Morrill: *Q.* Well, you did see him from time to time after the operation; is that correct, Doctor?

A.   That is correct, counselor.

Q.   Doctor, would you have any way of knowing the degree to which the man could extend his hand, his fingers, I mean, following your operation?

A.   I do not have it in my records.

Q.   Do you have any recollection at all?

A.   No, I don't.

Q.   Do you have any recollection that the hand got progressively worse in the months following your operation?

Mr. Weiss: Objection as asking for a nonmedical conclusion. I don't know what "worse" means.

Mr. Morrill: If it is not capable of being answered, I will rephrase it.

Q.   Can you answer the question?

A.   I would prefer that you rephrase it.

Q.   Do you have any recollection of the fingers involuntarily and progressively contracting to a greater degree after your operation?

A.   I think he progressed in flexion—flexion and contraction following the surgery.

Q.   That would be an involuntary flexion?

A.   Yes, sir.

Q.   In other words, the hand—the fingers—came closer and closer and closer to the palm; is that correct?

A.   That is correct.

Q.   How many months elapsed after that first operation, Doctor, before you decided that a second operation was in order?

A.   About 11 months.

Q.   As I understand it, you have no notes as to the degree of involuntary contraction of these fingers?

A.   I say, as I said before . . .

Q.   Is that question capable of being answered, Doctor, by a yes or no?

Mr. Weiss: He was about to answer it, I think. Technically now, Judge, we have a question on a question now.

Mr. Morrill: *Q.* Can you answer my last question, Doctor?

A.   What was your last question?

Q.   Will you read the last question back?

(Read by reporter: "As I understand it, you have no notes as to the degree of involuntary contraction of these fingers?")

Mr. Weiss: There are two questions pending.

The Court: Strike the latter question about "capable of being answered" and just present the question in chief—the main question. Do you now know the question, Doctor?

The Witness: I would like to have it read.

Mr. Weiss: It has got confusing.

The Court: All right, read it.

(Read by reporter: "As I understand it, you have no notes as to the degree of involuntary contraction of these fingers?")

The Witness: A. I do not see any evidence of degree in my notes here.

Mr. Morrill: Q. All right, Doctor. On the day of the second operation, which as I understand it was about 11 months later, do you have a note as to the degree of involuntary contraction on that date?

A. I do not see it on the operative notes as of May 8, 1961. There is present a note on May 13, 1962, at the time of the surgery. This is not . . .

Q. Was that May 13 or April 13?

The Witness: Your Honor, may I finish my answer without an interruption?

The Court: You may.

The Witness: Thank you. The date from the hospital record here is April 13, 1962. This is an operative record. It is not an office record, which the counselor asked for. There is a note saying, "Extension comes to about 30 to 40 degrees."

Mr. Morrill: Q. Can you demonstrate for the Court with your own hand, Doctor, the 30 or 40 degrees on that date?

A. (Witness demonstrating.)

Q. May I see the note that you were reading, Doctor; may I see your personal notes?
Do you remember this question being asked at that same deposition, Doctor, bottom of page 37:

"Q. Do your records indicate there that the degree—what the degree of flexion—the degree of flexion?

"A. I have a note of April 13, 1962.

"Q. What is that?

"A. That he flexes to one-half inch of the palm with his long finger and one-quarter inch of the palm with the fifth finger at the proximal interphalangeal joint, so basically, all these fingers were almost in the palm."

Do you recall those questions and those answers given?

Mr. Weiss: For the record, the same objection, if the Court please.

The Court: Overruled.

Mr. Weiss: And an additional objection, if this is an attempt at impeachment—well, I will reserve that until we see the next question, Judge. I will withdraw that part of it.

Mr. Morrill: Q. May I have an answer to my question?

A. May I have my notes back, Your Honor?

The Court: Yes.

Mr. Morrill: Q. Can I have an answer to my question, Doctor? I will be happy to give your notes back.

A. Thank you.

Mr. Morrill: Will you read the last question to the doctor that I gave, Mr. Reporter?

(Read by reporter: "Q. May I see the note that you were reading, Doctor; may I see your personal notes?

"Do you remember this question being asked at that same deposition, Doctor, bottom of page 37:

"Q. Do your records indicate there that the degree—what the degree of flexion—the degree of flexion?

"A. I have a note on April 13, 1962.

"Q. What is that?

"A. That he flexes to one-half inch of the palm with his long finger and one-quarter inch of the palm with the fifth finger at the proximal interphalangeal joint, so basically, all these fingers were almost in the palm.'

"Do you recall those questions and those answers given?"

The Witness: A. I have a note, I have a diagram here . . .

Mr. Morrill: Q. Doctor, may I have an answer to my question?

A. Yes.

Q. Now, Doctor, once again would you describe the results of your operation as a failure?

A. No, sir.

Q. Now again on April 13, 1962, I assume at that time, Doctor—this is the second operation—that you felt you had a reasonable chance of success in a reconstructive operation; would I be correct in that assumption?

Mr. Weiss: At this time, Your Honor, let me express this as a formal objection to this entire line of questioning. Number 1, this witness is not on trial. Number 2, we have an allegation of malpractice on a particular day, May 18, 1960, and a subsequent one of rehabilitation treatment constituting negligence subsequent thereto also encompassed in 1960. Whether an operation was done in 1962 or how an operation was performed in 1962, when whatever malpractice was accomplished was complete, has no effect on this claim; and therefore, I think it is just harassing this witness, sir.

The Court: Objection overruled.

Mr. Morrill: May I have my last question read, please?

(Read by reporter: "Now again on April 13, 1962, I assume at that time, Doctor—this is the second operation—that you felt you had a reasonable chance of success in a reconstructive operation; would I be correct in that assumption?")

The Witness: A. Yes, you would be.

Mr. Morrill: Q. And you have had other operations of this nature?

A. Yes, I have had.

Q. And you have had some success with other operations of this nature?

A. Yes, sir.

Q. Would I be correct, Doctor, had scar tissue not formed on that second operation, you would have had some improvement?

Mr. Weiss: What do you mean by the second? I'm lost; there have been three.

Mr. Morrill: Q. April 13, 1962.

A. I would have to have that read back, Your Honor.

The Court: I'm sorry, I didn't hear you.

The Witness: I will have to have that read back.

The Court: You may. Any time you have a problem about a question, you are entitled to understand it.

(Read by reporter: "Would I be correct, Doctor, had scar tissue not formed on that second operation, you would have had some improvement?")

The Witness: A. The question is completely unclear to me; there are too many variables in the question. You would have to be more specific in what you mean by improvement and what you mean by scar tissue.

Mr. Morrill: Q. Then I gather my question is incapable of being answered by yes or no?

A. I don't know what you gather.

Q. Well, do I understand you correctly, Doctor, that you cannot answer my question yes or no?

Mr. Weiss: He has already given his answer, counsel.

Mr. Morrill: I have not received such an answer.

Mr. Weiss: I believe, if the Court please, he has already answered the question the way the question is phrased; he can't give a proper medical explanation, and now counsel is asking him—well, what is he asking that is incapable of being answered?

The Court: Read the question, Mr. Reporter.

Mr. Morrill: My last question, please.

(Read by reporter: "Would I be correct, Doctor, had scar tissue not formed on that second operation, you would have had some improvement?")

Mr Weiss: I will withdraw my objection.

The Witness: A. It is incapable of being answered yes or no by me.

Mr Morrill: Q. Did scar tissue form as a result of the second operation, Doctor?

A. Some scar tissue formed.

Q. Would it be your opinion that that scar tissue would interfere with the motion of the tendons?

A. Partially, yes.

Q. Then once again, Doctor, if scar tissue did not appear after the second operation, would it be logical to assume that you would have had some improvement in the constructive repair that you attempted on your second operation?

A. We established yesterday, and you established . . .

Q. Doctor, may I have an answer to my question?

The Court: Doctor, I think if the question is intelligible, you are required to answer it to the best of your ability.

The Witness: I don't think it is an intelligible question for a doctor, and I cannot answer your question.

Mr. Morrill: Q. All right. Now, Doctor, I believe that you testified what you would like to see in the form of improvement from medical treatment to injuries such as received by the plaintiff; you would like to see an improvement to the degree where the function of the hand would be 50 per cent to 75 per cent of what it was previously; did I understand you correctly?

A. No, you didn't understand me correctly.

Q. Did you so testify yesterday that if a man got 50 per cent to 75 per cent return of function, this would be very satisfactory?

A. I testified to that, yes, sir.

Q. Now, if 50 per cent to 75 per cent return of function would be very satisfactory, Doctor, what would you call satisfactory?

A. I wouldn't use those terms.

Q. If you don't like the adjective or the elimination of the adjective "very," would you have some other way to describe what you would consider to be satisfactory?

A. No, I wouldn't have any other adjective.

Q. I believe you also testified that, in your opinion, this man had— now has—a hand with about 33 per cent of the function it had prior to the accident; am I correct?

A. You are correct.

Q. Doctor, can you say what degree of disability resulted to this patient with any reasonable degree of medical certainty?

Mr. Weiss: At any particular time?

Mr. Morrill: *Q.* As a result of the first operation performed at the Community General Hospital?

A. I would not be able to tell precisely.

Q. My question is not "precisely," Doctor. Would you be able to give us any estimate at all as to what degree of disability resulted from the operation at the Community General Hospital?

A. I can't answer that.

Q. Well, again, Doctor, referring to the same deposition, there was also another lawyer present who asked some questions, a Mr. Lee; do you recall that, Doctor?

A. I remember Mr. Lee being there.

Q. Now do you remember these questions being asked of you and these answers given?

Mr. Weiss: Which page?

Mr. Morrill: Bottom of page 56.

Q. This is a question relating to the operation at Community General Hospital.

"*Q.* Now can you state what effect these specific operations may have had on the plaintiff's subsequent condition, if you know?

"*A.* Well, I think it would necessarily increase his disability.

"*Q.* Do you have any idea as to what degree?

"*A.* This would be impossible to answer."

Do you recall those questions and those answers given by you?

Mr. Weiss: The same objection I made for the record as to the failure of submitting it for examination and signature to the witness.

The Court: Overruled.

The Witness: *A.* I recall those questions.

Mr. Morrill: *Q.* And those answers given by you?

A. Basically.

Q. Now, Doctor, I want to touch on the tourniquet for just a minute. There isn't any uniformity of opinion with regard to the use of a tourniquet in an operation such as this, is there, Doctor?

A. Is that your opinion?

Q. I'm asking you the question, Doctor.

A. There is uniformity.

Q. Is it true, Doctor, or not true that some competent surgeons would prefer not to close off the blood to tissue distal to the injury so that the tissue would have the proper blood and oxygen and nourishment?

A. Again, your question is inaccurately put and I cannot answer it.

Q. Is my question not capable of being answered, Doctor; is that your answer?

A. That is correct, by me.

Q. Doctor, does living tissue need oxygen and nourishment?

A. Yes, it does.

Q. All right; and is it possible, Doctor, that if oxygen and nourishment is cut off for an extended period of time, damage can result to living tissue?

A. It depends on your definition of an extended period of time.

Q. That definition, Doctor, would be a variable, would it not, among surgeons?

A. It is a variable among surgeons to a point.

Q. Now, Doctor, you also mentioned, I believe, that it was your opinion that the sutures that you found in the hand when you first opened this hand were larger than those you would normally use; am I correct?

A. That is correct.

Q. May I have plaintiff's Exhibit 2-A, please? Have you got your exhibits, Mr. Weiss?

Mr. Weiss: I think I took them—no, I thought I left them here. I'm sorry, I do have it.

Mr. Morrill: You will have to find it for me, Mr. Weiss. You marked it in there somewhere.

Mr. Weiss: All right.

Mr. Morrill: Q. Doctor, I show you what has been identified as plaintiff's Exhibit 2-A, which purports to be the Community General Hospital record, the operative procedure; is that correct?

A. Yes.

Q. Does that report indicate the size of the sutures used?

A. Yes, it does.

Q. And what size is that, Doctor?

A. 20 silk and 30 silk.

Q. Doctor, are there many competent surgeons that repair tendons of this nature with that size of silk?

A. Again, your question can't be answered directly because . . .

Q. Doctor, can you give me a yes or no answer?

Mr. Weiss: Let him finish his answer.

The Witness: The total answer . . .

Mr. Morrill: *Q.* If the question is not capable of being answered yes or no, please indicate it.

A. It is incapable of being answered yes or no.

Q. All right. Now, when you first saw the plaintiff in this case, did you take a history from him at that time?

A. Yes, sir.

Q. And what was your history, Doctor, with regard to the treatment received by this man?

A. All I knew was that he was taken care of at Community General Hospital initially.

Q. Is that the extent of the history that you took, Doctor?

A. That he was in the hospital about ten days, and shortly after the hospital stay, he stated that his hand became infected and the wound broke open and drained, and this drainage took three months to heal.

Q. Now, Doctor, is that history significant to you?

A. In what way?

Q. Let me ask you this: Does infection aggravate or cause scar tissue?

A. Yes, it does.

Q. And does infection impede healing?

A. Yes, it does.

Q. In fact, infection not only impedes healing, but has a strong counteraction?

A. That isn't always correct, no.

Q. Well, you would suspect that, would you not, Doctor?

A. I don't suspect anything; I'm a scientist.

Q. Well, you took a history that the man was being treated for an infection for three months following the hospital stay, didn't you?

A. No, I didn't.

Q. Oh, then what was the history again, Doctor; maybe I misunderstood?

A. I said that the man had infection for three months. I didn't say anything about treatment for three months.

Q. I see. Did you ask him if he was treated for the infection?

A. I don't recall.

Q. Would it be logical to assume he was being treated for an infection?

A. Not logical to me.

Q. Assuming the history to be accurate, Doctor, this infection of such a long duration would have an adverse effect on the surgery performed at the Community General Hospital, would it not?

A. I think that is true.

Q. And this infection, as I believe you said, Doctor, yesterday, as you so testified, can result from even the most ideal conditions; isn't that correct, Doctor?

A. It doesn't result from the most ideal conditions—it may occur in the most ideal conditions.

Q. Thank you. Did you take any history from the man at all with regard to the postoperative care, Doctor?

A. We took a history about his postoperative management, yes.

Q. And what was that?

A. That he received no rehabilitation.

Q. Well, then you did take more history than you just testified to here a minute ago; is that correct?

A. I testified to what I had in my notes.

Q. Well, where did you gain this additional information that you just told us about?

A. From my memory.

Q. I see. Then what the man told you with regard to no postoperative care was something that you remember now; is that right —no postoperative therapy?

Mr. Weiss: "Rehabilitation" was the word in his answer, I believe.

Mr. Morrill: *Q.* All right, let's use your exact word, Doctor. You distinctly remember this patient telling you that he did not have any postoperative rehabilitation?

A. Yes, sir.

Q. Now, in order for you, Doctor, to give us an intelligent opinion with regard to what end result this man has today, you must, in fact, base that opinion a good deal upon the history you took from the patient; isn't that correct?

A. In part from the history.

Q. So, as a matter of fact, you are basing your opinion in part on the fact that the plaintiff has told you that he did not receive any postoperative—what is the word?

Mr. Weiss: Rehabilitation.

Mr. Morrill: *Q.* (Continuing) . . . Rehabilitation?

A. That is a part of my analysis of the total.

Q. Would your opinion be necessarily different if the history given to you by the plaintiff or by your patient were different than what the facts are?

A. It would depend on the area it is different in.

Q. Incidentally, Doctor, you have no reason to disbelieve the operative records of the Community General Hospital with regard to the size of the sutures?

A. I wouldn't dispute it.

Q. I believe, Doctor, you testified yesterday that the first time you saw this patient the blood supply was materially diminished in his hand; is that correct?

A. That is correct.

Q. And you were able to determine this by coldness of the hand and pallor?

A. That is correct.

Q. You don't blame that condition on any treatment that he received at the Community General Hospital, do you, Doctor?

A. I don't blame anything, that is not my prerogative.

Q. Would you consider that the condition which you found with regard to the lack of blood supply in the hand would result from any incompetence?

A. It is possible it could be related to incompetence, yes.

Q. Now, Doctor, when you have an opportunity to see a patient very shortly after an injury of this nature, the blood supply would be materially damaged in this area, would it not?

A. Yes, it would be.

Q. And do you make any attempt to repair that?

A. Yes, I do.

Q. What is that?

A. I make certain that I have a good pressure dressing following surgery; that the patient is immobilized with plaster; that his shoulder motion keeps active and that he controls the venous stasis and edema that may occur in the fingers. This can cut down on the amount of damage to the oxygen supply, as you stated before, and this measure improves the circulation of the hand.

Q. Doctor, how do you repair the damaged blood vessels?

A. I showed you.

Q. How do you repair them?

A. I repair them if I need to repair them.

Q. Do you routinely repair blood vessels, Doctor?

A. I'm not going to answer unless you let me finish what I said.

Q. Can I have an instruction, if the Court please?

The Court: You may answer. Read the question, Reporter. The question, I believe, was: Do you routinely repair blood vessels?

The Witness: A. I do not routinely repair blood vessels.

Q. Do you repair blood vessels, Doctor?

A. On occasion.

Mr. Morrill: That is all I have, if the Court please.

V. Closing Arguments

Outline for Closing Arguments

FOR SUMMING UP THE EVIDENCE, a lawyer should develop a pattern and routine to make certain that he has covered the essentials. With the benefit of an outline, an experienced trial lawyer can with minimal preparation make an effective closing argument that will last well over an hour.

Important testimony bearing on the issues of the case, although apparent to the lawyer, may have been diluted with much triviality and may need isolating for the jurors. The lawyer should not, therefore, presume that the significant evidence has "stuck." The wheat must be separated from the chaff in a careful, logical manner to make certain that it is not overlooked. A suggested nine-point closing argument for either the plaintiff or the defendant follows:

(1) **Appreciation.**—There should be some expression of appreciation to the jurors for having fulfilled their function up to that point. Do not compliment them too profusely or they will feel you are trying to curry favor with them. A flowery speech about the glorious task they have done will do more harm than good. An example of a simple, but adequate, statement follows:

190

"On behalf of my client, John, as well as myself, I would like to take this opportunity to thank the jurors for the patience and attention they have devoted to this trial. We realize that sometimes the trial of a lawsuit moves slowly, and that this trial has taken a good deal of your time. Please be patient with us a little longer, as the case will soon be in your hands."

(2) **Review of Previous Representations.**—Review the facts as you represented them in the areas where there is no discord. Over 98 per cent of the facts in a lawsuit are not in dispute. This makes it possible for you to contend that the evidence has established the points as you represented them in your opening statement.

If your opponent has made a glaring misrepresentation, you can effectively mention it at this point. A review of the evidence establishing that it is a misrepresentation should not be gone into at the moment; it is enough at this point to merely remind the jurors that your opponent has distorted the facts.

(3) **Issues.**—The lawyer who is interested in getting to the heart of the dispute, one who feels that the evidence favors his side of the case, should narrow the issue down to the irreducible minimum. Make it as easy as possible for the jurors to make a decision by letting them know that the outcome of the lawsuit turns on this precise point. It is important that they accept this premise. You should give a logical, easy-to-understand analysis and should not move on to the next phase of the argument until you are quite certain that you have covered this phase in an understandable manner.

Limiting the issues is almost always the preferred tactic for the plaintiff's lawyer. The defense lawyer, on the other hand, should create as many issues as possible, unless he has strong evidence on the big point of the case. The more issues he creates, the more likely the jury is to feel that the plaintiff fell down on one or more of them. The more doubts that he can create the greater will be the chances of a verdict for the defendant.

In summary, it is usually better for the plaintiff to aim with a rifle and the defendant to aim with a scatter-gun.

(4) **Capsule Isolation of Conflicting Testimony.**—This is only for the lawyer who is interested in limiting the issues. Extreme care should be taken not to misstate the testimony of any witness on the precise issue of fact that is being pinpointed. There should be a completely fair appraisal of the conflicting testimony and the jurors should be told that whatever version they accept as accurate will decide the issue in the case.

(5) Analyzing the Witnesses and the Probabilities.—It is at this phase that each of the witnesses should be analyzed, together with the probability or improbability of the testimony each has given. On each conflicting point, the opposition witness should be analyzed first; then a contrasting analysis of the favorable witness should be given. Each witness can be analyzed according to the following pattern to make sure each persuasive point is covered:

A. Opposition Witness

(1) Any undesirable characteristics reflecting on the witness' credibility, such as looking at the floor, giving evasive answers, displaying an arrogant or hostile manner, exaggerating or making inconsistent statements in his testimony, or other characteristics contributing to a generally poor impression, should be brought out.

(2) His friendship with the opposing party, whether it be a social relationship, a kinship, or a business relationship—any evidence of prejudice or lack of impartiality—should be pointed out.

(3) Anything that would show that the witness has an interest in the outcome of the lawsuit should be covered.

(4) The improbability of the testimony should be analyzed. Point out the witness' lack of opportunity to observe the accident because of poor lighting conditions, his great distance from the occurrence, a momentary glance away, or any obstructions interfering with his view, a considerable passage of time between the occurrence and the time of testifying in court, or any physical impairment, such as poor eyesight or hearing. Comment upon any other valid points that attack the credibility of the witness as to what he says he saw or heard. Sum up the weak and inconsistent points of the testimony, being careful not to distort any part of it.

B. Favorable Witness

Any of the things that will add authenticity to a favorable witness' testimony should be covered in the same order as that used in the process of tearing down the opposition witness.

(6) Law.—It is a mistake to fail to cover the law in your closing argument. You should point out with confidence that, under the facts of the case, the law entitles you to a verdict.

Not only should the plaintiff's lawyer cover the law that he feels is favorable to his cause, but he should also anticipate the instructions that his opponent will rely upon. By anticipating these instructions and representing that, under the facts, the law is favorable to the plaintiff's side of the case, he can take a great deal of "sting" out of certain instructions when his opponent discusses the law.

The defense lawyer should take the position that the law favors his side of the case and answer each argument with confidence.

As mentioned elsewhere, the lawyer who has a strong case on the law should have prepared the jurors during his *voir dire* examination and opening statement by telling them that this is the most important phase of the lawsuit.

(7) **Special Problems.**—Any poison in your own case should be brought out and covered. Your client may be a convicted murderer or a target defendant, or he may have a disagreeable personality; but it may be that the law entitles you to the verdict, notwithstanding strong passions to the contrary. It is at this point that the jurors should be reminded of their duty and the promises made during *voir dire*.

(8) **Special Problems in Your Opponent's Case.**—Anything upon which fair comment can be made that is not redundant should be pointed out. This will be largely in areas where an inference can be drawn from the failure of the opposition to do something that would normally be expected, for example, his failure to put a party to the lawsuit on the stand or his unexplained failure to produce an important witness under his control.

(9) **Damages.**—The amount of time that the plaintiff's lawyer should spend on the damage argument will vary greatly. If the plaintiff has an excellent liability case and the real issue is the amount of damages, he could conceivably devote over 90 per cent of his argument to damages. On the other hand, there may be no dispute at all as to the amount of damages; you may have a situation in which the loss of income, the medical expenses, and the nature of the injury are admitted. If you have a serious question of liability and the defendant freely admits the damages, you may find it best to only touch on the damage argument. The plaintiff's lawyer would do well to keep his request for money damages down to a very modest figure if he is bucking a difficult liability case.

The defense lawyer should, likewise, devote the major portion of his argument to the more serious problem. If the defense lawyer finds himself defending a lawsuit in which the injuries are severe and the liability issue is precarious, he would be wise to direct his entire argument to the liability issue, rather than dignify the lawsuit by discussing the damages at all.

Advantage in Right to Open and Close

Inasmuch as the burden of proof rests with the plaintiff, it seems that fair play has established the practice of granting the plaintiff the

right to open and close the summation. There is no question that
this has two distinct advantages.

If the opening argument of the plaintiff appeals to the jurors and
they accept it, then there is a tendency to defend its acceptance
against contrary logic. Making an important decision is hard work
for jurors, who often have nothing more significant to decide than
what looks good for dessert on the menu. The average juror is like
anyone else; if he can in good conscience go along with the plaintiff
after a persuasive argument, he will not want to be brought back to
the point of indecision by the defense lawyer. But the defense
lawyer must drag him back to again face the struggle of making a
correct decision.

The other obvious advantage is that the plaintiff is the last one
to analyze the evidence for them and can answer all of the arguments
advanced by the defendant. This last opportunity may flop a juror
or two into the plaintiff's wigwam who had been struggling with
feelings of uncertainty, fully capable of going either way. There are
also those jurors who can be sold and unsold easily; this gives the
edge to the last one to close. Add this last type of juror to the others
in your camp, and it may well be enough to tip the scales.

In situations where there is more than one party on one side of
the lawsuit, the rules usually provide that they will argue in the order
in which their names appear in the pleadings. In a situation where
there are two or more defendants and the probability is that only one
will be hit with the verdict, then the last defendant to argue will have
a distinct advantage over his cohorts. When the defendants are
forced into a position of blaming each other for the occurrence, it
becomes almost a certainty that the plaintiff will receive the verdict.
Knowing this, each defense lawyer is faced not only with justifying
his own client's conduct, but also with joining forces with the plaintiff's lawyer to point out that his codefendant failed to exercise that
degree of care required of him. The last defense lawyer to speak has
an opportunity not only to meet the arguments of his codefendant,
but also to advance some of his own arguments, which his codefendant will have no opportunity to answer.

In this situation, the plaintiff's lawyer can have a decided effect
on the choice of defendant who will be tagged by the jury. He can
adopt the argument of the defense lawyer who has blamed the other
defendant. He will seem almost to be in a position of impartiality,
and by pointing to one defendant, he can create an overpowering
impression that his aim is true.

The defense lawyers are faced also with the problem of how to
handle damages. While each is desperately trying to throw the

liability "hot potato" into the other's lap, he will sacrifice some speed in getting rid of it by answering arguments on damages. The extent to which the defense lawyer can ignore the damage issue will be in direct proportion to the problem he is faced with in the liability issue. There are instances in which the plaintiff's lawyer, for one reason or another, may have pointed to one defendant as the real culprit. It would then be wise for the other defense lawyer to seize upon this opportunity and agree with the plaintiff's lawyer right down the line, staying completely away from the damage issue.

Your Words and Voice

Your speaking voice and manner of delivery are important factors in the art of persuading a jury. If skill in the use of words to move people is essential to this art, then its breath of life is the method of delivering these words. All successful orators have developed a pleasing technique for the delivery of words. Whether one agrees or disagrees with Franklin D. Roosevelt's political philosophies and the means for carrying them out, even his severest critics would have to admit that he had a voice that was easy to listen to. His popularity was in large measure the result of a voice that could stimulate and sway the voter even more than his words. It is difficult for a listener to concentrate on the speaker's message if he has an irritating voice, such as one that is too thin, too loud, or too soft, or if he has a vocal affliction or poor pronunciation.

Effective persuasion requires first that the lawyer create early a favorable impression of both the case and himself, and second, that he continue to maintain that impression throughout the trial. To have information or an awareness but to be unable to impart it through the correct choice of words or unable to convey it because of an ineffective delivery will interfere with moving a jury to the desired conclusion. If effort is made toward improvement along the lines of the following enumerated suggestions, there should be no reason why any lawyer cannot manage an effective delivery.

(1) Establish eye contact with the jurors. You will appear more sincere, and you will be better able to measure the success of your rationale, since the faces of the jurors will reflect to a degree their attitude of acceptance or rejection of your position. You also will avoid breeding thoughts in individual jurors about people who don't "look you in the eye."

(2) The tonal quality of your voice should be such that it is easy to listen to. A loud, blustering voice will distract the listener so that he is preoccupied with the flourish of trumpets instead of listening to the assessment of the logician. On the other hand, a weak voice that com-

pels the listener to labor in order to hear the words will cause him to become fatigued and to "tune out." The monotone is also difficult to listen to because the ear is accustomed to variations in the voice to express intensity of mood, such as hate, doubt, sincerity, or love. The speaker can hardly say, "then the defendant, while intoxicated, drove his car up over the curb onto the sidewalk, striking down Mary Smith," with the same tonal quality as "at the time of this occurrence, it was a pleasant, sunny afternoon." The same phrase, delivered with different tonal emphasis can detract from or enhance the clarity of the word picture in the mind's eye of the listener.

(3) The argument should be an extemporary presentation that permits the delivery to be spontaneous and genuine. Keep in mind that an extemporary argument is not to be confused with an impromptu argument. The extemporary argument can be well prepared, outlined, and even practiced orally before its delivery; it may even be desirable for a lawyer to write a few words that he can glance at during delivery to spark a thought and then carry on with his spontaneous argument. The impromptu argument, on the other hand, is given on the spur of the moment without any preparation.

It is the height of ineffectiveness for a lawyer to argue a case by reading his argument to the jury. This not only prevents a sincere, spontaneous delivery, but also precludes eye contact, as well as movement of the hands. If a lawyer wants to graphically emphasize the pain in the chest that his client experienced, he can place his hands on his chest as he talks about the pain incurred when the client struck his chest on the steering wheel. His hands will be free to touch other parts of the body to convey graphically the pain from introduction of needles into that area or to give a loud handclap to indicate the collision between the automobiles.

(4) When you have adequately covered the argument, *sit down*. Too many lawyers, because they have not used up their allotted time, feel it would be a shame to pass up an opportunity to talk further. This results in repetition, which is anticlimactic at best. While it might be desirable to repeat an important point in different words, you must be careful not to overdo it. Redundancy may begin to sound like insincerity or it may make it appear that you lack confidence in your position and are trying a little too hard to sell the jurors. If your argument becomes aimlessly wandering and rambling, it may even cause doubts to creep in where there were none.

> "In general those who nothing have to say
> Contrive to spend the longest time in doing it."
> —James Russell Lowell.

(5) Use words readily understood by the jurors. This does not mean that a lawyer is confined to shallow and artless words. What-

ever thoughts are expressed should not be weakened through fear of using the more meaningful word. Some words have an adhesive quality and will "stick" with the jurors when they retire to consider their verdict. With practice, an effective vocabulary can be developed that will bear fruit.

(6) Essential points, coupled with the lawyer's analogy, should be covered. To speak in platitudes is worse than to give no argument at all; even the dullest jury can see the obvious. It is the lawyer's function to make obvious that which is not obvious.

The Courteous Lawyer

Jurors are instinctively drawn to the lawyer who is courteous and who conducts himself as a gentleman. There will never be an opportunity for a more personal relationship between the lawyer and the jurors than during summation, with the possible exception of the *voir dire* examination. The jurors have observed the lawyer throughout the trial, which may have lasted several days. If he has earned their regard by consistently conducting himself as a gentleman, this will help immeasurably in persuading them to attach credence to what he has to say. He will eclipse his opponent if he is given the opportunity to contrast his admirable qualities with cankerworm conduct on the part of his adversary. Jurors cannot remove from their minds the assessments or opinions of the lawyers they have stored away. The lawyer is an indispensable and absorbing part of the case itself, and is identified as such throughout the trial. A sour, sulky, suspicious person can greatly improve his chances with the jurors by employing an affable lawyer who will be capable of offsetting the poor image that he projects. The combination of a personable client and a lawyer who have a fair case on the facts is a difficult one to beat. When the jurors like one side and dislike the other, they will without hesitation resolve every doubt in favor of the pair that they like. If the infatuation is strong enough, they may even consciously stretch a point or two with moral insensibility in order to justify giving the verdict to the side with which they feel rapport.

The summation provides an excellent opportunity for the lawyer to confirm that he is a gentleman of high principles who objectively sums up the evidence without any patent attempt to move the jurors through slippery practices and to demonstrate that there is no semblance of an appeal to passion or prejudice and no attempt to berate or defame any of the opposing witnesses or lawyers. There may be exceptions when the lawyer can assume an attitude of righteous indignation, such as when he has exposed a witness who obviously was lying. Assuming this posture of righteous indignation must receive the approval of the jurors; otherwise the honeymoon is over. He should try to draw the jurors' attention to the reprehensible conduct in a subtle way, without dwelling on it too long or too much (a gentleman does not engage in mudslinging). If he does engage in such conduct, it may backfire on him. Sometimes the ungentlemanly conduct can be rectified by gentlemanly apologies that will ease the psychological effect the situation may have had on a juror or jurors.

Paying Homage to the Jury

Flattery should be given to a jury in moderation, if at all. Jurors are quick to sense superficiality, just as is any person of normal intelligence. Believing that excessive admiration of the jurors' intelligence will flatter them into giving a favorable verdict is to engage in a forlorn hope. True, there are some who are overcredulous, but the number of people who have this pathological need to believe praise is too small to warrant using this method. If there is one characteristic more important than all others that a lawyer must possess in order to be a successful persuader, it is the ability to project sincerity. When a lawyer expresses admiration for the intelligence of a jury, upon what can he possibly base his opinion? The average juror recognizes this and will not be deceived; in fact, he will have a tendency to suspect the lawyer's sincerity in other things he may say or do. An expression of appreciation for the attentive and patient manner in which the jurors listened to the evidence will suffice.

ANALYZING THE LAW

Highlighting the Issues Raised in the Pleadings

Referring to the pleadings during closing argument can create a strong impression in the minds of the jurors and can segregate the issues probably better than any other method, if it is truly advantageous that they be isolated. Most jurisdictions permit this to be done, although a few require that the pleadings must have been formally received into evidence. The groundwork for this phase of the argument can be laid during the opening statement by informing the jury of the issues, as previously mentioned. The jury can again be reminded of the issues that were created by the pleadings. If the opponent's evidence was weak and failed to support representations made in his opening statement, the foundations of his case can begin to crack. The jury should be vividly reminded of this failure in order to insure the crumbling of those foundations, for example, by the comment "one ounce of performance is worth a thousand pounds of promises."

If you intend to read from the pleadings, then employ a little showmanship to heighten the importance of the document in the minds of the jurors. You can do this by walking over to the clerk during the course of the argument (having arranged this beforehand) and asking him to hand you the court documents known as the "Complaint" and the "Answer." Now, as you hold in your hands the official court documents, which were given to you from the court file by an official of the court, whatever points you make will be dramatically burned into the minds of the jurors. The jurors can be reminded, "These court documents are the very basis of the lawsuit. These documents, carefully prepared and drafted by both sides, have created the very issue that this jury is being asked to decide." At this point, with their attention focused on the issue, any chain of reasoning as to why that issue should be resolved in your client's favor can be most persuasive.

To illustrate this principle by way of an example, assume that the plaintiff in his allegations of negligence alleged, among other things, the following: "Contrary to an ordinance that was then and there in full force and effect in the Village of Sleepy Valley, the defendant carelessly and negligently drove his said automobile in excess of the posted speed limit of 10 M. P. H."

Assume that the plaintiff will later present convincing evidence such as skid marks, occurrence witnesses, and perhaps even a statement by the defendant himself that the speed of his automobile at the time of the collision was 25 M. P. H., the defense lawyer, if he makes a perfunctory denial of the allegation, can be beat over the head with his hasty answer. The jurors might well accept an argument that the speed limit is unrealistic and that violation of this speed limit is not, by itself, an act of negligence. By candidly admitting that the automobile was traveling in excess of the speed limit, but pointing out to the jurors that the test is what a reasonable and prudent person would do, you appeal more to their logic. The defense lawyer, when giving his rebuttal, will sound less sincere if the plaintiff has planted in the minds of the jurors the fact that the defendant, in the formal document called an Answer that he filed, had denied violating the speed limit. The argument of the plaintiff could be something like the following:

You will recall, ladies and gentlemen, that during the opening statements, it was explained to you that the function of the jury is to decide the facts. Another way of putting it is that the jury must decide what evidence is true and what evidence is untrue. It was further explained that these questions or issues that you folks are asked to decide are created by formal court documents. The plaintiff files a "Complaint," wherein he sets forth in some detail those things that he feels entitle him to a remedy under the law. These allegations properly inform the defendant of the reasons why the plaintiff feels he has a good and meritorious case against him. The defendant files a document called an "Answer," which either admits or denies the allegations made by the plaintiff. When the defendant denies an allegation or a claim, then there is an issue or question created that must then be decided by the jury.

Now, in the document that we filed, we claimed that the defendant was driving his automobile at a rate of speed in excess of the posted speed limit when the collision occurred. The defendant has filed his "Answer," denying that he was driving his automobile in excess of the speed limit. This, then, is a question that you folks must decide. Is the truth on the side of John, or is the truth on the side of the defendant? What is true or untrue can be determined on the evidence.

You will recall that Officer Smith testified that he arrived at the scene of the collision at exactly 3:05 P.M., which was five minutes after it had occurred. After rendering first aid, summoning the ambulance, and performing other investigative details, he took a tape measure from his police car and measured the skid marks of the defendant's automobile, which he found to be 47 feet. You heard further evidence that an automobile traveling 10 M. P. H. will lay down 17 feet of skid marks. You also heard testimony that an automobile traveling 25 M. P. H. will lay down 47 feet of skid marks. John testified that, in his opinion, the defendant was traveling about 25 M. P. H. when he first began to apply his brakes.

[It should be explained that John's opinion has value because of his opportunity to observe, his candor, and his forthright answers, together with whatever other qualifications you believe add value to his opinion. Also, the defendant's testimony should be reviewed, especially if there was any admission on cross-examination that he either was, or might have been, traveling in excess of the speed limit.]

Now, I submit that John would be entitled to a verdict on the basis of his testimony alone. Certainly he is entitled to be believed, and the reasonableness of his position would certainly seem to make it the more probable. Irrespective of the testimony of John, we have produced the police officer, who has no interest in this lawsuit and who completely supports the testimony of John. We produced this police officer; we are the ones who served a subpoena upon this police officer. We felt that the jury should hear all of the available evidence because the jury is entitled to base its decision on all of the facts—not just part of the facts. We submit that it is true that the defendant was driving in excess of the speed limit, and we further submit that the "Answer" filed by the defendant in which he denies he was driving in excess of the speed limit is untrue. Of course, I cannot presume to know what my opponent will say with regard to this question that you folks are asked to decide. He may, perhaps, admit that they were wrong when they filed their court document, although it would seem to me that they certainly must have given consideration to the truth or falsity of those claims we made before they prepared that document.

When the defense lawyer prepared the answer, he quite likely denied all of the allegations of negligence in the complaint as a matter of routine. Although at the time he probably never seriously considered that the plaintiff would not be able to prove that the defendant was driving 15 M. P. H. over the speed limit, he nevertheless denied it because it just isn't one of those things that a good defense lawyer ever admits. In addition to this, he justifiably believed that the speed limit of Sleepy Valley was ridiculous and that the jurors would share his sentiments; he also believed that the defendant was probably traveling at a reasonable rate of speed, considering all the circumstances, and that this, by itself, would never impress a jury as amounting to negligence.

After the plaintiff has made the foregoing argument, the defendant will be hard-pressed to explain why this official document he filed was incorrect. It would be tomfoolery to argue that the defendant was not exceeding the speed limit, when, Heaven knows, the evidence seems to put that fact beyond dispute. He may be able to wangle his way out of this dilemma by pleading a mistake, but, at best, there will be a question in the minds of the jurors about his candor. The plaintiff, on the other hand, has built up this manufactured issue out of all proportion, giving the jury the impression that the answer to this issue should decide the outcome of the lawsuit. But regardless of how nimble the defendant may be in explaining away the mistake, the plaintiff still gets the last bayonet thrust—the rebuttal argument. It could be something like the following:

It is interesting to note how my opponent changes his position with regard to the speed of the defendant's automobile. Perhaps it was only a mistake that the defendant denied he was traveling in excess of the speed limit, but it does seem ironic that such an important point as the speed of an automobile at the time of the collision would be the very point upon which they made their mistake. Now, however, they rectify the mistake by finally admitting that he was speeding. Now that Officer Smith, pursuant to a subpoena, has appeared here and testified under oath as to the skid marks, we finally have an admission that he was speeding. Regardless of what the speed limit was, please keep in mind, ladies and gentlemen, that the evidence establishes that the speed was two and one-half times the posted speed limit. Oh, it's easy to say, "We were mistaken when we filed our court document." It's easy to say, "We meant to admit we were speeding, but we made a mistake and denied we were speeding." They denied a lot of things when they filed the court document in answer to our charges. It is a fact, however, that when they did file their "Answer," they denied that the defendant was speeding, and it is a fact that they did not correct this mistake until after Officer Smith testified.

What would otherwise have been a rather insignificant point became fatal to the defendant's cause because of an unthinking Answer.

The Burden of Proof Is an Uphill Climb

An unmatched heritage enjoyed by the defendant is that he is not burdened with a requirement to prove anything. The American concept of evenhanded justice, which has been instilled in the minds of the jurors from childhood, is that if a person is accused of doing something wrong, it is only fair and just that the accuser be required to prove his accusations. Children learn at an early age, when they are most impressionable, through the mediums of television and movies that an accused is innocent until proven guilty beyond a reasonable doubt. When, as adults, they walk into the courtroom to serve as jurors, this feeling is there, subconsciously if not consciously, in spite of all the efforts the plaintiff may make to point out that the burden of proof in a civil case is quite different.

The defense lawyer should, therefore, remind the jurors at every opportunity, "It is the plaintiff who has the burden of proof in this case." On the *voir dire* examination, he has committed them to the position that if the plaintiff fails to meet this burden of proof, the jurors are duty-bound to find the defendant not guilty. In closing arguments, the jurors should be reminded by the defense lawyer that they each assured him that if the plaintiff failed to prove all of the things the law requires, they would then find in favor of the defendant, notwithstanding the natural sympathy everyone has for an injured plaintiff. Therefore, the defense lawyer always has a lion placed in the path of the plaintiff, which must be subdued before his client can be forced to pay five cents.

The plaintiff's lawyer, recognizing this problem, should strive to minimize the importance of his burden of proof by bringing it up immediately in his closing arguments. He should tell the jurors that there will be an instruction in the law as to the burden of proof that will outline the things he should prove. He should then take up each element, one by one, and explain why each of them has been proven. In this way, much of the solemnity will have been taken out of it before the defense lawyer gets a chance to explain that the plaintiff has this awesome burden. They will then be prepared to hear the instruction read by the judge; they will feel that they understand it and will not be quite so awed by their responsibility. After all, the plaintiff's lawyer explained how he satisfied all the requirements when he told them about it.

Strong on Law or on Facts, But Not Both

Every trial lawyer has taken on the task at one time or another of persuading a jury with a case that is strong on the facts but weak on the law, or vice versa. Each type of case requires a definite yet distinctly different approach with the jury. As previously pointed out, the lawyer will also be interested in having a different type of juror in each instance. Given a case strong on facts, but weak on the law, a plaintiff's lawyer will want a jury of people who can be moved easily by emotional appeal. The defense lawyer in this situation will want a jury that will be not only less emotional, but also less tolerant of minor infractions of the rules.

For example, many states have what is commonly known as a "guest statute," which, in effect, requires the plaintiff, in order to recover, to prove that the driver of the automobile in which he was a passenger acted in a willful and wanton manner. In a situation where the plaintiff can show a serious error of judgment or a negligent act on the part of the defendant driver, but he simply does not have the evidence to establish the willful conduct as required under the statute, we have a clear example of a case strong on the facts and weak on the law from the plaintiff's standpoint. Add to this a likeable, captivating plaintiff who has been seriously injured and a defendant who has one or more of those undesirable characteristics that can cause a jury to strongly dislike him. Now, for the sake of our example, if we assume that the evidence will establish only negligence, then the plaintiff is interested in having the jury conduct its own brand of justice, notwithstanding the law. The defendant is interested in having the jury set aside sympathy, put the saddle on the right horse by following the law, and turn this charming plaintiff out of court without a dime. From the plaintiff's lawyer's standpoint, it is obvious that his tactic should be to emphasize the hardship to the plaintiff. He cannot ignore or distort the law. The jury will expect him to show how the law is consistent under the facts so as to warrant a verdict for the plaintiff. The plaintiff's lawyer can be quite sure that the jurors want to find in his favor and that they are looking for a loophole whereby they can rationalize or correlate this crazy law with the facts, since they must satisfy themselves that in good conscience they can properly find for the plaintiff. The defendant, on the other hand, must emphasize the importance of the law. He can be quite sure that the jurors feel obligated to do their sworn duty by correctly deciding the case under the law. The defense, of course, on *voir dire* examination should have committed each juror to follow the law, regardless of what he thought the law ought to be, or even if he strongly disagreed with the law applicable to the case. The jurors should be reminded in the summation that they promised to follow the law and that they also promised, if the proceedings warranted it, to have the courage to find in favor of the defendant despite their natural sympathy toward the plaintiff. The jurors will find it distasteful to turn the plaintiff out of court without dispensing some reparation, but, on the other hand, they will likely feel compelled to find for the defendant according to their pledge on *voir dire*.

Not many cases fall into a category of pure law or pure fact, but will be made up of varying degrees of both. In the same lawsuit it is often found that there is a combination of strong points on law and on fact. It is effective to emphasize the law when it favors those issues and then switch to an emotional appeal when the facts are stronger. To illustrate this, assume that two automobiles collided at an intersection and that the plaintiff was a passenger in the automobile that failed to stop for a stop sign. Assume further that the defendant, who was driving the other car, entered the same intersection at an excessive rate of speed and that the collision resulted in serious injuries to the plaintiff. The law is quite clear that the negligence of the driver who failed to stop for the stop sign cannot be imputed to the plaintiff passenger. The plaintiff, however, is tainted by his driver's clearly wrongful conduct. The defendant, on the other hand, has committed a much less culpable act of negligence. Entering a guarded intersection at an excessive rate of speed is not nearly as culpable or outrageous as failing to obey a stop sign. Technically and actually, the plaintiff is entitled to a verdict since he cannot be guilty of contributory negligence as a matter of law. The excessive rate of speed on the part of the defendant constitutes a degree of negligence. As can be seen, this will not be an easy package to sell in order to avoid a compromise verdict. Great emphasis will have to be placed on the law if the plaintiff is to receive his full measure of damages. If the plaintiff's lawyer wants to emphasize the importance of the law, then a good portion of his closing arguments should extol the honor and glory of the law. He should emphasize the role of the trial judge, who has the grave function of acquainting the jurors with the law applicable to the case. The stage is then set for the jurors to receive these most important instructions in the law.

In many states, recovery in a cause of action under a "wrongful death statute" is limited to pecuniary loss to the next of kin or to the estate of the decedent. This will include loss of income, burial costs, and medical expenses if the deceased died following medical treatment for his injuries. Therefore, recovery for the death of a child is limited in scope. A tragic case creates an emotional problem in the minds of the jurors. For example, assume that a defendant who was intoxicated ran a child down in a crosswalk after failing to stop for a stop sign. During the *voir dire* examination, the defense lawyer insisted that each and every juror promise under oath that he would follow the law with regard to damages. The juror in his heart desperately wants to award the parents money for the terrible tragedy, and even more, he wants to punish the defendant. Even the most ideal juror, from the defense standpoint, will refuse to adhere strictly to the law and will to some extent compromise the law with his compassion. The defense lawyer must be careful to maintain a warm, sympathetic, and indulgent approach while tactfully reminding the jurors that grief caused by the loss of a member of the family is not a legal element of damages. The jurors will have a strong desire to inflict some punishment on the driver. The only apparent way open to them is through the size of their verdict. The defense lawyer should conjure up visions of the defendant's sleepless nights and his mental torment. If this thought can be subtly conveyed, it may satisfy, at least in part, the jurors' need to punish the defendant. Needless to say, the defendant should be adequately coached and cautioned about his attitude in the presence of the jurors. Should a juror detect unconcerned flippancy or anything related to callousness, the lawyer can be quite sure the verdict will be substantial.

A determination should be made at the outset by the trial lawyer as to how important the law is in relation to the facts of his case. If it is an important factor, he will have ample opportunity throughout the trial to emphasize its importance. The stage is set during the *voir dire* examination, when each and every juror is committed to specific positions. Each has promised that he will follow the law, even though he may disagree with it, and that he will not let sympathy, passion, or prejudice interfere with his sworn duty to follow it. Each juror is again reminded during the opening statements of his duty to be regulated by and to be consistent with the law. And again, during closing arguments, the juror is forcefully reminded of his allegiance and covenants. All of this is finally capped off by the judge's reading the law to him. With all this background, the juror may well vote in accordance with his duty, notwithstanding personal feelings to the contrary.

ANALYZING THE EVIDENCE

Using Sworn "Answers to Interrogatories"

It is sometimes necessary for a lawyer to rely on his opponent's sworn answers to written interrogatories. Ordinarily, one might assume that this type of evidence would be the best possible way to establish a fact; here we have, after due thought and deliberation, answers carefully prepared and signed by the other party under oath as to their accuracy.

The problem is that the significance of these answers can be completely overlooked by the jurors unless the background of the answers is sufficiently explained by the lawyer relying upon them. Regardless of any explanation given to the jurors during the opening statement or during the reading of the answers in the case in chief, the import of the answers should be thoughtfully explained to the jurors during summation. It is not sufficient to merely tell the jurors that it was not necessary to offer any evidence on a specific point because the other party had already stated it to be a fact by his sworn answers prepared before the trial commenced. If the answers are important to his case, the lawyer should hold them in his hands and flourish them before the jurors. He should give a step-by-step explanation of how these answers were prepared. It should be explained that these are facts that require no deliberation by the jury, and that this procedure saves everyone time; that the court and jury are not required to spend time hearing evidence where both sides stipulate as to certain facts. Answers to written interrogatories should not be used in lieu of testimony from a party to the lawsuit. From a psychological standpoint, damaging oral admissions brought forth from the other party while on the witness stand for the jury to hear will be more impressive. Any variation between the testimony of the witness and his answers to written interrogatories will mean that the opposing lawyer will have a banner to wave in front of the jury during summation as a symbol of the witness' obvious lack of veracity.

A Strong Opposition Witness

When the opposition has presented a strong witness who has testified in a believable manner, who is not interested in the outcome of the lawsuit, and who is apparently free from bias or prejudice, the natural inclination is not to mention him for fear the strong impression he has created will be further cemented in the minds of the jurors. As great as the temptation is to ignore him and hope that the jurors will forget about him, his testimony must be covered in the closing argument. There is usually at least some point that can be mentioned to help remind the jurors that he is, after all, only a human being who is subject to the same errors of judgment and observation as any other human being. Perhaps the importance of physical facts, such as photographs or the length of skid marks, should be emphasized and it should be pointed out that this evidence is irrefutable, whereas the testimony of a witness is always subject to human error, and that when the two conflict, certainly the latter should be disregarded. An imaginative lawyer can conceivably attack the problem from a unique and logical approach; necessity has no law. Perhaps an attack could be developed that, in spite of all his apparently accurate testimony, would demonstrate the improbability of the witness' statements. But, if this witness has testified to a crucial point in the case and every road to contest his accuracy has been blocked, then the lawyer, after receiving an adverse verdict, should find comfort in the knowledge that, after all, this case should have been lost. Perhaps it is naive, but I doubt that we would really want lawyers to be endowed with something more than mortal skill and capable of persuading juries contrary to truth and justice.

When Your Witnesses Are Outnumbered

When a lawyer finds himself in the position of having fewer witnesses to prove a point than does his opponent, he should give much thought to the type of argument that will best appeal to the jury. When the opposition has the advantage of having four witnesses to a lawyer's one to establish the color of the traffic light at the time of the collision, the lawyer would have to be naive not to recognize that this is a serious problem. This is especially crucial if the lawsuit is likely to turn on this single point.

If the outnumbered strategist feels that his lines have held up by means of other testimony, then this will be the place he must hit the hardest, because this precise battle will decide the outcome of the war. There is no use in his pretending that the problem is not there and ignoring it or passing over it lightly in the hope that strong evidence on other points will divert the jury's attention from it. Instead, the lawyer should aggressively assault the problem with all the logic at his command. He should also give consideration to generating arguments to use in the summation. He should analyze the areas where his opponent's witnesses are weak or vulnerable. A well-planned cross-examination, properly executed, not only can create instant doubt in the minds of the jurors, but also will provide the cross-examiner with much of his material for closing arguments. When the examiner compels the witness to make admissions on certain points, he is also preparing his closing argument. He will be able to argue to the jury that his opponent's own witnesses have established certain facts that are favorable to his client. Therefore, it can be seen that the anticipated answers given by a witness under cross-examination will be one of the cornerstones in the preparation of a closing argument that will have a logical basis for acceptance by the jury. Therefore, when a lawyer finds himself outnumbered on witnesses, he will almost certainly have to use the strategy of compelling the opposition's witnesses to help establish the truth. By forcing these witnesses to agree with him on certain propositions or compelling them to admit that these propositions are true, it will make it possible for him to argue to the jury that certain points have been established: "these points were established by testimony, not from our own witness, but from the mouths of the very witnesses produced by the other side." The other cornerstone used in building the argument will consist of exploiting any weaknesses in the other witnesses that can discredit their testimony. These weaknesses can be brought out by using the technique of analyzing the witnesses and the probabilities, as previously mentioned.

Therefore, the lawyer who finds himself outnumbered on witnesses should build his argument around a three-pronged attack: (1) the favorable points brought out by the opposition witnesses should be adopted; (2) their unfavorable testimony should be torn down; and (3) a detailed explanation should be given as to why the jury can attach credence to the testimony of his witness.

Witnesses Who Are Inconsistent

When a lawyer's witnesses have given inconsistent testimony on material points, he can be quite sure that his opponent will comment upon this fact, and he can be sure of the same treatment if he himself is vulnerable.

The plaintiff has the advantage in either event. If the plaintiff's witnesses have created a problem for him, he gets the first opportunity to be candid and honest with the jury by freely admitting the inconsistencies. He can then proceed to rationalize the problem to some extent by comparing the giving of testimony to parlor games that test the participants' ability to observe and retain certain facts. Probably most of the jurors have played the game where 20 or 30 different objects are laid on a table, and then, after being given a minute or two to study the objects, the participants are asked to write down as many of them as they can recall. Some remember quite a few, while others remember almost none. Many will write down objects that were not even on the table. Another parlor game involves having someone who is wearing an odd assortment of clothing run through the room unexpectedly and then asking the guests to write down all that they observed. Still another game involves having someone write a message on a piece of paper, fold it up, and then whisper the message to another guest. That guest, in turn, will whisper it to the next, and so on, until the last guest has heard the message. The last guest then repeats what he heard; then the message is read as it was originally given. The final message is usually so different from the original that there is no resemblance. All of these people were honestly trying to convey what they saw or heard, and yet the variances were remarkable. When an accident occurs, no one is prepared to watch it carefully for the purpose of remembering details so that he can accurately testify to the facts at a later date. An accident occurs and is over in a moment. During that brief moment, a witness gains a quick impression, but it can hardly be expected that two or more witnesses will remember the occurrence in exactly the same way. In fact, it would be highly unusual for witnesses to remember every detail exactly the same. If they did testify identically, their testimony would be subject to suspicion. Horace Smith is credited with saying, "Inconsistency is the only thing in which men are consistent."

After the plaintiff's lawyer has explained away, or attempted to explain away, the inconsistencies in the testimony, he is hardly in a position to criticize his opponent's witnesses on the same ground. If the inconsistencies of his opponent's witnesses are on a material point and are more significant than those of his own, he might be better advised to abandon this attempted explanation of his own witnesses' inconsistencies and hammer at his opponent's major inconsistencies. In making much of the inconsistencies of his opponent, he can interfere with any later attempt on the part of the defense counsel to explain them away. After pointing out the inconsistencies, he can say, "The defense lawyer cannot, in good conscience, stand up here before you folks and deny that his witnesses told inconsistent stories. What possible explanation can there be for two persons to come into court and tell two different versions under oath? Obviously, they both can't be right. One of them must be mistaken. He would ask you to believe one of them, but how are we to guess which one is accurate, if either of them is? Certainly, he would not ask this jury to base its decision on speculation, guess, or conjecture. Perhaps he has some clever explanation for the inconsistencies. If he has, I would certainly like to hear it."

As can be seen, the plaintiff's lawyer has a better opportunity to whitewash his own sins. He also has an opportunity, by implanting curiosity in the minds of the jurors as to what kind of "clever explanation" this lawyer will make, to put the defense lawyer in the uncomfortable position of having to justify his own sins.

The defense lawyer's answer, of course, to the plaintiff's lawyer's whitewashing his own witnesses, is to call it just that—an attempt to "whitewash." He can say, "No matter how much white paint the plaintiff's lawyer attempts to use, he cannot cover up the facts that he has the burden of proof and that his proof is inconsistent. Because of its inconsistency, this jury is justified in disregarding all of the testimony on that point." As to justifying the inconsistencies in his own witnesses, an explanation by the defense lawyer is certainly necessary. If a challenge was made, the defense lawyer can argue that it was only a trick, as why else would the challenge be made if his opponent was not well aware of its logical explanation?

Using the Evidence Deposition

As mentioned earlier, an evidence deposition may be a poor substitute for a real, live witness. On the other hand, it can work to the advantage of the lawyer who is relying on it. While a mere reading of the deposition lacks the punch of a persuasive witness who can be seen and heard, it also prevents the jurors from seeing and hearing a witness who has undesirable characteristics. For example, a witness who presents a poor appearance, who looks down at the floor while answering questions, who has an unpleasant voice, or who possesses other unpleasant characteristics that may affect his value should never be exposed to the jury unless it is impossible to prevent it. An effeminate man, an extremely masculine women, an overdressed woman chewing gum, a witness with a sarcastic voice, or a contemptuous, insolent youth are all witnesses that the opposition lawyer should be deprived of having the jurors see and hear.

For these reasons, a trial court should be most hesitant to permit an evidence deposition unless it can be clearly demonstrated that the witness is not available. However, if a lawyer intends to use the evidence deposition, he should get a commitment from the jurors on *voir dire* that they will give full weight and credence to the testimony given from a deposition—that they will give just as much weight to it as to a witness who appears in person to testify. In the summation the jurors should be reminded that they agreed to give full weight to this testimony and not to consider it any the less because of the manner in which this witness contributed his knowledge of the facts in order that truth and justice might prevail.

During the taking of an evidence deposition, the cross-examiner should attempt to bring out undesirable characteristics. While the record certainly will not reveal that the witness is shifty-eyed or overdressed or speaks with an effeminate voice, it can demonstrate that the witness was evasive, argumentative, or biased.

The routine way to have the jury hear the evidence deposition is to ask a person to take the witness stand and read the answers as if he were the witness. The rules provide that the individual playing the part of the witness should not unduly emphasize any words or phrases and should refrain from any conduct that would paint a picture in the minds of the jurors other than the spoken word. Because an individual wants to identify a voice with a specific person, there will be a tendency for the jurors to form a picture in their minds of what the person is like in physical appearance and manner. True, this will be an unconscious inclination, but it is impossible for anyone to accept a voice without doing this. Because of this inclination, there will be a strong tendency for the jurors to identify as the witness the person on the stand who is playing the part. For this reason, it would be wise to use a person who has desirable characteristics, such as a pleasant appearance and a good speaking voice—in general, a person who would be most likely to be accepted and liked by a jury of that locale and background.

Graphic Examples Help Cement the Point

When making a significant point, it is usually helpful to employ graphic words to give it a more adhesive quality so that it will stick in the minds of the jurors. The use, not only of graphic words, but also of motions with the hands and arms while making a point will help. For example, in referring to testimony that was not important or germane to the issues, many lawyers will say that it is "confusing the issues." It would be more likely to stick in the jurors' minds if the testimony was described as "merely muddying the waters." In referring to some unexpected and damaging testimony that hurt his opponent's case, a lawyer can say that it was a "damaging piece of testimony," but it would be more graphic to say that this testimony "blew them out of the water." A plaintiff, in describing terrible pain in the abdomen that resulted from an accident, can put both hands to his abdomen and bend over as if in pain. A lawyer can hold up his finger to show the length of a needle that was inserted into his client's spinal canal for diagnostic purposes.

An effective use of graphic words or demonstrations can conjure up a picture in the minds of the jurors much more vividly than can everyday words alone. For example, the defense lawyer can drive home the concept of contributory negligence through a simple demonstration. After taking a sheet of paper and tearing off a piece from the corner about the size of a fingernail, he can hold up the two pieces and compare them to negligence and contributory negligence: "If my client was negligent . . ." (showing them the large piece of paper), "and the plaintiff was negligent . . ." (showing the small piece), "then under the law, it is the sworn duty of this jury to find my client not guilty. It is not a matter of weighing which one was the most negligent. Before he can collect ten cents, the plaintiff must prove that he, himself, was not even guilty of that much negligence" (again showing them the small piece of paper).

How Many Issues Should Be Made?

In every trial, there are only a few really important points. Oftentimes there is only one. But there are usually many unimportant points, and the lawyer may find himself expending his energy on these false trails that merely divert the jury from the point that should decide the case. The argument should always come back to the major points so that the jury's attention is fixed on the deciding factor. This rule applies without exception to the plaintiff's lawyer.

The defense lawyer, however, may prefer to keep the jury occupied with numerous issues. If the question or questions that decide the case are close ones and the defense lawyer finds himself representing a target defendant, such as a large corporation, a taxicab company, or a bus company, then normally his best tactic is to not simplify the issues. By creating and nursing numerous side issues, he can make problems for the jury. "Troubles, like babies, grow larger by nursing," observed Lady Holland. One of these side issues might catch on and create enough of a problem in the minds of the jurors that it could swing them over to the defendant's side; whereas, if their attention had been focused only on the main issue, they might have given a verdict to the plaintiff. When the defendant has strong evidence on a major point, that is favorable to his side of the case, then he, like the plaintiff, should address himself to the significant point.

In a situation in which the plaintiff is attempting to simplify the issues and the defendant is attempting to complicate them, there will invariably be close questions of fact. The plaintiff's attorney normally should isolate the main issues for the jurors, explaining that the answers to these precise issues will decide their verdict. Then he should carefully take each issue and answer it for them by analyzing the evidence that demonstrates that a positive answer for each issue can give rise to only one conclusion—that the plaintiff has proven his case as required by the law, and is, therefore, deserving of a verdict. The defense attorney's approach should be to analyze the evidence from his client's standpoint, demonstrating that the question raised by the plaintiff should be answered in the negative. In addition, the defense lawyer should ask the jury, "Well, what about this question?," on a point that is favorable to the defendant, and then go on to say, "And, what about this question?," on another point favorable to the defendant. The defense lawyer can raise as many issues as his ingenuity can provide, and then he can invite the plaintiff's lawyer to answer each of the issues that he has raised.

ANALYZING THE LAWYERS AND THEIR RATIONALE

Bring Out the Bad Stuff in Your Own Case

When the plaintiff's lawyer rises to make his summation, he knows the weak points of his case quite well—almost as well as his opponent knows them. Aware of this, he can anticipate much of the argument that his opponent will offer, and he can be prepared to discuss the weaknesses openly and freely. He should not distort or hold back on those weak points, but, on the contrary, he should bring them out in the open and analyze them from the plaintiff's standpoint. He should point out the reason why they are not as weak as they appear to be, or why, in spite of these weaknesses, the plaintiff is entitled to the verdict. When the defendant attacks the same

weaknesses the plaintiff has analyzed, the jury already has the answers to his arguments; these arguments will be much less effective
if he is making a reply rather than bringing up the weak points for
the plaintiff to reply to. However, if the plaintiff's lawyer cannot
satisfy himself that the apparent weaknesses in his case are not fatal,
he should be prepared for an adverse verdict.

Defense Argument a Three-in-One Shot

A major problem of being a defense lawyer is that he must
accomplish three things during his summation and he gets only one
chance to accomplish all of them. The first thing he must do is argue
his own case; second, he must answer the plaintiff's argument; and
third, he must anticipate the rebuttal argument and answer it. I
know of no advantage in appearing only once before the jury on summation; therefore, I can only conclude that the plaintiff has a distinct
advantage. If we draw a parallel to boxers, the plaintiff gets the first
swing, and one effective swing can knock the defendant off balance,
but he must recover and come out fighting. However, the defendant
should not be content with merely defending himself; he should put
the plaintiff on the defensive in as many areas as possible by taking
the position that there are more issues than the plaintiff would have
the jury believe. He should point out why the evidence resolves those
issues in favor of the defendant.

If, on rebuttal, the plaintiff commits the sin of bringing up a new
argument that cannot be classified as a reply to the defendant's
argument, then an immediate objection should be made. It should
be explained to the jury that the defense will not have another opportunity to talk to them.

A Lawyer Changing the Testimony

There are times when a trial lawyer finds himself fervently
wishing that the evidence had gone in somewhat differently than it
did. He feels quite sure that just a point or two could have made
quite a difference and finds himself more apprehensive because the
evidence didn't come out exactly the way he had planned. This
desire to have it a little different may be so great that he is tempted
to alter it a little during his argument. This is nearly always a
mistake. In the first place, the jurors heard the evidence and probably
remember it, and they will resent his downright dishonesty. His
lack of honesty on one point will contaminate his entire argument.
It is not necessarily true that the perpetrator of this indiscretion will
lose the case as a result. In spite of the dishonesty of the lawyer, the
jury will still want to decide on the side of truth and justice. He may

have more than sufficient evidence for the jury despite the damage he has done to the case, but if it's a close one on the facts and his conduct is in contrast to that of his opponent, who may have impressed the jury with his fairness and honesty, any doubts will be resolved in favor of the opposition. His only hope lies in the possibility that his opponent will neutralize his mistake by committing the same sin. If both lawyers perform in the same manner, it will only confirm the suspicions that the jurors had all along—that lawyers are tricky, sharp, and engaged in a rather questionable profession. In this situation, the jurors will arrive at their decision without consciously attaching much importance to what either lawyer had to say. But after the jury has performed its function, its members may leave with their suspicions of lawyers confirmed. This type of trial lawyer will have done a disservice to the Bar in general. Fortunately, this is the exception to the rule, since most people who have had jury experience come away from their service with increased respect for the administration of the law as well as for lawyers in general.

In addition to the risk already mentioned, the lawyer who resorts to this tactic runs the risk of incurring an objection from his opponent and perhaps of receiving a reprimand from the trial judge as the objection is being sustained. If the objection is well founded, the erring lawyer must also suffer the embarrassment of having the jury see that his conduct was so improper that even the trial judge had to put a stop to it. On those occasions when the argument is apparently a proper one, the safest procedure for the trial court is merely to announce that the jury heard the evidence, unless he is quite certain that the objection is well founded. A mistake by the trial judge at this point will certainly be prejudicial to the innocent party, and quite often it will be sufficient to warrant a new trial if the verdict subsequently goes against the recipient of this erroneous ruling.

If there are shades of misrepresentation as to what the evidence was, the offending lawyer's incorrect assertions can be highlighted by his opponent's repeating those inaccuracies in the same words and then contrasting them by accurately stating the evidence. To use an example, assume that there was testimony by a witness that he saw the defendant drinking three martinis within the space of an hour and a half preceding the accident. The defense lawyer will justifiably feel that this evidence is certainly injurious to his case. If he was aware of this witness before the trial began, he was, of course, interested in selecting jurors who drink and then drive a car. This *voir dire* examination would have been conducted as previously discussed. The defense lawyer should tell the jurors that he acknowledges that his client should not have any roses pinned on him for this conduct, but that, on the other hand, it should be borne in mind that this is a common occurrence in the alcohol-conscious society in which we live. If the testimony with regard to the three martinis is more than the defense lawyer can live with, he should attack the credibility of the "three martinis" witness. However, in the absence of any other possibilities, an argument on that point could be as follows:

Now, ladies and gentlemen, there has been testimony that Henry had been drinking intoxicating beverages a short time before this accident occurred. We certainly made no secret of this fact, since the jury will recall that at the very outset, I said that the evidence would show that Henry had been drinking martinis. Not for one second do I stand here and offer excuses for Henry's drinking alcoholic beverages shortly before he drove that car. I would be the first to agree that this is a poor policy and one that should not be followed. To be completely safe, Henry should have taken a taxicab home after work, rather than drive his car as he has been doing for the past 25 years. This has been a long-standing procedure with Henry, just as with tens of thousands of other businessmen in this city. A tension-filled day at work followed by a drink or two at a cocktail lounge is a reality, and, like it or not, many of our good citizens do it.

The liquor industry spends literally millions of dollars each year to encourage us to drink its products, and one has only to circulate in our society today to observe the successes of this giant industry. It is difficult, at best, to move about in our society without having a social drink at a friend's home, a business meeting, or a party. People have learned through experience how much they can drink and still retain their complete mental faculties. How many people have driven their automobile to a friend's house for a party or social gathering, had a few cocktails, and then driven their automobile back home? [In selecting the jury, the defense lawyer will have made it a point to ask the jurors whether they drink alcoholic beverages, and if so, whether they have ever gone to a friend's home, where they have consumed alcoholic beverages, and then driven their car home.] The fact that a person has had a drink or two and was then involved in an automobile accident certainly does not mean that he was responsible for the accident merely because he had been drinking.

You will recall that during the *voir dire* examination I asked each and every one of you whether you would make the plaintiff prove that my client, Henry, was negligent in his manner of driving, and not merely assume that he was neg-

ligent because he had been drinking. The plaintiff in this case
has the burden of proving that Henry was negligent. That's
the question you folks are asked to decide—not whether Henry
had been drinking; that information was candidly and freely
volunteered by us at the very outset of this case. Now, there
has been evidence that Henry had one or two martinis, and
I submit that this, in itself, does not make Henry responsible
for, or legally liable for, this accident. The plaintiff in this
case must prove. . . .

As can be seen from the foregoing argument, the defense lawyer
felt that the testimony of the "three martinis" should be altered a
little to make a better set of facts. He had properly conditioned the
jury to hear this damaging testimony and he might well have persuaded them to accept his theory of the case in spite of the defendant's consumption of alcoholic beverages. But by misstating the
testimony, he not only let the jurors down, but he also let them know
that he felt three martinis was just one too many. The plaintiff's
lawyer on rebuttal can now highlight this in the following manner:

You have just heard my opponent attempt to justify the
defendant's drinking and driving habits. He would have us
believe that this is just as much a part of our way of life as
are motherhood and the American flag. Therefore, it follows
that there really isn't anything wrong with the defendant's
putting alcohol into his system and then getting behind the
wheel of a car. Maybe I'm not sophisticated, or perhaps I'm
even old-fashioned, but I don't think that drinking and driving
go together.

My opponent did say something, however, that I thought
was mighty interesting. In fact, it was so interesting that I
wrote it down in order to remember his exact words so that
I would not be guilty of misquoting him. He said "Now,
there has been evidence that Henry had one or two martinis . . . ." Now, I ask you, ladies and gentlemen, was that the
evidence? It seems to me that Mr. Johnson sat right there on
that chair yesterday and testified under oath that the defendant had three martinis—that is "three martinis"—not "one
or two martinis," but "three martinis." Now, Mr. Johnson was
not interested in the outcome of this lawsuit. He has nothing
to gain whether John wins the case or the defendant wins the
case. He was brought into this court under subpoena, and he
testified as to what he observed. Now, I'm not going into
everything he testified to, but certainly this jury must have
been impressed with the complete candor and forthright answers of Mr. Johnson.

Why, then, is my opponent so interested in bringing the number of those martinis down from three to one or two? I'll tell you why he's so interested. It's because he knows that when a person consumes alcoholic beverages his reactions are slowed down and he is dangerous behind the wheel of a car. Anyone who has had three martinis has absolutely no business getting behind the wheel of a car. My opponent obviously knows this just as well as anyone. Why else was he so interested in bringing down the number of those martinis? He heard the evidence of Mr. Johnson just as everyone else did in this courtroom. Mr. Johnson has placed the number at three martinis, ladies and gentlemen, and in spite of all the wishful thinking of my opponent, it will always be three martinis, not one or two martinis.

As can be seen from the rebuttal argument, the defense lawyer has given his opponent the perfect opportunity to highlight the misstatement of the facts. True, three martinis are an uncomfortable fact to live with, but one must live with the facts. Not only does a lawyer need imagination to persuade a jury, but he must be a realist. He must accept the facts as they are, since no amount of wishful thinking will change them, but those facts can be made palatable to a jury with the correct amount of seasoning.

If a lawyer is aware that he has a tendency to exaggerate to make a point or a tendency to overstate the evidence in spite of all his efforts to the contrary, then he should prepare the jurors for this when commencing his closing argument. He can state that, while he will try to be as objective as possible, he is, after all, like his opponent, a partisan, that he is interested in the outcome of the lawsuit, and that if, in his zeal or on behalf of his client, he inadvertently misstates any of the facts, they should "please disregard those misstatements," as he will not consciously stray from the evidence as he recalls it. A lawyer "caught cold" in stating something that would have been better left unsaid might also try humor in asking the jury's forgiveness. Perhaps a remark once made by Adlai Stevenson would be of value in this situation: "Man does not live by words alone, despite the fact that sometimes he has to eat them."

The Improper Argument

Improper arguments should be avoided not only because the lawyer using them runs the risk of being reversed even if he is successful in the trial court but also because the jury may penalize him for lack of fair play. An improper argument that is not objected to may be recognized as such by the jury, or its lack of propriety may be made obvious by the court's ruling in sustaining an objection made by the opposing lawyer. The adversary nature of a trial lawyer's profession usually prevents him from being truly objective. Because he has a strong belief in the righteousness of his cause, he is sometimes tempted to resort to an unprofessional attack on the opposition. Some of the more objectionable types of arguments are those that involve an unjustified appeal to passion or prejudice, those that appeal to racial or religious prejudice, and those that seek to arouse prejudice or sympathy by reference to wealth, large corporate size, and so forth. Some other objectionable arguments are those directed to counsel's conduct in objecting to evidence where the evidence was excluded by court ruling and those improperly singling out a particular witness because of his occupation, nationality or residence.

Know the Issue

Before the lawyer rises to make his closing argument, he should make certain that he understands the issues. It is important not only that he understand the issues, but also that he have analyzed them so that he is better able to address himself to these questions in a persuasive manner. Too often a lawyer progresses to his closing argument without asking himself just what it is that this fact-finding body is being asked to decide. It is too easy to jump to the conclusion that a sharp difference in testimony by opposing witnesses has created the ultimate or real issue that the jury must decide.

For example, let us assume that the attorney for the plaintiff had no difficulty in establishing that the defendant was negligent, and that the real point in establishing liability turns on whether the plaintiff, himself, was guilty of contributory negligence. This, then, is the real issue, notwithstanding a difference of opinion as to the speed of the plaintiff's automobile shortly before and at the time of the occurrence. It is conceivable that the jurors might well accept the accuracy of the defendant's testimony with regard to plaintiff's speed—perhaps they might even reject contrary testimony by the plaintiff. It is further conceivable that, notwithstanding their complete acceptance of the defendant's opinion, they would not be persuaded that this excessive speed constituted contributory negligence, but would, in fact, come to the conclusion that the speed was reasonable under the circumstances. The plaintiff's lawyer, in electing to take a firm stand on the conflict in opinions as to his client's speed, may focus the jurors' attention so sharply on this side issue that they may consciously or unconsciously gain the impression that this is the question that decides the outcome of the lawsuit. By attaching such significance to that point, he can throw himself off as well as the jurors. The jurors should be told exactly what the real issue is. The testimony or evidence, combined with their own common sense and everyday experience in the ordinary affairs of life, might resolve the question of contributory negligence in favor of the plaintiff.

There may be situations, however, where the skilled trial lawyer will prefer to divert attention from the real issue, such as where the weight of evidence tends to favor the opposition. In this situation, he may deliberately attempt to magnify the importance of a relatively minor issue or even to create an issue of his own. If a battle to the death can be commenced on such an issue, the opposition may be thrown off balance and the jury misled completely by something that would otherwise have been nothing but a side skirmish. Therefore, before a course is set in closing arguments, it should be determined how the evidence went in so that it can be decided whether the heart of the case should be isolated and whether it can bear careful scrutiny.

Failure of Opponent to Fulfill a Promise

If the opposing lawyer fails to produce evidence, through the tesimony of a witness, exhibits or otherwise, that during his opening statements he promised to produce, this should be mentioned. This promise to produce may have been forgotten by the jurors for one reason or another, and their memories should be refreshed. It might be that the opponent promised to produce a certain witness who never appeared, or perhaps that he stated that a witness would testify to certain facts and this did not, in fact, occur. This failure could be quite significant in the minds of the jurors, who might even interpret it to mean that the testimony would have been adverse.

More Than One Lawyer

When more than one lawyer appears and argues on behalf of a party to a lawsuit, there will probably be both advantages and disadvantages. An obvious advantage, of course, is that the resourcefulness of two minds is available for persuading the jurors. There will then be more than one approach to analyzing the evidence, a variety of methods of highlighting points that will appeal to different jurors, or different slants in answering an opponent's argument. A different personality may appeal more to certain jurors, a choice of words may have more persuasive value with some jurors, and, of course, there are numerous other similar advantages. In cases where the verdict could be substantial, the presence of more than one lawyer is usually justified in the minds of the jurors, and there can be significant value in the persuasiveness of a team. The attention of the jurors and, therefore, their receptiveness, begins to wane after one lawyer has talked for a considerable length of time. The jurors, by this time, have become accustomed to his manner of speaking and his choice of words; since they have satisfied their curiosity to some extent, they may permit their minds to wander. At the midway point, another lawyer is a complete change of pace; he can recapture their attention with a fresh approach.

The disadvantage of having more than one lawyer is obvious. It is human nature to sympathize with the "underdog." For this reason, the lawyer who is a member of a group must cover this problem. He has the jurors committed that such a situation will not influence them, as previously mentioned. A reminder of their commitment, together with an admonition that justice is nourished on truth, and that the number of advocates does not affect the truth, will help. This can be a real problem and should not be overlooked.

Is the Jury Spellbound?

When making his closing argument, the lawyer should keep in mind the fact that the jurors are not nearly as interested in the outcome of the lawsuit as he is. The parties to the lawsuit and their lawyers, as well as the key witnesses, have all been intensely interested in even the smallest details. This may delude the lawyer into thinking that the jurors feel the same way. "No man was ever so much deceived by another as by himself," said Greville.

Jurors are interested in discharging their duties, but it should be kept in mind that the trial of a lawsuit does not compare with an exciting novel or a television program, which is designed to capture and hold the attention of its audience. A trial can move very slowly for jurors who must wait while the lawyers argue out some point in the judge's chambers and then return for a long and tedious examination of a technical witness, who is not there for the purpose of entertaining them. How many of us have gone to a lecture or a religious service and found our minds wandering to other subjects? The lawyer, when making his closing argument (which might take an hour and a half), may feel sure that the jurors are listening to him because they are looking directly at him and following his brilliant analysis of the evidence. But the truth is that probably a good percentage of them are "tuned out." After 45 minutes of listening to a lawyer drone on about his case, I suspect that half the jurors are not following him; their minds are somewhere else. It is difficult for most people to give their complete attention for an extended period of time to a subject in which they are not personally interested. For this reason, a lawyer should not stand in one place while giving his summation. He should move around. He should also vary the tone and volume of his voice when he is delivering his argument. His delivery should be broken up with such things as picking up an exhibit and then walking over to the jurors and holding it up for them to see or walking over to the blackboard and pointing out various

items. A paradox in making a point with the jurors is that a loud
voice is not as effective with them as is a change of pace to a very
soft voice. A sudden change to a soft voice will capture and hold
their attention better than a shouting voice. If the jurors must strain
just a little to hear the voice, it is more likely to register.

Don't Force the Jury to Guess

The most undercompensated element of damages in a personal
injury lawsuit is pain and suffering. It is easy to add up the medical
expenses, loss of income, property damage, and other damages when
the jurors find that liability does exist. This is more than likely the
first and only time that they will find it necessary to determine in
dollars and cents how much "hurtin" the plaintiff has had, or may
have in the future. If the defendant is a "nice guy," but apparently
was guilty of an error in judgment, it is almost a certainty that the
jurors will underevaluate the pain and suffering unless this element
can be graphically demonstrated. In this situation, the jurors may
feel that there is no need to penalize the defendant, who was not
guilty of prejudicial conduct. In addition, since they are uninformed
as to the magnitude of the pain and its effects, they can hardly be
expected to accurately evaluate this intangible. An inadequate image
will be created in the minds of the jurors if the plaintiff simply uses
undescriptive and totally inadequate words, such as, "I had terrible
pains in my shoulder, neck, and back for two years"; one juror may
recall a stiff neck he had a week before when he woke up in the
morning after he apparently had slept in the wrong position, while
another juror may have another minor complaint that he will associate or identify with that of the plaintiff.

Should Charts Be Prepared in Advance?

Charts and blackboards can be used during the closing arguments
to convey the message through another of the five senses. In itemiz-
ing the damages in order to justify the total amount, it may be that
the spoken word will be sufficient, but a message carried to the
brain through two senses will register more indelibly. It is probably
more effective to write down each element of damage and assign an
amount of money to it at the time the argument is being made, as
a jury is more likely to follow the argument with greater interest if
it appears to be spontaneous. This is not to say that charts carefully
prepared in advance of the argument are not effective. As a matter
of fact, they have at least one advantage, since the defense lawyer
will be less inclined to mark up charts during his closing argument.
There is nothing to prevent the defense lawyer from erasing figures
the plaintiff's lawyer has put on a blackboard and writing in a zero.
At the same time, he can explain to the jury that the plaintiff is

entitled to no more than the figure he has inserted on the blackboard because the plaintiff is guilty of contributory negligence. The plaintiff's lawyer can prevent this by stating that he has spent a good deal of time preparing the charts and that he would appreciate it if the defense lawyer refrained from mutilating them or marking them up. At the same time, he can invite his opponent to use his own charts or blackboard if he so desires.

EXAMPLES OF CLOSING ARGUMENTS

It is difficult to give an example of a closing argument because of the unlimited ramifications in any given case. In spite of the great publicity given some trials, the fact remains that most lawyers usually try typical "bread and butter" cases. Most cases go to verdict because there is a dispute as to liability and the injuries are substantial enough that the case is not settled.

By way of example, we will take a case that answers this description: Where a child is injured when he darts out from between parked cars, it is always difficult for the plaintiff to succeed. In the absence of any evidence as to wrongdoing on the part of the driver or unless he is an unpopular defendant, the trial usually results in a verdict for the defendant. Miraculously enough, it seems that most child-dart-out cases do not result in terribly serious injuries. There may be fractured collarbones, fractured arms, and sometimes even a skull fracture, but children being what they are, they mend quickly and usually make a complete recovery.

For our example, let's take a six-year-old child in a state where the law excuses him for any negligence, and let's take an unpopular defendant, such as a taxicab company. If the plaintiff's lawyer is modest in his request for money damages, he will improve his chances for a verdict. The strategy for the defense lawyer is probably to ignore the damage issue because of the danger of dignifying it. After all, if something does go wrong, and the jury enters a verdict against the defendant, it won't be a large one. Any effort to reduce the amount of the verdict may result in the jurors' thinking in terms of a "guilty" verdict. Effective arguments for each side might be something as follows:

May it please the Court, counsel, ladies and gentlemen of the jury. It is at this stage of the proceedings that the lawyers for both sides deliver what is known as a closing argument or a summation. You will be retiring shortly to consider your verdict. At this time, I would like to thank the jury, on behalf of both my client, John, and myself, for the consideration and patience that you have displayed for both sides of this case. We who are trial lawyers, as well as His

Honor, Judge Broadbeam, know that juries are extremely conscientious and that they work hard at the task assigned to them. We know that you folks are struggling to make a correct decision in order that fairness and justice may prevail.

The task that you folks must now address yourselves to is to decide whether the Fast-Wheel Taxicab Company was negligent in the operation of its taxicab through the conduct of its agent and employee, Joe Heavyfoot. As to little six-year-old Jimmy Terror's emerging from between parked cars in front of his house, everyone will certainly agree that this is exactly the foolish type of thing that a six-year-old child can be expected to do. Every parent knows that regardless of how many times he tells his child not to go in the street, it will happen from time to time. It isn't necessarily that the child is disobedient. The problem is that he doesn't have the maturity that comes from experience in life. Children sometimes become so preoccupied with imaginary dragons or Indians that they completely forget where they are or what they're doing. These years of childhood are the happy, carefree years. Children's minds are not burdened by the cares and problems of an older person. They are intent on the fantasy or plaything of the moment. Every adult knows this to be true. Sometimes an adult's memories fade and he forgets what it was like to be six years old, but the parent of a six-year-old is reminded of his own childhood when he observes his child at play. To put it another way, six-year-old children are simply not responsible. This fact is so well known that we pass laws to protect six-year-old children. We have such a law in our state. At the conclusion of this case His Honor will instruct you in the law with regard to the duty of care required of a six-year-old child.

You folks will recall that when we first started this trial yesterday, we lawyers, as well as the judge, asked each of you quite a number of questions. Before you proceeded to answer those questions, each of you was sworn to answer well and truly all questions put to you by both Court and counsel. I believe I explained that we lawyers were not permitted to discuss the law with you at that stage of the proceedings. Each of you was asked, however, if you would follow the law as His Honor would instruct you at the conclusion of the case. Each of you answered that you would follow the law, even if the law was different from what you thought it should be or understood it to be. Each of you, therefore, promised under oath that you would follow the law of our land as given to you by the judge. The judge will shortly advise and instruct you as to what law is applicable to this particular case. I believe that His Honor, Judge Broadbeam, will instruct you that at the time of this occurrence (as well as presently) there was a law in our state that provided that a child under the age of seven could not be held responsible for any negligent conduct on his part. It is the sworn duty of this jury to follow that law. There may be some of you who will not favor that law; however, let me remind you that it is your sworn duty not to let your personal feelings influence your verdict in this case. It is not my function to persuade you as to the wisdom of the law; I can only remind you of your sworn duty to follow the law. If I seem to have dwelt too long on the subject of your sworn duty as jurors, please forgive me. I would feel derelict in my duty toward little Jimmy and his parents if I did not cover this point adequately.

The jury will also recall that I asked each of you whether you could give little Jimmy a fair trial. You each assured me that in spite of any personal experiences you may have had with regard to children's emerging from between parked cars, you could give Jimmy a fair trial. It isn't simply a question of saying that a thing like this can happen to anyone driving down a street. It's true that Jimmy did a foolish thing. As adults, you certainly wouldn't come out from between parked cars without first looking. But as adults sitting in judgment on little Jimmy, you cannot judge him by the same standard of care that you would use to judge an adult. As a matter of fact, the law says that Jimmy is incapable of exercising care for himself. He is just too young and immature to be expected to use good sense. It is, therefore, the duty of an adult to realize that children will be children and to protect them against their own folly.

The Fast-Wheel Taxicab Company had a duty toward Jimmy as it drove that cab down the street Jimmy lived on. Incidentally, just to avoid any misunderstanding with regard to the corporate taxicab company, I believe His Honor will instruct you that the corporation can act only through its officers, employees, and servants. Any knowledge these people have automatically, by law, becomes knowledge to the corporation itself. Therefore, whatever knowledge its driver, Mr. Heavyfoot, had or whatever negligent act Mr. Heavyfoot committed automatically, by law, became the knowledge or negligent conduct of the corporation itself. Now, you heard the testimony of Mr. Heavyfoot. He has been driving a taxi-cab in this community for a good many years. He has driven on Jimmy's street many times in the past and admitted that he knew that a good number of children lived in the area. Children being children, he well knew that they could be expected to do the very thing that little Jimmy did in front of his house. Mr. Heavyfoot and his corporate employer had a duty to little Jimmy to be especially careful when they drove down his street. They had a duty to keep that cab under control so that they could bring it to an absolute stop in the event of just such an occurrence as this. If the Fast-Wheel Taxi-cab Corporation had been exercising care for Jimmy, Jimmy would not have been injured and we wouldn't be here today. I submit that the evidence clearly shows that this taxicab corporation failed in its duty toward little Jimmy. Mind you, the driver of that taxicab testified he didn't even see Jimmy until he was three feet from him. It was only then that he proceeded to put his foot on the brake. He obviously didn't even have his foot on the brake at the time his fender struck little Jimmy's head.

Now, it's true that the speed limit on Jimmy's block is 25 miles per hour. Mr. Heavyfoot says he was doing about 20 to 25 miles an hour. I believe His Honor will instruct you that there is a law in our state covering this situation, which I will paraphrase. In essence, this law says that regardless of what the speed limit is, a person shall not drive faster than what is reasonable with regard to the conditions prevailing at that time. I submit that even if we were to accept the driver's estimate as to the speed he was traveling at the time of the accident, it would be an unreasonable speed. The conditions prevailing at that time were obvious to this corporation. The conditions prevailing were that children lived in the neighborhood and therefore played there. The conditions prevailing were such that a person exercising ordinary care would have driven at a lesser speed, so that he would have complete control of his vehicle in the event of just such an occurrence as we have here. This taxicab corporation is subject to the same law as any other motorist. Just how Mr. Heavyfoot was driving that taxicab is for you folks to decide. Incidentally, I believe that His Honor will also instruct you that in considering the evidence in this case, you are not required to set aside your experiences in the ordinary affairs of life, but you are to use those experiences in deciding the reasonableness of the facts in this case.

Now, there isn't any question that Jimmy was injured. Even this taxicab corporation has to admit that Jimmy was injured. There's no dispute that Jimmy had a skull fracture and he was confined to the Community Hospital for four weeks. He suffered a great deal with headaches, and it was a frightening experience to be away from home for such a long period of time. Fortunately, Jimmy came out of this accident without any apparent permanent injury. It was an unfortunate experience for Jimmy and one that will leave an indelible mark of horror on his mind. The only thing that justice can do for Jimmy now is to award him money. The assigning of a sum of money to compensate Jimmy for those elements of damages applicable under the law in this case will be the duty of this jury. Each of you assured me that you would award Jimmy money damages if the evidence indicated that he was entitled to compensation. Each of you also assured me that there was nothing distasteful about awarding a sum of money for an injury, and that you would fairly and adequately compensate him in the event the evidence indicated that he was entitled to compensation. Pain and suffering is a lawful element of damage, and certainly Jimmy is entitled to be compensated in that regard. What is fair compensation? This is something that only you folks can answer. The hospital and medical bills total $1,496. This is an easy sum to ascertain because all we have to do is add up the doctor and hospital bills to have them received into evidence. May I suggest a figure of $7,000 as compensation for this unpleasant experience. The total verdict that I would respectfully suggest would, therefore, be $8,496.

Thank you for your attention. My colleague will now have an opportunity to make his summation. Then I will have another opportunity to answer the arguments advanced by him.

The closing argument for the defendant's lawyer might be as follows:

May it please the Court, counsel, ladies and gentlemen of the jury. Joe and I would also like to thank you for your consideration and attention. We realize that yours is not an easy task. It is a rewarding experience, however, and we feel sure that you will go away with a renewed appreciation of law and order. Please be patient with us a little longer, as the case will soon be in your hands.

The jury will recall that when we made our opening statements yesterday, I represented to this jury that certain facts would be established. I said that Joe, here, has been with us for a good many years. He has driven a taxicab in our community under all types of weather conditions and in all parts of the community. He had driven down Oak Street in the past, and on the day of this accident, he was operating his vehicle just as he had many times before that day. He was familiar with the posted speed limit and was observing the law on that fine, clear, sunny afternoon. The driving conditions were excellent, and he was operating his vehicle in a completely reasonable manner. As he drove along, maintaining a proper distance between his car and the cars parked to his right, a child darted out from between parked cars directly in front of his vehicle. The only way that this accident could have been avoided was either to have Joe operating that taxicab on some other street or to have the child not dart out from between the parked cars. Driving within the speed limit of 20 to 25 miles per hour is neither more nor less than what would be expected from any person operating a motor vehicle there. The driving conditions prevailing at that time were excellent. For a child to dart out from between parked cars when the driver is only three feet away makes this a completely unavoidable accident on the part of Joe. Most people will go through a lifetime of driving without having to undergo such an unnerving experience as this. Fortunately, with Joe's experience he was able to somehow swerve his cab to the left so that the wheels did not pass over this child's body.

Counsel for the plaintiff made the remark that Joe did not even have his foot on the brake at the moment of impact. I submit that it would be physically impossible for Joe to get his foot on the brake in such a short period of time. Counsel for plaintiff knows this and is only attempting to muddy the waters.

Regardless of any effort to muddy the waters, and regardless of how clever his rationalization may be, keep in mind, ladies and gentlemen, that this vehicle was being operated in a reasonable manner, well within the speed limit. Also keep in mind that this child darted out from between parked cars when our vehicle was only three feet from him. Even if Joe were going only five miles an hour, he could not have avoided this accident. Counsel would have you believe that Joe was driving that vehicle in a fast or careless manner. Keep in mind that there hasn't been one shred of evidence presented to substantiate such a conclusion. Quite the contrary, the evidence—in fact, the *only* evidence—was that the vehicle was being operated well within the speed limit. Counsel would have the jury completely ignore the evidence, and in the face of all evidence to the contrary, come to the conclusion that our vehicle was speeding. He says that we knew that children lived in the neighborhood. I submit that children live in every neighborhood of the community and that there was nothing more special about this street than any other street, other than perhaps a business street, and that type of street has no relation to the facts in this case.

You folks will recall that yesterday when we were asking questions, I also asked a number of questions pertaining to your fairness. You will recall that I agreed that we all have sympathy for anyone who is injured. I think that we especially have sympathy for an injured child. We would be less than human if we didn't have sympathy for the injured plaintiff in this case. But you agreed with me that sympathy does not decide a lawsuit. You agreed that we had a right to defend ourselves and that you would give us a fair trial—the same as you would give anyone else. You assured me under oath, that you would give my client a fair trial; that if you had had any unpleasant experiences with taxicabs or had any preconceived feelings about taxicabs, you would not let those feelings interfere with your sworn duty to be fair to both sides. You assured me that if the plaintiff failed to prove his case, you would have the courage not to award him damages; that you would find us "not guilty" if the evidence failed to prove that we were guilty of negligence; that you would not ignore the law and the evidence and enter a verdict awarding damages merely because we are a corporation.

I am sure that you folks would agree that if juries ignored the law and evidence, our jury system as we know it would be completely valueless. If juries were to assume the role of Robin Hood in redistributing the wealth, our society would be one without law and order. If we did something wrong, then we should pay for it. If we were guilty of negligence, and our negligence was the cause of the injury to this child, then we should be held responsible, just as anyone else would be. If, on the other hand, the injuries that this child received were caused by his darting out from between parked cars, then it is the duty of this jury to find us "not guilty." We lawyers have great faith and confidence in our jury system, and I am sure that this jury will perform its duty.

Epilogue

"My business on the jury's done—the
    quibblin' all is through—

I've watched the lawyers, right and
    left, and give my verdict true."—Will Carleton, "Goin' Home To-day."

PROBABLY NO SOCIETY, regardless of how sophisticated or dedicated its motives, will ever be able to devise a fact-finding system that will result in "pure justice." In our never-ending attempt to improve our system of justice, it is doubtful that we will ever find the perfect system, because any system must rely upon human beings. Justice must, necessarily, fail at times, just as man must fail at times in his never-ending struggle to find the truth. All of us, regardless of our philosophies or experiences in life, must, therefore, necessarily agree that our trial-by-jury procedure can be improved upon. It is perhaps conceivable that someday a superior system of establishing the truth may be devised. It is not beyond the realm of possibility that someday our society, under its democratic processes, may scrap our entire jury system and substitute a procedure made possible through the discoveries of medical science. The civil trial lawyer may find that the public will prefer to receive unquestioned truth from the mouth of every witness through the use of a harmless truth

230

serum. It cannot be said to be beyond the realm of possibility that the use of this system can be successfuly advocated, if it, in fact, will prevent our "lady of justice" from making a mistake from time to time.

One of the unknowns in the problem of jury persuasion that is virtually undiscussed in this book, as well as in any other book on this subject, is what happens to the jurors *after* they retire to consider their verdict. The probable reason for the void in this area is two-fold: first, the sanctity of the jury room prevents any reliable study whatsoever; and second, there is nothing that anyone connected with the lawsuit can do after the jury has begun its deliberations. The experienced trial lawyer, however, is troubled on occasion by a verdict that seems incongruous with the attitude displayed by the jurors. How many times has a lawyer, during his closing arguments, observed a nod of the head from several of the jurors, indicating what appears to be their complete agreement with his analysis of the evidence? This tacit approval seems to give advance notice that they are looking with favor upon his side of the case. However, not infrequently he may be stunned to find that the jurors will bring in a verdict completely contrary to what he has read into their attitude.

The reason for this seeming "upset" is that the closing arguments did not end when the jury retired to consider its verdict. On the contrary, the evidence was being argued and analyzed in the jury room by a juror who was determined to persuade his fellow jurors. There is no way to silence or answer the arguments of a juror who either intentionally or through ignorance erroneously analyzes or misstates the evidence. Fortunately, it appears that most juries are composed of individuals who remember and interpret the evidence accurately. Therefore, the erring juror is usually not influential with the others, and he can usually be persuaded to vote with those jurors who are well grounded. When the jury takes a position contrary to that which would normally be anticipated by reasonable men, then perhaps justice was ruptured by a forceful, articulate juror who had ulterior motives. Fortunately, this type of person is indeed rare, and his presence can readily be detected during the *voir dire* examination by the careful trial lawyer. The well-educated juror with a convincing demeanor who is possessed of a deep-rooted prejudice must be identified and removed, or our "lady of justice" will run the risk of being raped in the jury room. The author knows of no precedent giving an unsuccessful litigant a second "bite at the apple" if one or more of the jurors has satisfied a pathological desire to abort justice.

"The jury, passing on the prisoner's life,
  May in the sworn twelve have a thief or two
  Guiltier than him they try."—Shakespeare, "Measure for Measure."

The trial of a lawsuit should never be considered as involving a "bag of tricks." All of the techniques described in this book are intended only to assist the lawyer in guiding the jury toward truth and justice. The casual reader may have come to the erroneous conclusion that a trial lawyer, through the skillful use of deception, can move a jury up the stream against a torrent of truth and righteousness. Lawyers who consistently work with juries know that this is not the fact. They have learned that integrity and sincerity, together with conformity to basic, common sense rules of persuasion, will create a better chance of success. There is nothing that occurs from the time the prospective jurors are herded into the courtroom until they sign their names on the verdict that does not contribute in some part toward the ultimate verdict. From the jurors' very first impression, for example, the apparent attitude of a party to the lawsuit or that of his lawyer, to the reasonableness of testimony, every single detail will play a part. There is no one segment of the trial that stands by itself; each becomes a part of the whole. During *voir dire* examination promises were extracted from each juror that were important to the entire case. These promises or commitments may again be brought up during the closing argument. The testimony elicited on either direct examination or cross-examination may well have been highlighted by letting the jury know in the opening statements what was coming. The importance of this evidence can again be dramatized in the closing argument. If a lawyer is capable of performing brilliantly on any one segment of a trial but that ability is contrasted with his mediocrity for the balance of the trial, his persuasive ability will be poor, at best. Not only are all phases of the trial closely interrelated, but each phase is dependent upon the others. The segments of a lawsuit can be likened to a wheel whose spokes all meet at the hub. The wheel is functional because, as a complete unit, it has design and purpose. No one spoke is superfluous, although the wheel may be functional without one of the spokes. As in a wheel, one of the segments of a lawsuit could be omitted and the lawsuit might still be successfully concluded. There is a point, however, at which a lawsuit will collapse, just as a wheel will, if a sufficient number of segments are neglected or omitted.

From the very first word spoken to the very first prospective juror through the last word uttered in the summation, every word that the lawyer speaks should be deliberately designed to persuade 12 men and women that one position is more probably true than not.

Our jury system has proven itself through the test of time, and almost all men and women who are concerned in one way or another with jury decisions will speak out in favor of its continuation. However, the system has been under attack from various quarters, but it will almost always be found that those who would abandon the jury system are those who have had little personal acquaintance with it. Let those who would destroy and bury the jury system know that there are dedicated disciples who must first be overcome. Let us, therefore, resolve that we will never be complacent about our jury system, either in its present posture or at any time in the future but that we will nourish it and care for it as a living, breathing thing. Justice thus will survive.

Index

235